7845

320.01

D1437381

WITHDRAWN FROM STOCK

This book is due for return on or before the last date shown below.

7 JAN 1991

10 APR 2000

F 8 JAN 1992

10 MAR 1993

- 8 NOV 1994

19 MAR 1997

27 APR 1998

29 MAY 1998

Don Gresswell Ltd., London, N.21 Cat. No. 1208

DG 02242/71

Politics and the pursuit of happiness

Politics and the pursuit of happiness

an enquiry into the involvement of
human beings in the politics of
industrial society

Ghiţa Ionescu

Longman

London and New York

Longman Group Limited
Longman House, Burnt Mill, Harlow
Essex CM20 2JE, England
Associated companies throughout the world

Published in the United States of America
by Longman Inc., New York

First published 1984

British Library Cataloguing in Publication Data

Ionescu, Ghiţa
    Politics and the pursuit of happiness.
    1. Political science
    I. Title
    320′.01   JC257.I5

ISBN 0-582-29549-1

Library of Congress Cataloguing in Publication Data

Ionescu, Ghiţa.
    Politics and the pursuit of happiness.

    Includes index.
    1. Political psychology—History.   2. Ideology—
History.   I. Title.
JA74.5.I55   1984   320.5′09   84-3899
ISBN 0-582-29549-1 (U.S.)

Printed in Great Britain at the Alden Press
Oxford, London and Northampton

Contents

Preface

The idea of this enquiry grew slowly, but overwhelmingly, in me as I continued my study of the comparative problems of the politics of industrial societies, liberal or communist. The more I dug into the logic of these problems, the more evident it became that its surface roots were entwined with the deepest roots of the significance of politics in human life. In other words, that only by re-asserting the order of priorities between the existence of individual human beings and their co-existence with other human beings, can one assess the ultimate significance of politics in human life. This applies also, or indeed especially, to human beings in industrial societies which, by virtue of their intrinsic functional interdependence, constantly increase political involvement.*

Socrates's 'know thyself', Christ's 'love thy neighbour as thyself', Shakespeare's 'the fault, dear Brutus, lies not in our stars, but in ourselves' all reaffirm, in the great moments of European culture, the principle of the priority of the self. But when European society entered into the industrial age this principle was subverted by the new ideological manner of thinking, the principle of which is, on the contrary, the sacrifice of the self to public, collective or historical finalities. With so many ideologized human beings pursuing, in an increasingly materialistic way, the 'chimaera of public happiness', to use Rousseau's phrase, no wonder industrial society advanced towards its present crisis.

The exposition of this idea, it seemed to me, required a premiss as broad and old as the original teachings on the meaning of human life, and conclusions as precise and modern as the present crisis in industrial society can inspire. Concomitantly, the more I saw the subject expanding the less I felt justified in turning my hand to it. Several times I almost abandoned it. Yet always direct or indirect, fortuitous or expected, encouragement

*My own efforts to discover the essential characteristics of the politics of industrial society as a whole, were preceded and helped by the works of Raymond Aron, Daniel Bell, Bernard Crick, Ralf Dahrendorf, Karl W. Deutsch, S. E. Finer, Carl J. Friedrich, Ernest Gellner, W. J. MacKenzie, Giovanni Sartori, Andrew Shonfield, and Edward Shils, most of whom were also valued friends.

helped me to persevere with it. I would like here to acknowledge — in chronological order — all those who played a part in the final realization of this book.

At the very beginning, when I had grave doubts whether such a far-fetched scheme would make sense to anyone but myself, a significant little event set my work in motion. Guy Garfit, the publisher of political books at Longmans, whom I had not met before, though he told me that he had been my student long before at Manchester University, proposed that I should write a book for Longmans on a familiar subject. Although tempted, I declined the offer on the grounds that I wanted to concentrate solely on a quite different subject. When he asked me what this subject was, I answered quite casually 'The Tragic Sense of Politics', the first title I had given to my project. To my astonishment he inquired whether this would be an expansion of a lecture he had once heard me give on the significance of Unamuno's *Tragic Sense of Life* for our attitude to politics. Since that time, he added, he had read a great deal of Unamuno. I had given that lecture only once in one particular year, and I was struck by the impact it had made on at least one student. I signed the contract soon after, thus committing myself formally to writing this book. Since then, Guy and his editor, Fiona Lipson, have shown great patience and understanding.

A second favourable circumstance arose as a result of a visit to Paris, to discuss one of my working hypotheses with François Furet, the president of the Haute École des Sciences Sociales, whose book, *Penser la révolution française* had greatly impressed me. My hypothesis was that Jacobinism lay at the root of ideological politics. M. Furet thought that the idea was worth further and fuller exploration, and proposed that we should organize at his Institute a joint seminar which met weekly for over four months, and the details of which are given on p. 71. I want to thank Professor Furet for this generous intellectual hospitality.

I would also like to thank Professor J. B. Skemp, whose brilliant translation and interpretation of Plato's *Statesman* — that curiously under-valued work — had led me, and surely many others, to re-discover it. He was kind enough to examine very thoroughly the presentation in this book of Plato's tragic sense of politics.

As I progressed with my work, sometimes in hope, sometimes in despair, I was greatly helped by friends whose judgement I trusted and to whom I submitted either the whole or parts of the manuscript. Above all, I must thank three good friends who spared the time to read through the whole manuscript. Sir Ian Gilmour read the text twice, made many most valuable comments and criticisms, and helped me to express my own ideas, with which he by no means always agreed, as lucidly as possible. Professor Isabel de Madariaga discussed the theme of this book with me from the moment of its inception and took an active and helpful part in all its different stages. I shall never be able to thank her enough. The generous and pertinent comments made on the whole of the final version by

Professor Harvey Mansfield Jr. of Harvard University, reached me just as the manuscript was being sent to the printers. I was however able to take account of many of his remarks. If I have not always followed the good advice of these three friends the fault is mine.

Another friend, Dr Margaret Canovan, commented on the third version, but I had no opportunity to show her the fourth, which was reconstructed with her comments in mind.

The comments of my friends Ernest Gellner, Pierre Manent, and Geraint Parry (in alphabetical order), on a summary of the book, also proved valuable.

Mrs Joan Titterton who has been for years my secretary in Manchester University, undertook the gruelling task of typing the first three versions, with innumerable changes, and Mrs Judith Hicks typed the final version. Both deserve my full and remorseful thanks.

Valence, my wife, had to put up with the longest period yet of the disorder which pervades the house when I am writing a book. But our long conversations on the themes of this book illustrated the contrast between the serenity of Christian philosophy and the agitations of politics.

G.I.

To the memory
of
Don Salvador de Madariaga

Introduction

The working hypothesis of this enquiry is that ideological politics, nowadays practised in all industrial countries, is incompatible with the essentially functional industrial society. The working definition of the function of politics adopted in this enquiry is: the regulation of the co-existence of human beings within a unit of rule, with a view to improving it in the present and in the future. It is assumed that the improvement depends on the extent to which the regulation is guided by the observance of laws; and on how much it reduces the part coercion plays, and hence increases the part which participation plays, in that lawful regulation.

The essentially functional character of the industrial society is incompatible with the ideological approach. Yet since human history suffers from the same duality as human life, it so happened that functional industrial society and ideological politics (see Chapter 3) were born at almost the same time, the dawn of the nineteenth century. Of course this was not simply accidental: the same epistemological break produced the antagonistic twins. Moreover, ideological politics offered for a while to the human beings in countries ripe for industrialization,[1] beliefs, which although factitious, encouraged them to effect, by reform or revolution, the social and political modernization required by the industrial society.

But since the beginning of the twentieth century at least ideological politics have become increasingly inadequate as a means of regulating the co-existence of human beings in an industrial society, and hence they have become dysfunctional. This is a likely explanation of the present crisis of political credibility in all industrial societies, capitalist and communist alike. For there can be only one reason why the contradiction between ideological politics and the functional industrial society came to a head almost at the same time in both regimes. The year 1968, the year of the

[1] Industrial countries are the members of the Organization for Economic Co-operation and Development *and* the members of the Council for Mutual Economic Assistance (CEMA or COMECON) with a few exceptions on each side. See also for the communist industrial societies my book: *The Politics of the European Communist States* (1967) and for the liberal ones: *Centripetal Politics* (1977).

students' revolt and of the revolt in Czechoslovakia, can be taken as the high point of the manifestation of the new disbelief in the optimistic promises of ideological politics in both systems of industrial societies. That the symptoms of the crisis were more easily seen, and its treatment more overtly sought, in the expressive liberal regime than in the repressive communist regime does not alter the premise that both are affected by some comparable troubles.

The origin of ideological politics is to be found in the extension at the end of the eighteenth century, by way of ideologization, of the belief that happiness can be provided by politics, that the happiness of human beings depends on politics. One of the first formulations of this creed in European politics is to be found in article 1 of the Declaration of the Rights of Man in France in 1789, which stated that 'the goal of society is human happiness'.[2] Once the industrial society had started to function in its specifically materialist way, the belief that it could dispense happiness was further strengthened by the exciting availability of material comfort and by the consequent increasing need for public co-ordination, which was conferred on the state. The second series of promises started when Marx's followers pledged that Communism would bring about full equality and to each according to his needs. In the twentieth century all politics in industrial society are based on the promissory technique, i.e. they promise different kinds of happiness to be achieved with different ends and means.

There is nothing wrong, of course, with the pursuit, or even as Bertrand Russell has put it, the 'conquest' of happiness.[3] As will be discussed at great length in Chapter 2 the acknowledgement of an original tragic sense of life, and consequently of an original tragic sense of politics, does not exclude a perception of real human happiness; on the contrary, real happiness is based on man's perception of his entire destiny, from birth to death. To try to defeat the tragic sense of life by pursuing pleasure and avoiding pain is to lie to oneself. Provided that happiness is defined as the ultimate interior experience of one particular human being, and as his or her ultimate self-achievement — 'One day or a short time, does not make a man happy' as Aristotle used to say — the pursuit of happiness is bound to be one of the major impulses in life.

What is wrong, however, is to present happiness as a material object, which can be publicly dispensed, as a reward for belief in an ideology and for the rendering of political services. What is even worse is to make the specific promise that the prospects of fundamental changes heralded by the stunning advance of the natural sciences, can be expanded, by way of ideology, to change the human condition as a whole. Whereas the natural sciences and their precise philosophical interpretation limited future prospects to the changes which could be made in the conditions

---

[2] For the differing conceptions of the relationship between happiness and politics in the American and French Revolutions, see pp. 19–20.

[3] Bertrand Russell: *The Conquest of Happiness,* London 1953.

of life of mortal human beings, the ideological philosophies (see pp. 24–26) deformed the prospects of change in two ways.

First, they expanded them with promises of complete human happiness, of changes in the human condition as a whole. Condorcet, the most luminous exponent of the neo-Rousseauian ideas of the French Revolution went so far in his predictions of human progress as almost to presage the abolition of human mortality by science. Bentham, once he had adopted the radical ideas of the French Revolution, defined the purpose of human existence, and of government, as the pursuit of happiness and the avoidance of human pain. Marx explained human happiness as the end of human alienation and promised that this goal could, and should, be achieved through the communist revolution.

For, and this is the second deformation, the ideologies conditionally linked the availability of 'happiness', for either the 'greatest number' of men or for the 'human species' as a whole, to the political action which men should themselves conduct in accordance with the instructions and prescriptions formulated by the respective ideologies. By doing so the ideologies not only burdened science with a promissory philosophy heavier than it could bear, but also burdened politics with a Messianic commitment which is outside its range. As stated in the working definition the function of politics is to regulate the public co-existence of contemporary human beings.

But the ideologies, by mixing the public role of politics with the pursuit of human happiness, an elusive and essentially *private* concept, made of politics the key to all human endeavour. They subordinated implicitly and explicitly all human destinies to the ambition of politics. The result was trebly counter-productive: politics became hypertrophic, incapable of achieving many of the innumerable tasks with which it had thus been overloaded. Secondly, the minds of individual human beings were distracted from their purpose of individual self-achievement into a phantasmagoric demand for happiness to be distributed, individually or communally, by political institutions and procedures. This second effect led to the third: gradually the concept of politics took precedence over that of law – that supreme moral law which in the past even Caesars, kings and emperors were deemed to serve and observe. The ideological communities, with their eyes fixed on the promises of the future, gradually neglected or even rejected the moral laws, provided they could obtain happiness.

To substantiate its critical analysis this enquiry adopts a historical and at times allegorical approach. It attempts to show that as a result of the triumph of science in the epistemological conflict between science and religion – unnecessarily provoked by the Church of that time – several seemingly disparate elements emerged simultaneously. The development of the exact sciences led to new discoveries and to their application to the material betterment of the human condition. In the sphere of culture, much expanded by education and information, this led to the development of the belief in progress, and in the sphere of the economy to the belief in the magic power of industry. Each of these spheres was following its own independent course in the developing industrial society; and politics, whose traditional function was to regulate the co-existence of human beings with the aim of improving it from generation to generation, was now also called upon to regulate and co-ordinate the activities of these different spheres.

But politics itself was born, or at least reborn in the wake of the 'great transformation', to use Karl Polany's expression. To be sure, in the past, rulers of all kinds had regulated to a certain extent the co-existence of human beings, guided by, or invoking some supreme law or laws. But they were right not to use the Greek word 'politics' — which was frowned upon until the eighteenth century — because they did not have a *Polis*, the institution which rendered possible, indeed compulsory, the participation of the members of the community. But as industrial society was advancing to its modern, participatory form, everyone acquired in principle a right to participate in policy-making. This was democracy.

Democratic politics was first proclaimed during the French Revolution. Chapter 3 elaborates on the association between politics and ideology which began during the French Revolution, and on the operation of ideologization. For it was then that the respect for the 'laws' of the Graeco—Judaic—Christian heritage of European culture was exchanged for that of the 'will' of the community. Finally, it was at that time that the concept of democracy revealed its ambivalence, when it was deliberately and explicitly shifted by its Jacobin leaders from constitutional government to revolutionary government. That ambivalence was eventually incarnated in the two types of industrial society, indeed the two types of democracy, political and economic, which confront each other in the modern world, the welfare—liberal and the communist—dictatorial.

At this point, in order to express the line of its argument more clearly, this enquiry sets out to construct two types of industrial society, seen as systems of political happiness. That, of course, is not what they are called, but that is what they are in reality. One is the utilitarian—liberal system of political happiness, deriving from the English ideological philosophy of hedonistic utilitarianism (later transformed into pragmatism in America) and from the liberal ideology of progressive permissiveness. The other is the communist—dictatorial system of political happiness, deriving from Marx's ideological philosophy, which acquired political viability only when thoroughly transformed into Marxism—Leninism.

Both ideological philosophies are materialistic, in the sense given to the word since Helvétius. But they use materialism for political purposes; and they replace the spiritual independence of man's conscience with such materially conditioned substitutes as 'interest' or 'class consciousness'. They also relativize traditional virtues, including the *vertu* of the French Revolution. Both are based on a conditional promise of human happiness, either present or future — conditional in so far as its achievement depends on the exactitude with which the 'method' is followed and the dedication with which the 'party' is supported. Although both ideology and ideological political parties appeared only in the nineteenth century, they were to prove the most efficacious vehicles of the new politics.

The enquiry then follows the rise and fall of the ideologies of the systems of political happiness. They rose during the period in which they helped to demolish the remnants of the *ancien régime*, which was obstructing industrialization and the advent of the industrial society. They enjoyed a brief period of uncontested domination in the early part of the twentieth century, when more and more people expected the state, or a party, to dispense happiness. Their dysfunctional decline became manifest already by the First World War, when the concept of progress suffered from the epistemological developments in the fields of science, culture and economics and the professional optimism of ideological politics became increasingly illegitimate. Moreover two opposed promissory systems were now engaged in a political duel which itself gave rise to the third, and highly imitative, ideology, namely Fascism or Nazism. This in turn led to the Second World War. This then was followed by the global ideological 'cold war' launched by the communist system, liable at any moment to slide into a global ideological nuclear war. The blatant dysfunctionalism of the systems was now leading to possible human disaster instead of to the politically dispensed human happiness first promised.

This enquiry might give the impression that like most modern 'critical' political theory, of the Orwellian or of the Frankfurt school type, it is an exercise in 'a plague on both your houses'. That it points to some fundamental similarities between the two systems might seem to give grounds for this assumption. Yet too much critical political theory from, say, C.B. MacPherson in the 1950s to Habermas in the 1970s has concentrated its fire exclusively on the negative aspects of liberalism and has suffered as a result from a certain lopsidedness. Few modern thinkers, with the notable exception of Raymond Aron and Karl W. Deutsch, have dared to embrace the crisis of the whole of industrial society in one single perspective. It is the comparative exercise made in the light of the functioning of the industrial society, which explains the partiality shown here towards the liberal system. In comparison with the communist system it is more human (Althusser's recent demonstration, in Marxist terms, that Marxism is anti-humanist confirms this point); it is pluralistic and therefore more suited to the pluralism of industrial societies; and it is 'open' in Popper's sense, and therefore much more predisposed to reform, reorientation and self-correction than the communist system, so hermetically enclosed in its heavy structures that it might take an explosion to change them; finally it is decidedly less aggressive than the communist system, which at least since Stalin launched the 'cold war' in 1947, has manifestly increased the ideologization and counter-ideologization and hence the present explosive trend.

In view of the specific defects of the communist system, the natural remedy envisaged by this enquiry into the present crisis of politics would be more feasible in the liberal system. The remedy is described as natural because it consists simply in bringing politics back from the two delusive paths it followed when it separated itself from ethics and the moral laws, and when, *after virtue*[4] it started to follow in the dark the illusions of ideologization. The natural solution would therefore simply consist of the reintegration of politics within ethics – and disideologization. Disideologization however is not a kind of de-briefing, brainwashing, recantation, or disintoxication. It is both a political and a moral operation. In political terms disideologization means convincing the people, the new sovereign, that although it makes the laws, the laws must derive from higher and more permanent moral laws. Obviously, this political solution cannot be reached unless the 'people' themselves change, unless human beings disoriented by ideology, exteriorized in their pursuit of exterior goods, are themselves reorientated to the givens of the human condition.

The moral solution is therefore the return to interiorization, facing one's own self alone, which is the existential priority. This would be much easier if people could still choose, as Aristotle would wisely advise them, the contemplative life. But in an essentially, and unprecedentedly participatory society as we know industrial society to be, this is even less possible. Most human beings must participate in the functioning of society, because otherwise it would not function. But functional participation is the other side of the coin of political participation: if I do not approve of the way the enterprise is going, I can bring it to a halt.

In communist systems participation is replaced by mobilization – coercion replaces voluntary action, which is the conceptual condition of participation. When Lenin 'put the lid on opposition' in 1921, he himself recognized that he was putting it on all opposition for good – or for as long as the seething pot could be controlled. But in the liberal industrial society, participation is both a moral right and a moral duty. It is a moral duty because I am materially involved by the interdependent nature of society in most of its developments. And it is a moral right because I am ultimately free, in my involvement, to observe the moral imperatives.

The real reconciliation between interiorized man, the man fully integrated in himself, and man as a political participant, might be found in what is the ultimate object of disideologization, namely the achievement of 'disinterestedness' in both the mental and the moral process of political participation. Interest vitiates all judgement, as Kant reminds us, and political judgement must be the purest of all judgements.

I have tried to explain here what this book is about; but perhaps the reader may be helped if I were also to indicate the four major respects

[4] Alastair MacIntyre: *After Virtue*, London 1978.

in which the approach of this enquiry into the involvement of human beings differs from the approaches of ideological politics and political theories; and then to indicate where I agree with and where I differ from other authors who before me have examined the incompatibility between ideological politics and the politics of the industrial society.

The four major respects in which the approach of this enquiry differs from that of ideological politics are as follows:

1. While there is no question that good political judgement and decision-making requires a *logical* framework within which to assess the ever-alternating order of priority of the issues to be considered and their interrelatedness — it is argued in the enquiry that, on the contrary, because *ideological* frameworks direct all issues towards a single goal those issues are squashed together and amalgamated into one pre-conceived judgement.

2. As seen in the working definition, while the function of politics is to regulate and improve the regulation of co-existence of human beings within a unit of rule, it is argued here that politics is only a *circumstance* — good or evil, limited or overwhelming — in the actual existence of a human being.

3. The action of regulating public affairs is bound to attract those human beings with a vocation for proposing and conducting courses of action. This has led and is increasingly leading to a professionalization of the political function — as described by Max Weber — which to the extent to which *it does not vitiate, let alone violate, the political judgement of each participant in the functioning of the industrial society* is concordant with its manifold divisions of labour.

4. Although a principal purpose of politics is the continuous improvement of the co-existence of human beings, it is illogical, let alone immoral to try to achieve that improvement to the detriment of the existence of the individual human being himself, or even of his own political judgement.

Coming to other authors who have examined the incompatibilities between ideological politics and the politics of the *industrial*[5] societies:

Although like Raymond Aron, Edward Shils and Daniel Bell, in the 1950s, I detect an element of disideologization already among people in industrial societies, this is not another book about 'the end of ideology'. I wish it were. But today, in the 1980s, the ideologies reign supreme. Having captured domestic politics, they have now taken a strong hold on international politics, from which the fate of the whole of industrial society depends. From this point of view this book is a critical history of ideology to date, with the avowed aim of strengthening in its readers their own sentiment that politics in both types of industrial society is

---

[5]Specified, so as to separate it from Michael Oakeshott's broader theme of the overall incompatibility between ideology and politics.

now going through a grave crisis of credibility, and of explaining why and how.

Although Ronald Inglehart's important book *The Silent Revolution*[6] was the first significant attempt to confirm by scholarly, empirical means, a change which began with the generation of 1968 in the orientation of the inner direction of many people in industrial Western Europe away from the materialism of their parents — it is on the definition given by Inglehart to materialism that the premises and the conclusions of my book differ from his. One symptom of a genuine estrangement from materialism is, in the classic conception, putting duty above pleasure. While it is true that the kind of happiness preached by the leaders of the post-1968 generations differed from the hedonism of their parents, theirs was nevertheless still a pursuit of hedonism, though the pleasures were different. And progressive permissiveness reached its utmost heights precisely under the aegis of that generation, thus incurring the danger of weakening the moral sense in society still further.

Nor is this book another plea for depoliticization. Although the concern that 'politics should not become a soteriology' has been expressed by Jacques Ellul in his *L'illusion politique* (1966), this book follows a line of thought different from his, in stressing that what industrial society needs is *more* rather than *less* politics. But the politics should be of a kind which would provide the participant with the impartial judgement and the disinterested moral stand which alone would help him to find the right path. So instead of being an indictment of politics itself, this book attempts to take a stand *In Defence of Politics*, to paraphrase the title of Bernard Crick's book, and make it read: In Defence of the Politics of Industrial Society.

I only read Alasdair MacIntyre's *After Virtue, a Study in Moral Theory* when I had already completed the first draft of this book. *Mutatis mutandis* the two books share the premises of what he calls 'The failure of the Enlightenment projects' to replace the ancestral rules of morality by some new teleologies; and of the consequences this failure has had on the conduct of modern society. But the conclusion of his book that 'what matters at this stage is the construction of local forms of community within which civility and the intellectual and moral life can be sustained through the new dark ages' must seem inadequate in this book's perspective of the interdependence of human beings in industrial society. What matters in its perspective is to try to reassert, above the present public auctioneering of happiness, the individual's tragic sense of life which alone situates the existence and the co-existence of human beings in their true perspectives, and to try to improve in this way the regulation of that co-existence.

---

[6]Ronald Inglehart: *The Silent Revolution, Changing Values and Political Styles among Western Publics*, Princeton 1977.

Chapter 1

How the meaning of the words politics, happiness, and society has changed

The use of the word happiness in connection with politics may strike one as an exaggeration. No one explicitly asks an authority to provide him with happiness, and no constitution lays down that the state is obliged to dispense happiness to its citizens.

One can argue, of course, that the idea that politics should bring happiness to human beings derived first from Greek political philosophy and notably from Aristotle's maxim that a good government is that which makes its citizens happy. But that would be playing with words, what is more, with ancient Greek words. For never, not even in modern Greek, have the concepts of politics and happiness meant the same thing in modern languages and to modern mentalities as they did in the Greek of Aristotle. Politics, for him, meant the decision-making processes in the selective, oligarchic, racist, male-dominated and slave-based *Polis*. And the concept of happiness, to express which Aristotle used at least a dozen interchangeable words, was taken in general by him, not to speak of Socrates and Plato, to mean the enjoyment in one's conscience of the interior goods which are mainly of the resort of ethics, as distinct from politics.

But playing with words is one of the principal occupations of political theory. Each work, in that discipline, has to start with the presentation of its semantic credentials. Concepts do need to be redefined in each case, according first to the historical background upon which they are projected, and second to the idiosyncratic twist given to them. In this work it is assumed that two ancient concepts, that of *politics* and that of *happiness* have, in the last decades of the eighteenth century, entirely changed the meaning which they had preserved with some inevitable variation during the whole period of the early Graeco—Judaic—Christian tradition. It is also assumed that since, and because of, that change, these concepts have revealed an interrelatedness and experienced a cross-fertilization which had not previously been observed. This is understandable because the change of meaning, and hence of the interrelation, of these concepts was made possible only through the intermediary of several new, historically unprecedented, concepts which all appeared at the same time at the end of the eighteenth century. From among these new concepts, the following: *industrial society*, *ideology*, with its components ideologization and ideological party, *intellect* (see pp. 90–92), *interest* (see pp. 114–18) and *capitalism* entered the vocabulary of politics also only in the eighteenth century – not of course in that order, but, on the contrary, in so disorderly a fashion that no one has yet been able to establish which of them has been a conceptual chicken and which an egg.

Once this assumption that the concepts must be redefined is agreed on between the author and the reader, then it is incumbent upon the former to inform the latter of the specific idiosyncratic sense he is giving to the newly defined concepts, politics, happiness, ideology, and industrial society.

POLITICS

The broad working definition of politics proposed in the Introduction stressed its aspect as the regulation, by coercion or by participation, of the co-existence of human beings in industrial society. This definition can be grasped more clearly if the notions of *human beings*, *regulation*, and *participation* are further developed.

HUMAN BEINGS

In a general sense 'human beings' means exactly what it says, i.e. living men and women. But when more precisely analysed, it might sound like a series of pleonasms – existence, human, and beings, all pointing to the mortality of man. The fact is that politics comprises only living people and only as long as they are alive. Once dead, they are physically cut off from the enmeshment of regulating activities which is the ambit of politics.

This extraordinary platitude would not be recorded here if, on reflection, it did not strike one that the missing factor in modern political science, and in social science in general, is precisely the mortality of man. The units of conceptualization and of statistical quantification are abstract and permanent categories or prototypes called men, Frenchmen, Americans, citizens, voters, workers, women, blacks, urban and rural dwellers, etc. It is true that within each category the objects of investigation in the natural sciences *are* interchangeable: atoms, figures, celestial bodies, animals, plants, parts of the human organism, etc. But the specific individual man, who is meant to be the object of investigation of the social sciences, dies, or as Unamuno would insist '*above all* – dies'.

It is within this death-bound time that real human beings must regulate their ephemeral co-existence. Nothing that mortal men regulate in their public life can attain finality. Rightly, the House of Commons acknowledges that its sovereign decisions cannot be binding on future Parliaments. Wrongly, the French and the Russian Revolutions, the two absolute and therefore apocalyptic revolutions, proclaimed that they were shaping the future for centuries. For never has history witnessed such Icarian failures as that of these two apocalyptic revolutions in these two particularly hubristic centuries. In actual fact, these failures have only served to lead to the rediscovery of the tragic sense of politics by modern men.

REGULATION

Hence also the choice of the expression 'to regulate' in defining politics as the regulation of the co-existence of human beings. The expression 'to regulate' was chosen with two considerations in mind. On the one hand, 'to regulate' is used in preference to the phrase 'to solve'. For politics, and especially politics as understood in the context of this work, never solves the problems facing the community. The community itself is after all in a constant state of intragenerational transition, and the problems change so constantly that they can never be really comprehended, in the double sense of the word. New human beings face new problems or the same problems in a new context. They can only regulate them for the time being. On the other hand, the problems of human co-existence produce conflicts between different rights, obligations, and above all between the points of view of different categories of people living together. The use of a neutral expression like 'to regulate' implies that the ultimate decision can be taken by different means and by different procedures, ranging from persuasion to participation.

Different kinds of 'regulation' are necessary in order to establish the co-existence of human beings. The regulation of relations between individuals is achieved by civil customs and laws. Relations between the individual and the community as a whole, of which he is a member by 'association' or by 'contract', or with the institutions of that community, are regulated by public or constitutional laws.

The laws themselves whose role is to prescribe the regulations and to indicate how they should be made to work, are made by the individuals of the community, or by the community of individuals; and yet the laws also originate from some supreme, ancestral and unwritten Laws,[1] Commandments, Customs or Virtues, which correspond also to the permanent aspiration towards the good which is engraved in the conscience of human beings from their mysterious origin. Conscience, Virtue, Law,

---

[1] Or, as expressed by Antigone: 'Nor do I think your edicts were so wrong/That any mortal man should override/*The gods unwritten and undying laws*/Their life is not today and yesterday/But always, and none knows from whence they came/I would not pay the price before the gods/Of breaking these for fear of any man'. (My italics.)

Right, and Justice are as closely linked together in the moral field as Religion, Ethics and Politics are in the interdisciplinary field.

All the activities of human beings, public as well as private, collective as well as individual, are limited by the boundaries of human life. This is why whatever the size of the sphere of politics, the political activities of human beings, because they are only mortal, constitute only a finite set of permutations, from the fundamental few discerned by Aristotle to the innumerable computer permutations of the modern mathematical analysis of political facts. Human life is bounded — to use Karl Jasper's expression — by space-limits and by time-limits. Man's geographic knowledge has now extended to the entire planet on which he lives. There is no corner of the earth, no mountain peak, no fathom of the sea and no height of the atmosphere which has not been explored by man or by his instruments. The planet is by now truly a 'global village'. Moreover man's knowledge of life on earth has at the same time been dramatized by the discovery, as a sequel to the recent explorations of the moon and the planets, that there is life only on earth — that the space-limits of the earth are therefore also the limits of life. But when it comes to the time-limit, then death remains the unchanged limit of human time.

There is a great difference between the space-limits and the time-limits of the sphere of politics. Their evolution, in the last two centuries or so, has been different, indeed opposed. The space-limits have continuously expanded.[2] The sphere of politics has grown both in terms of territorial size and in terms of the intensification of interdependence — that is the dependence of any political decision in any one place or unit of rule on the decisions taken in innumerable, unidentifiable, other places or units of rule. The art of government has increasingly become the art of power-sharing at all levels, whether external or internal, in decision- and policy-making processes.

But whereas the space-limits of the sphere of politics have expanded to this extent, the time-limits of the sphere of politics have remained almost the same.[3] 'Almost' because it is true, according to world statistics, that the average human life-span has been prolonged in the last century or so by some ten years. And 'almost' because given the 'acceleration of history', that is the rapid succession in time of major political

---

[2] Causing in the exercise serious misunderstandings of politics. People have tried to apply first to large countries like France, and then to all powers of the world, the model of democracy which Rousseau derived from the examples of minuscule political units like Sparta or the Canton of Geneva. Rousseau's controversial concept of the general will was so diluted in these large circumfusions that whatever sense it had in his original vision, became nonsense when applied to ever-larger nation-states. Voltaire's annotation on the copy of the first edition of *Le Contract Social*: Could M. Rousseau tell us how the million inhabitants of Paris alone could be assembled in permanent sittings of policy-making? — revealed almost at once the impracticable foundations of Rousseau's concept.

[3] Though political decision-makers are constantly faced with the need to take a longer time-scale into account in specific fields, e.g., energy or pollution.

developments, a man living, say, between 1914 and 1984 has witnessed, if not experienced, hundred times more changes in the world than a man living between 1844 and 1914.

But, much as politics may have interfered with, or indeed buffeted, a person's life, how much of his life-span of seventy years, or of the forty years of his maturity, can a human being in a liberal democracy, be expected to devote to politics without sacrificing his vocation, his family and above all his own individuality? The contradiction between the maintenance of his own integrity and increasing political pressures is obvious: modern man must make the choice, described by so many modern philosophers at the different stages of the evolution of mass society, between politicization and the weakening of the self under the pressures and constraints of the mass society. This enforced choice has been denounced at almost equal intervals of thirty odd years by Unamuno[4] before the First World War, by Karl Jaspers[5] before the Second World War, by David Riesman[6] soon after, and by Jacques Ellul[7] in the 1960s. They all sadly observed that the consciousness of the individual was being increasingly diluted in order to contribute to the growth of mass consciousness.

But the community, or society, is not composed only of the activities of individuals *qua* individuals. It embraces entire occupational ranges of activities in which individual human beings are engaged, and which form distinct functional spheres, each with its own specific contribution to the productive activities of a society. Socrates, via Plato, was always eager to remind politicians that without such activities there would be no human community — and that without a human community there would be no politics. But once that community exists, politics, as the regulation of the co-existence of human beings, should also regulate the co-existence of those functional 'spheres' or ambits such as for instance, the sphere of science, the sphere of economics, the sphere of labour, the sphere of education, etc. Each of these spheres functions independently — and yet all of them are essentially interdependent. The larger and the more developed the society the more striking the contrasting independence/ interdependence of the functional spheres, culminating in the great cacophony of the advanced industrial society.

Unlike the classic descriptions — that is from Henry VIII's Act 24(1532) to Sir Ian Gilmour's book[8] in 1969 — which show how the 'body politic' encompasses the society, this enquiry endeavours to show how (industrial) society encompasses politics.

The ambit of politics in the industrial society is situated at, and formed by the intersection of the other ambits (see p. 14). In principle, it ought

---

[4] Miguel de Unamuno: *The Tragic Sense of Life,* Madrid 1912, London 1930.
[5] Karl Jaspers: *La situation spirituelle de notre époque,* Paris 1961, Berlin 1930.
[6] David Riesman: *The Lonely Crowd,* New Haven, 1952.
[7] Jacques Ellul: *L'illusion politique*, Paris 1966.
[8] Ian Gilmour: *The Body Politic*, London 1969.

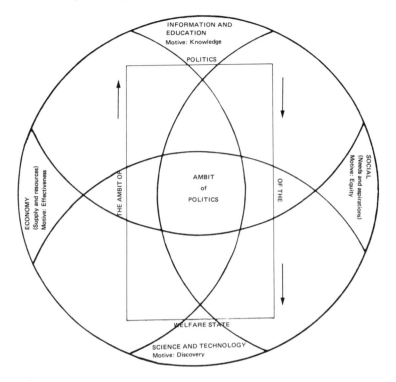

THE AMBITS OF THE INDUSTRIAL SOCIETY.

to regulate the co-existence of these spheres not only directly through laws or constitutional procedures but also indirectly, as an umpire, or at least an intermediary, when the conflict between some or all of those spheres brings the functioning of the society to a stop.

The role of umpire is the more fitting one for politics because in the order of decision-making politics comes first. Since it regulates the functioning of the other spheres, in cases of conflict the latter must subordinate their activities to the decision of the regulatory sphere.

Already, as the diagram shows, the welfare state expands the ambit of politics over the others. In the totalitarian state politics encompasses all the ambits of the industrial society.

PARTICIPATION

Everybody is involved in the functioning of an industrial society — either by mobilization or by participation. The characteristic element of participation and notably of political participation is personal voluntariness. The fact that I might be involved in a political action does not mean that I myself am taking part in it — neither in the decision which led to it, nor in its implementation — if I were not constrained. Neither Stalin's Kulaks nor Hitler's Jews could be said to have *participated* in the political action which led to their death.

Political participation must bear the hallmark of voluntariness. Even the exercise of a vote in a quinquennial or quadrennial general election must be exercised or indeed *not* exercised, in total constitutional freedom if it is to have a true significance of participation.

Democracy in an industrial society is measured by the amount of participation it produces. In theory the economic democracy of the communist industrial societies is based on the direct participation of the producers in the economic decision-making processes. In theory the political democracy of the liberal industrial societies is based on the indirect participation of the voters and their representatives in the political processes.

The proof of the urgent need to 'regulate' the economic and social activities of the industrial society by modern participatory politics was provided by the economic crisis of the 1930s. What was then diagnosed as the 'contradictions of capitalism' (the communist system was only beginning its industrialization) were in reality the contradictions between old ethics and politics and the new society.

One of the real trends of 'convergence' in both types of industrial societies, liberal and communist, is the public demand for increased participation. The recent action of the Polish trade unions and the 1968 action of the Czechoslovak trade unions demonstrate the necessity for the communist industrial societies to allow real participation in the economic processes if those societies are to function. In liberal industrial societies the same problem is seen from the other end: representative governments, elected on the basis of political representation, find it increasingly difficult to govern without the participation in policy-making processes of the socio-economic groups.

The regulation of the co-existence of human beings is synonymous with participation in the industrial societies and with political participation in the liberal industrial societies. The corollary of the involvement of most human beings in the working of those societies is the political condition that most should also have their say in the processes of decision-making.

HAPPINESS

As we have seen there is a considerable difference between what the Greeks, the Romans and the Jews understood by happiness, and the eighteenth-century European and American concept of happiness. Above all there is a great gulf between the popular and the scholarly understanding of the meaning of the almost magic formula 'the pursuit of happiness', let alone of happiness itself, the meaning of which, as Sir Isaiah Berlin has remarked, 'is so porous that there is little interpretation that it seems to resist'.[9]

The Greeks and, for different reasons, the Christians had expressed grave doubts as to whether happiness could be achieved on earth. In the dialogue between Polus and Callicles in the *Gorgias,* Callicles maintained a brutally hedonistic conception of happiness. He was countered by Socrates's precept that 'when acting, do not let any consideration come before moral considerations'. The principle that moral considerations condition happiness led, even in Greece, to many other meanings of happiness. These range all the way from Aristotle's belief — that the 'contemplative' life is 'happier' than the active one, and that in the mixture which he himself described in Greek as happiness the 'interior' goods prevail over the 'exterior' (material) ones in so far as they filter the latter through the moral conscience and limit them accordingly — to Antigone's cry: 'And if I die for it, what happiness!' where 'it' represents the moral consideration, the accomplishment of the moral duty.

Over the centuries a number of warnings have been issued against the belief that happiness is the supreme good, and making the pursuit of happiness the main object of life. These were:

— The Greek reminder that since fate is so unpredictable no one can consider himself happy until he draws his last breath. The positive corollary of this warning is that true happiness is the result of conducting one's life with a continuity of virtue which is clear in one's own eyes and confirmed by one's reputation in the eyes of others.

— The Christian belief that happiness is unobtainable on earth and can only be the reward in heaven for those who have lived virtuously and have been granted the grace to win their salvation.

— The tragic sense of life, to use Unamuno's expression, of which more later, or Hegel's 'consciousness of unhappiness' (*unglückliche Bewusstsein*) in the face of the absurdity of the human condition, the irreconcilable contrast between its glory and its misery, which Pascal has so firmly situated at the centre of man's questioning of the universe.

— Kant's imperative assertion that the purpose, the end of one's existence, must be moral, for 'not every end is moral and that of personal happiness, for example, is not moral. The end must be an unselfish one'.[10] And further, 'thus it can by no means be said that I

[9]Sir Isaiah Berlin: *Four Essays on Liberty*, Oxford 1969, p. 121.
[10]*Kant's Political Writings,* ed. Hans Reiss, trans. H.S. Nibet, Cambridge 1970, p. 65.

class as happiness every state which I *prefer* to all modes of existence. For I must be certain that I am not acting against my duty. Only then am I entitled to look around for happiness in so far as I can reconcile it with the state I know to be morally (not physically) good. . .'.[11] Or 'Happiness embodies everything that nature has given us and nothing else. But virtue embodies that which no one but man can give or take away from himself.'[12]

Kant's attitude to the pursuit of happiness differs from the three which preceded it in time, and has a greater modern relevance, because it was during the last half of the eighteenth century that the 'pursuit of happiness' first invaded the moral life of human beings, followed by the politics of happiness. The premises of human thought and behaviour were radically altered by the orientation of late eighteenth-century philosophy towards secular happiness and the proclamation in and by means of the French Revolution that the achievement of public happiness is the aim of the individual (see Ch. 4). Ernest Gellner has perceptively described Kant, in a broad metaphysical context, as a 'refugee from a catastrophe who arrives, nobly carrying but the two or three beings dearest to him'.[13] In the context of this enquiry, that moral catastrophe was the quickening of the pursuit of public happiness just before, during and after the French Revolution among ever larger numbers of people. This is not to say that most people since then have done no more than pursue happiness, not even in the materialistic industrial societies which are the framework of this enquiry. But it does underline the fact that since the last decades of the eighteenth century the pursuit of happiness has become the dominant motivation of public life. It is the pursuit of happiness which dictates the line to be followed by public authorities, and it is the *Zeitgeist,* imbued with this doctrine, which describes the philosophies which have reservations about this kind of pursuit of happiness as either reactionary or inhumane.

The great change in the *Zeitgeist*, with which this enquiry is concerned, occurred when two such heterogeneous notions as happiness and politics came to be fused together, crushing in the exercise the moral values which, before that fusion, were essential to each of them. For happiness is an uncertain notion, the only certainty of which is that it happens in the most interior conscience of the individual human being, while politics, on the contrary, is the sum of external relations between human beings.

As already mentioned one of the major causes of this change in human mentality and behaviour was the industrial revolution, and one of its major results was the emergence of the phenomenon of ideology, with its two necessary accompaniments, ideologization of the individual, and the

---

[11] Ibid., p. 68.
[12] Ibid.
[13] E. Gellner: *The Legitimation of Belief*, Cambridge 1973, p. 188.

17

organization of the ideological political party. These two concepts must also be explained in the context of this enquiry.

INDUSTRIAL SOCIETY

In the history of the West the industrial revolution, which began first in England, and then, after the French Revolution, spread to much of the continent — played a determining part in the political, social and economic changes which marked the great divide between the *ancien régime*, and the constitutional regimes which ushered in the modern Western democracies. The first, or primary industrialization, which is what is usually understood by the term industrial revolution, so affected human behaviour that it created a new type of society, the industrial society. Raymond Aron, one of the first to study this subject systematically, spoke of industrial societies as those states in which industrialization had been effected.[14] But when he used the singular 'industrial society' he referred to industrial society as a whole, comprising the whole group of industrialized states. The generic noun is obviously more correct for a number of reasons. In the first place the industrial society in all its stages, political types, and geographic situations differs so fundamentally from the non-developed or underdeveloped countries that its parts unite in a homogeneous logical and terminological whole. Secondly, the industrial revolution spread so rapidly in Europe and the United States that it marks a clear dividing line in time in the history of the world: before and after industrialization. Thirdly, it also effected changes in space. For the process of industrialization is eminently transnational. It expands over national and continental boundaries, creating transnational linkages as powerful if not more so than national linkages. It thus separates the world into two economic parts: the developed and the underdeveloped countries.[15]

[14] See his *18 Lectures on Industrial Society,* London 1961. In the text Aron uses the plural 'industrial societies' both when he refers to different types of industrial societies and to different states which have been industrialized.

[15] Thus, in the article 'The importance of international economic linkages' in *OECD Economic Outlook*, July 1983 (pp. 16–21): 'The perception of most (OECD) countries singly that many of their problems flow from abroad is correct: but for the OECD countries as a whole it is not true that most problems originate abroad. Many originate *within* the OECD area, and are transmitted from one country to another by strong economic linkages. And others, which appear to emanate from outside the OECD area, are in fact often traceable back to earlier developments within the OECD area' (italics in the text). As for the economic contrast between the two worlds two figures from the World Bank's *World Development Report 1981*, show that the share in the 1980 world population of all developing countries was 73.6% and of the industrial market economies 15.4%. On the other hand, the share in world GNP of the developing countries was 21.5%, of the industrial non-market economies 17.4% and of the industrial market economies 64%.

The connection between the political and cultural revolutions of Western Europe and the United States and the industrial revolution derives from the expectation of perpetual progress which developments in scientific thought had encouraged among eighteenth-century intellectual élites, and which had afterwards extended throughout the rest of the world under European influence. Industrialization, and the achievements of the industrial society confirmed the prediction of constant progress made by the prophets of happiness of the late eighteenth century. Material happiness, palpable happiness, exterior happiness had been grasped at last. The great question however still remained: how to make *all* human beings, or at least those people who dwelt in industrial societies share in the material happiness which had now become available. 'The industrial revolution', writes Karl Polanyi, 'was merely the beginning of a revolution as extreme and radical as ever inflamed the minds of sectarians, but the new creed was utterly materialistic and believed that all human problems could be resolved given an unlimited amount of material commodities'.[16]

The idea of material and technical progress, which in reality more than surpassed the expectations of past and even sometimes of present science fiction writers, animates students of industrial society even today; whereas other writers still deplore its coming in history. Thus Daniel Bell, an outstanding analyst of industrial society, defines 'its quality of life as measured by the services and amenities. . . which are now deemed desirable and possible for everyone', whereas to Polyani, the industrial revolution was 'an avalanche of social dislocation', the dangers of which were 'never really overcome'. Between these optimistic and pessimistic views one might choose perhaps to take an intermediate stance, an as it were objective view of the industrial revolution, which allows for the dualities inherent in most human creation.

Even in the two major characteristics of industrial society, the primacy of knowledge and incessant economic growth, the ambivalences can be detected at once, namely the gigantic material progress, overshadowed by disturbing signs of spiritual regress.

KNOWLEDGE

The increasingly rapid broadening of the base of knowledge, both in terms of literacy and in terms of professional qualification, produced two major ambivalences. One is the ambivalence of the accessibility of knowledge; the second is the ambivalence of the use of knowledge or of the applicability of human knowledge to human purposes.

The ambivalence of the accessibility of knowledge is probably the most dramatically visible of all. One of the greatest hopes harboured by men,

[16]Karl Polanyi: *The Great Transformation. The Political and Economic Origin of Our Time*, Beacon Paperback 1957, p. 40.

in the age of secularization and rationalism, was that more human beings would be taught to know all that can be known, and all that is to be known would one day become known. Illiteracy has now been almost wholly eradicated in most industrial countries (at least to the extent that most people are taught to read, write and count). But while basic knowledge has spread, the highest levels of knowledge have become more rarefied and inaccessible than ever before. The quality — not to speak of the quantity — of scientific and technological discoveries has increased so much that it has gradually, but infallibly, gone beyond the capacity to understand of the average cultured person. As science has continued its search for truth, the very meaning of that truth, and the language in which the search was conducted, has become incomprehensible to the ever larger number of people of average culture. The almost exclusive use of mathematical symbols has marked the further divorce between the material comprehensiveness and the immateriality of the problems explored thenceforward by human science.

This progressive separation between knowledge and understanding and between human beings and their sciences has only increased the frustration of modern people. If truth cannot be digested by the average intelligence, it still had to be fed with something, be it quasi-truths or myths or indeed with ideologies.

The second ambivalence of modern knowledge lies in the practical application of the findings of science. This is the point at which science branches out into technology, and technology subsequently leads to industry. Pure science is indifferent to the application of its results to human purposes. It does not care whether its own work has any use or indeed any meaning for man; it does not care whether the uses to which human beings put it will improve or worsen the human condition — foster or destroy human life. On the other hand, man's ingeniousness has been able to turn many scientific discoveries to account in practical applications designed to make life easier.

But human civilization is one thing and human nature another. The neo-Hegelian and Marxist interpretations of the practical developments of science as the transformation not only of nature by man but of the nature of man himself is exhilarating. Man cannot fly by himself like a bird, or plunge into the fathoms of the sea like a fish, or land on the moon, but he can now do all these things with the machines he has invented and made. But this transformation is, alas, valid only for the physical nature of man. The moral nature of man has still not changed, not even that of educated communist man. Communist and capitalist societies alike have produced aeroplanes, submarines and spacecraft which have achieved feats of exploration; but they have also produced nuclear bombs and missiles and human misery, even if different forms of human misery.

ECONOMIC GROWTH

People in industrial societies still believe that industry can magnify the 'growing' capacities to incalculable proportions. By means of machines, that is to say of applied science, industrial production will — as it has gradually done until now — reduce the physical human effort (pain) of physical productive work and increase the quantities and qualities of consumable goods (pleasure). It was this idealized type of industrial society which was portrayed by Saint-Simon in his early descriptions of a society in which no moral or social difference was made between the capital-providing producers and the labour-providing producers, or between producers and consumers, all of whom were seen as united in one common endeavour. But the socio-economic cleavages and conflicts generated by capitalism, a historical phenomenon parallel to industrialization, led even the ageing Saint-Simon to see his image of a homogeneous industrial society breaking up into ambivalences.

One was the ambivalence implicit in economic egalitarianism. As it developed, manufacturing industry required increasing numbers of 'workers'. This created a new form of reward 'in cash', and a new social mentality of 'buying' one's needs and wants. The medieval sentiment that men should share in poverty and humility (power was then not yet dissociated from wealth), was replaced by the new feeling that all men should share in work and in its rewards. In the new materialistic ways of thinking, aspirations to equality implied 'levelling' which, in Tocqueville's words, 'reduces men to prefer equality in slavery to inequality in freedom'. In turn the pursuit of 'levelling' leads to the creation of a central organization, that is the state, as the supreme controller of that operation. The Russian October Revolution was the triumph of state-induced levelling.

Nevertheless, growth was stimulated in all industrial societies and by any means. Yet this led to the dilemma of the limits of growth. The *absolute* limits of economic growth had always been present in the minds of pessimistic economists, from Malthus to the Club of Rome. But the *relative* social limits of growth, that is of the uses of the products of economic growth 'once the mass of the population has satisfied its main biological needs for life-sustaining food, shelter and clothing', was a new and different variation on the theme of scarcity in a capitalist society. Fred Hirsch defined it as 'the social limits of growth'.[17]

The third ambivalence of growth is that it requires the increased involvement and participation of greater numbers of people in the decision-making processes of industrial production. Four trends converge in this ambivalence: the increase in numbers of industrial workers employed; contrary to the previous trend, the increased requirement for technical qualification among industrial workers; the consolidation of the sectorial interest-groups of industrial society into massive corporations; and more visibly since the Second World War the 'evaporation of property', to use Schumpeter's expression, from the entrepreneurs or owners of industrial enterprises to their management. The cumulation of all these trends, but most notably of the second and third, has imposed the participation in

[17]Fred Hirsch: *The Social Limits of Growth*, London 1977.

the process of production of all categories of, by now, specialized industrial workers as a *sine qua non* condition. This in turn required the consultation and participation of the entire technostructure,[18] in most processes of decision-making. The purpose of this consultation is simply to obtain the assent of those who will have to implement a decision before it is taken — for a decision which cannot be implemented is not a decision. The political consequences of what seemed to be a purely industrial relation have changed the entire character of modern politics in industrial societies. The problem of 'participation' is rightly considered to be central to the modern political crisis — and the same problem, expressed by the same word, affects both contemporary systems of industrial society equally. In May 1968 'participation' was the slogan on the posters and in the chants of demonstrators both in liberal Paris and in communist Prague.

But it is the expression 'involvement' which describes accurately the interrelatedness between the people in industrial society and that society. The industrial society has attained the highest density of interdependence known to history. Its specific transnational interdependence has already been mentioned; but the internal interdependence within an industrial state is even more characteristic. The industrial society is a functional grid in which all functions, even the most modest (think how a local strike by busmen, postmen or railwaymen gradually affects national and transnational relations) are enmeshed in a tight chain of reactions. Functionalism, urbanization, intense means of communication, notably information, and centralization around the state institutions have, and will increasingly have the effect of *involving* individuals in the activities of society to a previously inconceivable extent. His daily life, as much as his destiny, is conditioned by the functioning of the society around him, while his own activity also conditions to a certain degree that functioning. This creates a mutual involvement — the concept of which is different from participation to the extent to which the latter contains in it an element of voluntariness. Involvement is less than voluntary, it is circumstantial.

We are touching here also on another theme of this enquiry: the distinction in the politics of industrial societies between political and ideological, and particularly between political judgement and ideological judgement. Given that there is no way in which the human being in an industrial society can avoid being involved in its functioning (unless he opts out in the search for a hermitage, a 'commune' or other forms of individual escapism) it follows that his political participation ought to be given voluntarily. He must be alert to the public and professional developments — and as these developments, in an interdependent society, form endless concentric circles, his political attention must be stretched

[18]Galbraith's name for the decision-making 'groups' in modern industries, which comprises all those involved through their special roles from all echelons of managements to all specialized workers and foremen.

to comprehend their connections. His political judgement[19] therefore should also be as sharp and detached as possible. This also depends on how far he succeeds in avoiding the ideological deformation of his judgement by the processes of ideologization, concepts to be explained in the next section of this chapter.

IDEOLOGY

Ideology was born when the apparent conflict between the epistemology of religion and the epistemology of science came to its climax at the end of the process of the secularization of society in the nineteenth century. Since that time modern men have tried to speak publicly in the language of one or another science, esoteric and rigid as this language always is; but this is not the language in which men speak to themselves, within themselves; and especially of men who until then used the language of faith. A vacuum was thus formed within man which his intellect could not fill. Science and reason could not fill the vacuum left by the many-sided attacks on the credibility of religion; the basic need for faith was thus exposed like a raw nerve. There were several reasons why science was unable to fill this vacuum. One is that scientific knowledge itself was always esoteric and has become increasingly so. It is *directly* intelligible only to an ever-shrinking number of minds, and it has become incomprehensible to the multitudes. Theology too was always incomprehensible to the multitudes. But whereas faith is beyond understanding, scientific and rational thinking can be communicated only through comprehension. Secondly, unlike religion, which by its very nature offers to men a cosmogonic explanation, science imparts only fragments of knowledge which it can prove. It declares that many mysteries, indeed the principal mystery of the life of man, may well elude its investigation; and in any event it is not bound to provide men with either certainties or consolation. And reason, whose essential function is to analyse critically the meaning of things, replaced the reassuring reflexes of faith by the corroding reflexes of doubt.

It was in this crisis that ideology was born, claiming that it could provide the method by which happiness could be ensured for all on earth. Each ideology offered a general promise, and by doing so, it enlarged the promissory mechanism of politics, transforming it into ideological politics. Ideologies also offered to the divided man a new understanding of life and man's role in it. Man would then find new faith in reason and reason for new faith.

But the 'reason' ideology actually offered and offers is a pseudo-reason

---

[19] See below, pp. 220 ff.

because since it is essentially promissory, it seeks to provide human beings with a substitute for faith; while ideological faith is a pseudo-faith because it is based not on the acceptance of mystery, but on theoretical pseudo-reasoning and on allegedly scientific evidence. Moreover, instead of making man search his soul, as faith does, ideology makes him submerge his consciousness in the consciousness of the collectivity, either of the present community or of the human species or, indeed, of human history as a whole. For ultimately, ideology is based on a distinct kind of philosophy, the ideological philosophy.

Benthamism and Marxism are the two great ideological philosophies which engendered the two great ideologies: Utilitarianism and Communism — as distinct from socialism (see below Chapters 6 and 7).

The incompatibilities between philosophy and ideological philosophy are numerous. Philosophy is submitted to the learned, ideological philosophy is beamed to the populace. Philosophy is demonstrative, ideological philosophy is persuasive. Philosophy is ironic, ideological philosophy vulgarizes. Philosophies might lead to the formation of schools of thought, ideological philosophy must lead to the formation of active organizations. Philosophy is detached, ideological philosophy is militant. Philosophy is interrogative, ideological philosophy is dogmatic. Philosophy demands to be critically read, ideological philosophy is prepared for mass-ingestion. Philosophy exists by itself, unlike ideological philosophy which can only exist when it is shared, when it undergoes ideologization.

'Ideologization', a not particularly elegant neologism but which expresses unmistakably the operation of spreading the slogans of an ideology as widely as possible, is actually more important than ideology itself. As I shall insist later, whereas ideologization can exist without an ideology, ideology cannot exist without ideologization. For the very process of ideologization so deforms and dilutes the original principles of the ideology that at the end those principles become in the minds of the converted something quite different from, and more often than not, opposed to what they were intended to be in their origins. As John Plamenatz[20] has so acutely perceived, 'ideology exists only when it is shared by a group of people'. Whereas authentic philosophies can exist without being shared by multitudes or indeed even by many individuals or groups, ideology exists only when it is shared among many. That *sharing* is the essence of ideologization — or the action whereby sets of slogans, explicitly derived from and attributed to a political philosophy, are injected into the minds of human beings with the double effect of (a) providing them with a *Weltanschauung* and a reason for pursuing the 'goal' of happiness, present or future, individual or collective and (b) making of that pursuit the main justification of their passage on earth, that is transporting their interior and spiritual selves on to the plane of

[20] John Plamenatz: *Ideology*, London 1976, p. 56.

exterior and more often than not materialistic (hedonistic or historical) achievements. Thus the materialistic verb is turned into materialistic action.

Because it needs to be shared by ever-increasing groups of people, philosophical ideology needs to go through the process of ideologization, that is the propagation of its precepts by all available media of communicaton, in order to become an ideology – a code of *action* (as distinct from a code of religious or ethical *behaviour*) used to guide individuals and multitudes who endeavour to achieve on earth the happiness which they have been promised.

Ideology cannot exist without ideologization, whereas ideologization can proceed even if it be progressively separated from the initial and authentic ideological philosophy or even indeed without any philosophy at all. The progress of ideologization does not depend so much on the content of the ideology as on the modern means of communication. The world-wide reduction in illiteracy and the ever-increasing world-wide volume of information, by means of printed material, but above all through television, radio and the transistorization of the world (transistors and television can be used by illiterates) create the optimum condition for ideologization.

In this sense it is significant that the first ideology, or rather what some people now restrospectively call the Jacobin ideology (see Ch. 4), was in reality an exercise in ideologization without a specific ideology behind it.

Historians who speak freely of the Jacobin 'ideology'[21] take the term in the broad sense of a set of popular beliefs injected into a historical culture by social, economic and political developments. But this, in some respects, is anachronistic, both in form and in substance. In form because the word 'ideology' was only invented in 1775 and then in a quite different context: as the science of ideas. It was never used by the French revolutionaries; it was made more popular by Napoleon who used it in a pejorative way: *'les idéologistes'*. And it is anachronistic in substance because ideologies, as we will argue later in this book, derived from the materialistic philosophy of Helvétius, whereas, to the extent that it derived from Rousseau and Rousseauism, the official and popular 'credo' of the French revolutionaries was idealistic, even if not fideistic, as illustrated by Robespierre's attempt to establish the cult of the 'Supreme Being'.

---

[21]Thus Albert Soboul: 'Jacobinism, which permeated both the theory and the practice of the revolutionary government, was characterized by an *ideology* deriving from Rousseau and by certain political attitudes and techniques'. (*A Short History of the French Revolution* 1789–1799, University of California 1965, p. 106). Or Marc Bouloiseau, 'L'idéologie Jacobine' an entire section of his book *La république Jacobine*, Paris 1972, pp. 38–40. F. Furet, however, prefers to speak of 'ideology and the militants who were its bearers', and attributes the entire phenomenon of politicization which then took place, to 'the formidable logic which reconstituted in a secular form the psychological certainty of religious beliefs': 'The French Revolution Revisited', *Government and Opposition,* Vol. 16, No. 2, Spring 1981, pp. 200–19.

If one therefore cannot speak of a Rousseauian Jacobin *ideology* – one can nevertheless confidently speak of a Jacobin system of ideologization.

The deformation of their ideological philosophies by means of ideologization was also the fate of Benthamism and Marxism, and was, in the exercise, one of the causes of the universal moral crisis, to be examined in this book. Bentham's 'pursuit of pleasure' *might* be invoked by the millionaires of the capitalist world in their insatiable quest for luxury and 'refinement', by the consumerist society as a whole and, last but not least, by the addicts of sex, pornography, and drugs in that society. And Marxism *is* invoked by brutal Stalinist regimes – in primarily agricultural countries, situated in other continents than industrial Europe or America, from the Russia of 1917 to the Cuba of today – and by terroristic gangs of desperadoes in Western Europe and America who no longer believe in the ineluctable revolutionarism of the 'working class' and therefore try to produce 'revolution' artificially through sheer terrorism.

THE AMBITION OF POLITICS

The ambition of the new, ideological politics was, in the intoxicating atmosphere of progress of industrial society, to promise political happiness to human beings.

It is true that promises of political happiness were made, directly or indirectly, in the verbal excesses of political rhetoric in all countries and in all epochs. Whenever in the history of European civilization political leaders have competed for the favour of the people, they have been lavish in their verbal promises of 'happiness' to their supporters, by patronage or other ways of sharing the spoils.

But this was entirely different from the explicit ambition of modern politics, as first presented in the French Revolution and then in the two major ideologies of the nineteenth century, to claim that the happiness of mankind depends on politics and on politics alone, and so to expand the ambit of politics in theory as well as in practice, and take possession of the realms of ethics, philosophy, and religion as well.

There is no doubt that such ambitions were nourished by hubristic political leaders and philosophers even before the advent of the autonomy of politics. But it is also significant that these kinds of hubristic ambitions have always been denounced by tragedy. From Aeschylus's *Oresteiea*, to Shakespeare's *Julius Caesar* and Schiller's *Don Carlos*, tragedy has warned politics not to allow its ambitions to lead it to overstep the bounds of the human condition. The most explicit warning was given by Shakespeare. 'But as he was ambitious I slew him', exclaims Brutus after he had forestalled Caesar's attempt to go beyond the limits of the laws.

But with the coming of the secular sentiment of 'freedom' of the existence of human beings and of the regulation of their co-existence, and with the optimistic trends of thought simultaneously fostered by the material progress engendered by the industrial revolution, new hopes were dangled by politics before human eyes. The result of these new expectations was that human happiness was equated with public happiness and later, in a rather syllogistic way, with political happiness: happiness is a public matter; all public matters are political; *ergo*, happiness is political.

But the question is: should people consider politics as an end to which they must dedicate, by all means available, their own self and upon which they ought to mould that same self? The question has been central to political philosophy from its very inception. The response of societies and individuals in Europe and later in America and in other parts of the world, falls, in a very simplified way, into two different periods. Again, if we simplify deliberately, in the first period which runs from the fourth century BC to the eighteenth century AD, the happiness of man was seen as a supremely private state; the public and political circumstances might contribute to its achievement, or, on the contrary, they might endanger it to the point of annihilation.[22] Hence, it was the duty of man, through his own participation in its regulation, to prefer and, if possible, create circumstances which were favourable to the self-realization of the individual. This was even more evident after Christianity proclaimed its faith in an immortal life after death, transcending the *Civitas Terrena* of the mortals.

During the period which, in political history, began with the English Revolution and continued with the American Revolution and with the most complete and explicit of all, the French Revolution — the answer to the question was turned upside down. Now — that is, in the spirit of the French Revolution — human beings had to serve their social environment through their dedication as 'citizens' to the public cause; only by their voluntary submersion in that society could they achieve happiness. The moment in history when that question was publicly asked is described either as the proclamation of the autonomy of politics, or the birth of modern politics or, in the terminology of this enquiry, the birth of the systems of political happiness. This assertion will be fully examined in Chapter 3.

The equation of happiness with politics presents another ambiguity which lies in the concept of *public* human happiness: does this imply that the 'public' factor provides the opportunity for individual human beings to achieve their own happiness, or does it imply that the 'public' factor dispenses uniform happiness uniformly, to be shared out by the

---

[22]'Les actes de quelques hommes ont pour des millions d'hommes des consé-quences comparables à celles qui resultent pour tous les vivants des perturbations et des variations de leur milieu... L'intelligence et la volonté affectant les masses en tant que causes physiques et aveugles — *ce qu'on nomme politique*'. (Italics in the text.) Paul Valéry: *Regards sur le monde actuel*, Paris 1945.

community among the individuals which comprise it, the sharing out being itself a condition of that happiness?

Hannah Arendt has exposed the contradiction in this ambiguity by pointing to the contrast between the meaning of public happiness as it was conceived in the American Revolution and as it was conceived in the French Revolution. She wrote:

> The men of the revolution were able to discover the sharpness of the distinction between the private and the public, between private interests and the common weal, only in the course of the revolutions during which the two principles came into conflict with each other. The conflict was the same in the American and the French Revolutions, though it assumed very different expressions. For the American Revolution it was a question of whether the new government was to constitute a realm of its own for the 'public happiness' of its citizens, or whether it had been devised to serve and insure their pursuit of private happiness more effectively than the old regime. For the French Revolution, it was a question of whether the end of revolutionary government lay in the establishment of a 'constitutional government' which would terminate the reign of public freedom through a guarantee of civil liberties and rights, or whether, for the sake of 'public freedom' the Revolution should be declared in permanence.[23]

What is implicit in Hannah Arendt's exposition but must be made explicit if the argument is to reach its full coherence, is the fact that the French revolutionaries had an absolute belief in the *autonomy of politics*, whereas the Americans had only a relative belief in that autonomy (and the English revolutionaries disbelieved in it completely). This fundamental difference arose because whereas the English and the American Revolutions took place within a Christian conception of social and political organization, the French Revolution was in its very essence anti-Christian. The affirmation of the absolute sovereignty of the will of the people was only made in the French Revolution; and it represents the claim to the outright autonomy of politics. If there is no other sovereign either on earth or in heaven, it follows that men can and must organize their *co-existence* according to a will which is general and which yet supersedes their individual wills, for it now enacts their rights to life and liberty. And if there are no eternal laws, mortals can make any laws they wish.

From this point of view, at least, it can be said that the French Revolution did mark, if only symbolically, the beginning of modern politics, of the autonomy of politics — or, in the terminology of this enquiry, of the conflict between the tragic sense of human life and the ambition of politics to provide political happiness to mankind.

When Napoleon, the dialectical heir of the French Revolution and of the Jacobins, told Goethe, at Erfurt in 1801, that 'had Julius Caesar

[23]Hannah Arendt: *On Revolutions*, London 1963, p. 130. See also Chapter 4 below.

been given more time he would have made mankind happy', he was expressing consciously the new ambitions of politics and subconsciously the tragic sense of politics. It was also during the same conversation that Napoleon exclaimed 'Nowadays politics is Tragedy'.

The supreme desire to transform the miserable human condition has given their absolute hubristic character to the two truly apocalyptic revolutions in history, 1789 and October 1917. These two revolutions were absolute not only because they expressed the grievances of peoples in revolt against oppressive regimes, but because they expressed even more profoundly the atavistic sense of Apocalypse: the sense that the power of the ruler who oppresses mankind is evil, and that once his rule is overthrown, the liberation of men from all the evils of the human condition will follow. Luigi Vallauri[24] went so far as to equate the pursuit of eschatological liberation with that of political liberation; he argued that while Resurrection is the religious category of radical transformation, Revolution is the political category of radical transformation. And one of Malraux's Spanish civil war heroes in *l'Espoir,* when asked to define the purpose of Communism, answers at first sight incongruously: 'Our modest function is to organize the Apocalypse'. With this short-cut Malraux alluded to the aim of professional revolutionaries to channel the apocalyptic longings of men in revolt towards the dour discipline of the 'organization' — a key concept in Leninist political philosophy.

Characteristic of the apocalyptic vision is the absolute contrast between total present evil and total future good, between the tribulations of today and the pure glory of tomorrow. In order to make the future look more luminous the present has to be painted even blacker than it is; in order to do full justice to the unhappiness of men living in the present the future must be portrayed as a bountiful provider of happiness. Ideological politics has never been able to shake off its apocalyptic origins.

[24] Luigi Lombardi Vallauri: 'Résurrection et révolution' in *Religion et Politique,* Aubier-Montaigne, Paris 1970, pp. 261–6.

Chapter 2

From the fall of the past to the ascent towards the future

Death is a far more poignant mystery than birth for the man who thinks about the human condition. A final and bitter reflection might lead him to conclude, like the chorus in Sophocles's *Oedipus at Colonna*, that 'nothing surpasses not being born', meaning that rather than go through all the phases of a death sentence, culminating in one's execution, it would be better to be spared it all. Yet, while man cannot know that it is better not to be born before he is born, he will soon know, once he is born, that he will die. Hence his obsession with what seems such an unjustified finality, in which life is given only to be taken away, a being is constructed only to be destroyed. This is the principal obsession of all humans ever since their spirituality was first aroused, and indeed modern biology confirms that human consciousness was only awakened by awareness of the fact of death.[1]

The thought of mortality and the resulting sense of insecurity **have** always overshadowed the activities of the human mind. They have **origin**ated in the immemorial myths of a separation from the cosmos, of the abandonment of mankind by the Gods, of the expulsion from the Garden of Eden. An inborn nostalgia for a pre-history, when men had no history precisely because there was no death, or time, which is the agent of death, is the mainspring of this sentiment of mortality.

Although all historical epochs and all cultures in five continents have shared this nostalgia, the degree of poignancy with which people have reacted to intimations of mortality has varied according to the time and

---

[1] In their enquiry on *The Self and its Brain*, (Springer International 1980), Karl R. Popper and John C. Eccles refer, for their 'argument for interactionism', to the theory of the American biologist Theodosius Dobzhanski, who interprets the appearance of ceremonial burial customs as 'the first clear indication that this primitive (Neanderthal) man had now developed some spirituality' (p. 404). Commenting separately on this scientific theory, Karl Popper writes: 'I agree with Dobzhanski who wrote: I am not only alive but aware of being alive. Moreover I know that I shall not remain alive forever, that death is inevitable. . . I possess the attributes of self-awareness and death-awareness' (p. 101); while John C. Eccles writes: 'When the first self-awareness came to mankind it was linked with death-awareness' (p. 158).

the place.[2] The distinctiveness of European culture lies in its particular sensitivity to human fate. But within the history of European culture — which understandably in this political enquiry begins with the Greeks — the Greek and Roman polytheistic cultures not only differed in their attitudes to death from the monotheistic Judaic and Christian cultures, but also from each other, just as Judaism and Christianity were eventually to differ.

The Greeks and the Romans accepted mortality as a fact-of-the-Gods, perhaps even as a caprice-of-the-Gods from which they had no hope of redress, possibly because, as Nietzsche surmised, they had no belief, or, rather, as H.F.D. Kitto has more disturbingly maintained, because they did not even have a word for 'God', as we mean it. For *Theos* has a wider and, as it were, more pantheistic meaning than God. But the great difference remained that between the immortals and the mortals some lesser or even demi-Gods might help mortals to improve the quality of life on earth, or indeed to *survive*, but would not assist them to return to the Olympus of the immortals. And moreover Prometheus would be punished for his complicity with men. Plato argued that the soul can survive, thus stating the duality body—soul. But in order to do so, the mortal must meditate upon his soul, while it still inhabits the body. Therefore he must not immerse himself too much in the active life and he must cultivate the virtues. Even the more practical Aristotle, concerned as he was with man as a political animal, still regarded the virtuous, contemplative life as the best.

Both Plato and Aristotle believed that courage, or fortitude, was a most necessary human virtue, and that it should be fostered by education so that in future men could be better prepared to live and to live in common. Fortitude helped the Romans, who like Aristotle were more practical, to extend their conquests throughout the world and to establish laws and institutions so solid that they would serve humanity after the Roman Empire had passed away. Although glory on earth ranked high in their ambitions, they too envisaged death resolutely and in consequence practised suicide with equanimity.

The monotheistic relationship with, or belief in, one single God, of the Jewish people, introduced a direct element of hope. The Jews believed that their God, whom they must not offend by ignoring or rejecting his commandments, would guide them through their march in history. Christian monotheism offered the hope of vanquishing death through the death and resurrection of Jesus Christ to all men of all peoples, or at least to those men who passed through the valley of tears preparing themselves by faith in Christ and the observance of Christian virtues for the life after

---

[2]Frank Borkenau once divided civilizations into 'death denying', 'death defying', 'death accepting', and 'death transcending'. Quoted in J. MacManners: *Death and the Enlightenment, Changing Attitudes to Death among Christians and Unbelievers in Eighteenth-Century France*, Oxford 1981, p. 2.

death. Yet, in a paradoxical sense, the fact that hope and consolation were available only after death made human life on earth seem even more tragic. Indeed it seemed so tragic that the less the Christian regarded his life, and the more he concentrated on the salvation of his soul in the after life, the easier was his passage through life. This is why, coming back to politics, the Christian was advised to render unto Caesar that which is Caesar's and unto God that which is God's. But what social theologies now forget is that the balance in the Christian context was necessarily tilted in favour of God. Pascal was most adamant on the danger of being 'diverted' from the concentration upon one's death by the *divertissements* of life, of which the ambitions of politics were among the most tempting. 'The only thing which consoles us for our miseries is diversion, and yet this is the greatest of our miseries. Diversion amuses us and leads us unconsciously to death' wrote Pascal in *Pensées* (No. 71).

The climate of religious belief began to break up with the Renaissance and the advance of scientific knowledge. Knowledge punishes. It was when Adam ate of the tree of the knowledge of good and evil that he was expelled from the Garden of Eden (as Oedipus had been punished for trying to acquire the knowledge of the sphinx). The second fall of man, in the Renaissance, also came about through the attempt to scale the heavens in pursuit of knowledge. The old sense of mortality, combined with the new confidence in science and material progress, the signs of which soon became apparent, led to a resigned concentration on the means and ends of human co-existence in godless solitude on earth.

This led also to a re-evaluation and rediscovery of 'politics', the very name of which had not been used by the kings, emperors and popes of the Middle Ages, and had been virtually banned. It is from the fifteenth century onwards, between Machiavelli and Hobbes, that the primacy of politics came to be seen as a consequence of the weakening of religious faith which until then had held society together. The corruption of the Church, the Reformation and the counter-Reformation, the religious wars, all contributed to undermine the previous dominance of the religious outlook on life. If religion led to civil and international war and to social disorder, then the pursuit of order must fall upon politics. We shall see later why and how philosophical materialism was added to this political reasoning.

The continuing progress of scientific knowledge encouraged confidence in the powers of human reason. The greater wealth provided by industry and commerce allowed the upper strata and the 'bourgeoisie' − burgesses, Bürgen, bourgeois − who in urban surroundings were among the first to feel the benefits of the improvement in material conditions of life, to aspire to something vaguely called happiness, *le bonheur, felicità*. Much of European thought in the second half of the eighteenth century was dedicated to finding ways in which men could be provided with prescriptions for individual happiness within the framework of human society and of the Christian virtues on which that society had been founded for eighteen centuries. But the idea of making happiness dependent on politics was still far from being conceived.

From the next chapter onwards we shall try to retrace the triumphal penetration of this idea, first expressed at the end of the eighteenth century, into the accepted public mentality of the twentieth century. But before doing so, we must consider four other prototypical attitudes to happiness which, although very different from each other, have in common the absence of the Christian belief in the possibility of happiness in after-life, as well as of the ideological belief in politically induced happiness. What they also have in common is a certain degree of awareness of the tragic sense of life.

These four attitudes are:

1. The absolute tragic sense of life and its political postulates.
2. The tragic sense of human necessity and the political conclusions to be drawn from it.
3. The eudaemonistic pursuit of happiness against a still tragic background.
4. The prospect of a public happiness requiring the immolation of the tragic sense of life of the individual.

UNAMUNO AND THE TRAGIC SENSE OF LIFE

The list of competitors for the best description of the tragic sense of life in the history of literature is formidable, since it comprises at least the Greek tragedians, Plato, St Paul, Spinoza, Pascal, Sénancour, Kierkegaard and among moderns Heidegger, Sartre, Camus and Beckett. Yet with an obvious disregard for chronology, in my fallible opinion, the most personal, indeed obsessional, description of the tragic sense of life at its starkest is to be found in the work of Miguel de Unamuno.[3]

[3] A second reason for the choice of Unamuno is that in the history of existentialism he has been unjustly neglected, when one considers his originality, both in the sense that he is uniquely authentic and that he is at the origin of modern, post-Kierkegaardian, existentialism. Some of the reasons why he has been persecuted will be found in the following pages. But for the reader who, partly because of that persecution, does not know much about him, here is a short bio-bibliographic description. Born 1864, d. 1936, Unamuno became professor of Greek (1891) and of Comparative Philology (1900) in the University of Salamanca and Rector in 1901. He became one of the best-known writers of the 'generation of 1898', the group which turned a critical eye on Spain after its defeat in the war with the United States in 1898, leading to the loss of the remnants of Spain's colonial empire. Never at ease either with the constitutional monarchy or with the dictatorship of Primo de Rivera, Unamuno was banished to the Canary Islands in 1924, and subsequently spent six years in exile in France. After his return to Spain in 1930 he was re-appointed Rector of the University of Salamanca. Briefly a deputy in the Spanish Cortes, he was increasingly alienated by the Republic and at first welcomed the rising of General

Miguel de Unamuno was a poet, philosopher, novelist, dramatist and journalist but, except perhaps for his journalism, all his work was linked indirectly with the theme of the tragic sense of life, which is dealt with directly in the work of that name, *The Tragic Sense of Life among Men and Peoples*, and in *The Agony of Christianity* (two long philosophical essays); in 'The Christ of Velazquez' (a poem); and *Mi religión*, which are examined here for that reason.

The central idea which Unamuno expounds in these writings reflects the deep contradiction within himself, which tore the fabric of his genius apart, namely the irreconcilability within each individual of his faith in God with his revolt against the human condition, or death.

The tragic sense of life is the *memento mori*, the reminder of mortality and of how ephemeral is man's existence. As such it is *the* fundamental thought or sentiment. It is at the origin of all religions and philosophies. Individual men, peoples and nations, indeed whole *Zeitgeists* may have concentrated to differing degrees upon this primordial thought. This can be explained by the extent of the consolation, or of the 'distraction' which some faiths and some systems of thought offer to their followers.

The Christian religion offered, once and forever, the sublime answer to man's question to God: 'Why did you make me mortal?', when God sent his only Son to share in the death of man, who, because of His sacrifice, could now share in His Resurrection. But this answer is available only to those who keep their faith in Jesus Christ. Even for Christian pessimists like Pascal and Kierkegaard, faith was their salvation.

But just as existentialism is probably the most acute and cogent expression of the tragic sense of life in the history of philosophy, so Unamuno is its most acute, poignant and cogent exponent within the corpus of existentialism. Because of the time in which he lived, and because of his conflict with the Roman Catholic Church, Unamuno's battle with his faith is more dramatic than that of either Pascal or Kierkegaard. Whereas Pascal finds consolation in his faith, Unamuno who had held faith as the supreme inspiration of all his work finds nevertheless that faith is vulnerable to corroding doubts. Unamuno's work has also an

---

(Footnote continued)

Franco. But he very soon saw through it and his criticisms led to his removal from the rectorship and confinement under house arrest in Salamanca, where he died on 31 December 1936. Among his most important works are the essays: *Vida de Don Quijote y Sancho*, Madrid (unless otherwise stated), 1905; *Mi religión y otros ensayos*, 1910; *Del sentimiento trágico de la vida en los hombres y los pueblos*, 1913; *La agonía del cristianismo*, Paris, 1925; Poetry: *Rosario de sonetos líricos*, 1911; *El Cristo de Velázquez*, 1920; novels: *Niebla*, 1914; *La tía Tula*, 1921; *San Manuel Bueno, mártir y tres historias más*, 1933; theatre: *Fedra*, 1921; *Medea*, 1933; *El hermano Juan o el mundo es teatro*, 1934; *Teatro (Fedra, Soledad, Raquel Encadenada, Medea)* Barcelona, 1954.

On Unamuno see also Martin Nozick: *The Agony of Belief*, Princeton 1982, which reached me when most of this book was written, but proved particularly useful.

essentially poetic character, which brings it closer than that of any of the other masters of existentialism to the sublime expression of the tragic sense of life, which *is* poetry, or as Heidegger once said, more *Dichtung* than *Denken*.

Unamuno's philosophy starts where his faith can take him no further. The fundamental contradiction in this mind 'of strife and contradiction' lay in his religious beliefs. Unamuno thought and affirmed that he had reconciled these supreme contradictions in his two major books, *The Agony of Christianity* and *The Tragic Sense of Life*. But the Catholic Church, twenty years after his death, thought that he had not. Unamuno's description of his own personal religion is moving in its sincerity. 'And so' he writes, in his book *Mi religión*,[4] ' "What is my religion?" I shall answer: My religion is to seek truth in life and life in truth. My religion is to struggle with God, from dawn to dusk, as, it is said, He struggled with Jacob.' For in the background of his faith there had already set in, perhaps indeed it was always there, *the* doubt: 'I assert and believe as poet, as creator [but] deny, disbelieve as a man, as a Christian.'[5]

His disbelief was caused by his revolt against death, a revolt which could not be appeased even by the Christian promise of salvation. 'I dread the idea of having to tear myself away from everything sensible and material, from all substance.'[6] His favourite quotation comes from Sénancour's *Obermann*, 'L'homme est périssable. Il se peut; mais périssons en résistant et si le néant nous est réservé, ne faisons pas que ce soit une justice.'[7] He finds in that reflection the essence of his doubt: 'my own self *might* have to be destroyed for ever'; but he also finds his natural reaction to this doubt: 'but in that case I shall fight against this injustice; I shall perish fighting against it, resisting it.' Unamuno expresses this thought with even greater lucidity when he says that 'The remedy is to consider our mortal destiny without flinching, to fasten our gaze upon the gaze of the Sphinx, for it is thus that the malevolence of its spell is discharged.'[8] This, interwoven with the principle of suffering, as the external reaction of the spirit against matter, generates the major theme in Unamuno's philosophy, which I describe as the *Agony*, the word being taken in its current sense, but also in the Greek sense of the word *Agon*, a struggle or contest. Yet such a fight against destiny does not conform with Catholic faith.

J.L. Aranguren has suggested that Unamuno's thought came very near to Protestantism. But, although the young Unamuno was interested in Luther and Calvin and of course in Kierkegaard, he denied this, at least formally: 'The Puritan sentiment' he says, is 'the preoccupation with sin

[4]Miguel de Unamuno: *Mi religión*, Espasa Calpe, p. 10. (My translation.)
[5]Miguel de Unamuno: *La agonía del cristianismo*, Espasa Calpe, p. 23. (My translation.)
[6]*The Tragic Sense*, pp. 52–53.
[7]Ibid., pp. 59, 255 (as motto to the chapter 'The practical problem'.
[8]Ibid., p. 58.

and predestination.'[9] Indeed, even for Protestant existentialists, from Kierkegaard to Paul Tillich, the forgiveness of sins constitutes the ultimate principle. Starting from a premise almost identical with that of Unamuno on the tragedy of death, Tillich warns: 'Do not deceive yourself about the seriousness of death — not death in general, not the death of somebody else, but your own death — by nice arguments for the immortality of the soul.' But he then continues: 'The Christian message is more realistic than these arguments. It knows that we, really we, have to die; it is not just a part of us that has to die. And within Christianity there is only one argument against death: the forgiveness of sins.'[10] But, as if he had heard Tillich's argument, Unamuno gives an almost brutal reply when he exclaims: 'What is important for man is not to die, whether he sins or not.'

Behind Unamuno's internal struggle lies not a struggle between two religious faiths but the supreme conflict between religious faith and human revolt. Unamuno's mind is a battlefield where this perennial conflict fought one of its most formidable contests — and in the history of existentialism it is, as I have already intimated, the equinoctial point where the tortured faith of a Pascal and a Kierkegaard turns towards the sombre atheism of Heidegger and Sartre.

The modern schools of existentialism are, in many respects, born out of the epistemological crisis of the very beginning of the twentieth century when science, or at least physics and biology, admitted that scientific investigation would never penetrate the mystery of the life and, especially of the death, of the human being. Hence Heidegger's and Sartre's total and militant atheism (and hence their unholy and uneasy alliance with the two contemporary atheistic political systems: Nazism in the case of Heidegger, Communism in the case of Sartre, and hence also Gabriel Marcel's admirable but difficult attempt to build up a Christian existentialism).

But whereas Pascal was writing at the very dawn of the scientific revolution, and was himself a great mathematician, and Kierkegaard was writing at a high point in the history of the idea of progress, and therefore fought especially against the complacent, arch-confident, neutrality of 'bourgeois—Philistine' society, Unamuno was already caught up in the turmoil of the crisis of knowledge and consciousness which broke out at the end of the nineteenth century and the dawn of the twentieth century. Martin Nozick is right to visualize him as the immediate successor of Nietzsche and Dostoevsky. 'With Nietzsche' writes Nozick, Unamuno 'suggests a new level of heroism that incorporates despair and yet surpasses it.'[11] But whereas Nietzsche had in view the heroism of the pre-Socratic, and pre-Christian thinkers and tragedians, Unamuno's agony is that of a man who clings to his faith in spite of its inability to console him. Like the

[9]*The Tragic Sense*, p. 59.
[10]Paul Tillich: *The Shaking of the Foundations*, London 1962, p. 179.
[11]Martin Nozick: *The Agony of Belief*, Princeton 1982, p. 203.

Greek tragic heroism, he knows the tragic fate of mortals. But he knows it after having experienced the Christian faith.

Having been flung by history in the twilight of the hope of human progress and of materialistic and 'scientific optimism,' Unamuno still addressed himself to God and to his beloved Jesus, and mocking the progressist atheists and the confident scientists it was still to God that he addressed his cry of despair against death, his own death. The fate of his work is also more dramatic than that of Pascal's, because later and almost surreptitiously, long after his death, the Roman Catholic Church placed three of his most important books on the Index: *The Tragic Sense of Life, The Agony of Christianity* and the novel *San Manuel Bueno, Martyr.*

While logically, and presumably even more so theologically, one can understand the reasons why the Roman Catholic Church condemned these three books, it is less easy to understand two circumstances in which that decision was taken: why so late, that is twenty-one years after the author's death and forty-four years after the publication of the first of the three banned books? And why only those three out of a corpus of some hundred titles, many of which are as controversial as these three? Was this second circumstance a recognition that Unamuno's spirit was caught in such a conflict with itself that it could produce in the Church's opinion works of dangerous influence — but at the same time also works of divine inspiration, as, for instance, the long poem on *The Christ of Velazquez* (1920) 'considered as the most important religious poem written in Spanish since the Golden Age'[12] with its deeply felt prayer:

> You are the first-born of the dead
> You are the fruit, death-ripened,
> of the Tree of Life, which never dies
> from which we have to eat if we should wish
> to be set free from yet a second death.
> For you have made of death, which is an end,
> the principle and sovereign of life —
> White death wrapped in a black cloak
> Astride a yellow horse;
> Death, Empress of History
> whose scythe cuts down all men and
> moulds them with a conqueror's avidity.
> Man is the son of God and God the son of man.
> Thou Christ, with thy death gave to the universe
> human finality.   (My translation)

But the answer to the question of how a man who 'denied' faith could write this fervent poem of pure Christian love — written and published seven years after *The Tragic Sense of Life* — and which the Roman

---

[12]Nozick: op. cit., p. 178.

Catholic Church could only at great cost to itself eliminate from modern Christian poetry and philosophy, brings us back to the examination of Unamuno's perpetual and fundamental dilemma, between his adoration of Jesus and his revolt against the human condition. This original duality arguably divided everything else around and in him, and made him see the positive and the negative as interchangeable. Yet while this might be true as regards his wordly interests, it is untrue as regards his ultimate 'confidence in God' as Julian Marías rightly describes it. For there is in the background of Unamuno that ultimate option for faith, that *fidelidad*, that *fundamento* which transcends his philosophy, including the political philosophy which can be reconstituted from it.

Unamuno is sometimes described as a precursor of the modern sense of revolt. This description is false, when one compares the dull, materialistic and destructive negativism which derives today — that is, after Camus — from the sense of the absurd, with the noble, spiritual and constructive consequences Unamuno draws from the tragic sense of life. Four concepts of Unamuno's philosophy have a direct relevance for political philosophy. They are the concept of *agony* or the urge to action and to creativity; the concept of *happiness through suffering*; the concept of the *fraternity of man through death*; and the concept of *transpolitics*.

AGONY

This is the word which best expresses both as the pangs of death and as a struggle or contest, Sénancour's philosophy of *périr en résistant*. The agonist's life is a long fight against death through creativity and suffering. This is why it is wrong to interpret Unamuno's tragic sense of life as 'a hysterical lament that man is not immortal'. Far from being a 'hysterical lament' — as Sidney Hook[13] thinks — *The Tragic Sense of Life* is a resolute call to action. Sloth, in all its guises is the worst danger for man. Indeed it is the materialistic danger.

> The origin of evil, as many discovered of old, is nothing other than what is called by another name the inertia of matter, as applied to the things of the spirit — sloth. And not without truth has it been said that sloth is the mother of all vices, not forgetting that the supreme sloth is that of not longing madly for immortality. Consciousness, the craving for more, more and always more, hunger of eternity and thirst of infinity, appetite for God — these are never satisfied. Each consciousness

[13]This sentence is one of the few which makes direct reference to Unamuno's tragic sense of life in Professor Sidney Hook's *Pragmatism and the Tragic Sense of Life* (New York 1968). In spite of its title this collection of essays amounts to a pedestrian defence of the American philosophical school of pragmatism, which could be made without ill-treating Unamuno in the process. It ridicules Unamuno's 'tragic sense of life' in the early pages and Unamuno has only two entries in the bibliographical index.

seeks to be itself and to be all other consciousness, without ceasing to be itself: it seeks to be God. And matter, unconsciousness, tends to be less and less, and tends to be nothing, its thirst being a thirst for repose. Spirit says: 'I wish to be! and matter answers: I wish not to be!'[14]

This long passage is one of the clearest formulations of Unamuno's agonistic philosophy. Everything that distracts us from our urge to *be* ourselves, which means both to know ourselves and to act according to ourselves, is sloth, is the desire to rest or to forget. The sole object of Unamuno's teaching is, on the contrary, to awaken the spirit, to cudgel the brain in order to make the self know itself, and once it has forced itself to struggle, to extricate itself from the surrounding torpor leading to death. Herein lies the original unmistakable difference between the philosophies of matter and those of the spirit. For all materialistic philosophies, hedonistic or 'historic', try to teach man to forget his spirit either by drowning it in the glut of sensual pleasure, or in the mythical absorption in collective or historical dedications. In contrast all philosophies of the spirit teach man that suffering is a condition of his self-realization.

The achievement of the self or self-realization does not need to be glorious. The glory resides in the perfection pursued and achieved by a man who simply creates anything, whatever it may be. Unamuno's favourite example of the glory of creativity regardless of the humble status of the creator is the one often quoted of the shoemaker. He compares the shoemaker who makes shoes with just enough care and attention to keep his clientele, with the shoemaker who looks after his customers' footwear so well that they will feel a definite loss when he dies — when he is 'dead to them', not merely 'dead' — and they feel that he ought not to have died: 'he shod them for the love of them and for the love of God in them'.

Unamuno's emphasis on the achievement of the self through perfection[15] comprises two distinct themes: the first is the 'hunger for

---

[14] *Tragic Sense*, p. 211.

[15] In a strangely topical passage of *The Tragic Sense of Life* Unamuno expresses his concern with the professionalization of work in common. 'Working men group themselves in associations, they form co-operative societies, and unions for defence, they fight justly and nobly for the betterment of their class, but it is not clear that these associations have any great influence on their moral attitudes towards their work'. The whole passage, written in the first decade of the twentieth century, shows an almost prophetic foreknowledge of the problems of industrial relations in the last few decades of the twentieth century. It should also, however, be read, in its depth, as a forewarning against the consequences necessarily following on the corporate and collective way of life. Unamuno's discourse is addressed to man himself, to man now submerged in 'units' or 'groups' of production, and systematized into the daily routine. He was fully aware of the monotony of industrial labour which he contrasts unfavourably with the work of the labourer in the field 'who has a clearer conscience of the social value of his work'. Boredom is the danger against which Unamuno raises his voice, because the man who is bored rapidly falls prey to sloth and dissolution in material discontent. Yet it is only recently that modern industry has recognized that boredom with mechanical, monotonous, anonymous work is a major cause of 'alienation' of the workers in factories and assembly lines.

immortality' which manifests itself through the pursuit of perpetuity in love for others; the second is the suffering entailed by creation and for the love of God.

The pursuit of self-achievement at the basic level of the creative work of society is not the same, for Unamuno, as the 'hunger for immortality' of those who want to inscribe their name on the records of history, through the fame of their deeds or of their works. He clearly acknowledges despair as the impulse towards this kind of pursuit of immortality. 'I believe' he says, 'that many of the greatest heroes, perhaps the greatest of all, have been men of despair and that by despair they have accomplished their mighty works'.

HAPPINESS THROUGH SUFFERING

Suffering is an essentially Christian value. Given that at the end of his life the greatest pain will be suffered by mortal man in the hope of thereby achieving eternal happiness, the Christian not only accustoms himself to the idea of suffering and especially to the suffering inherent in all forms of labour, but also sees happiness as the dialectic reward of suffering. In the human condition happiness cannot be obtained without preliminary suffering. Thus T.S. Eliot's credal-like verse:

> Pain is the opposite of joy
> But joy is a kind of pain
> I believe the moment of birth
> Is when we have acknowledged Death
> I believe the season of birth
> Is the season of sacrifice.[16]

The idea of suffering derives directly from that of the liberation of the spirit, or of the consciousness, through work, and leads directly to that of Jesus's supreme sacrifice. So, at one end, 'Suffering is a spiritual thing' says Unamuno, 'It is the most immediate revelation of consciousness. . . A man who had never known suffering whether in greater or lesser degree would scarcely possess consciousness of himself. . . Spirit finds itself limited by the matter in which it has to live and acquire consciousness of itself. . . Suffering is simply the obstacle which matter opposes to spirit.'[17] But, at the other end, this abstract statement is related directly to the incarnate sacrifice of God. God is revealed to us because he suffers with and for us. 'This was the scandal of Christianity among Jews and Greeks, among the Pharisees and Stoics. . . the scandal of a God who becomes man in order that he may suffer and die and rise again.'[18]

Avoidance of pain is a widespread urge among people in modern

[16]T.S. Eliot: 'The Family Reunion' in *Collected Plays*, London 1962, p. 82.
[17]*The Tragic Sense*, p. 209.
[18]Ibid., p. 203.

industrial society. It runs from avoidance of pain in the form of refusal to consider the existential problems of the human condition itself, to avoidance of the pain required by efforts to work and to create. This is where Unamuno's tragic philosophy differs so profoundly from Sartre's existentialism. The 'freedom of choice' degenerates into Sartre's political 'commitment', on the one hand, and hedonistic promiscuity on the other. He wrote:

> The existentialist on the contrary is annoyed by the fact that God does not exist, because with him there disappear also all possibilities of finding values in an intelligible heaven; there can no longer be an *a priori* good because there is no longer a perfect conscience which would conceive it; nowhere is it written nowadays that the good exists, that one must be honest, that one should not lie, precisely because we are now on a plane where there are only men. Dostoevsky has written that 'if God did not exist everything would be permitted'. This is the starting point of existentialism.[19]

But Unamuno's starting point is just the opposite. He starts from the identification of men, of every man, with the God who was made man so as to suffer with all men, and with the duties which derive from this identification.

FRATERNITY OF MORTALS

'With all men' — it is in the new sense that he gives to fraternity that Unamuno's voice joins in so vibrantly with those of Tolstoy, Dostoevsky, and in our own day Malraux and Herbert Butterfield in what is the principal social consequence of the tragic sense of life. Inspired by it Tolstoy spelled out in French in *War and Peace*, the maxim of this fraternity: *'Après tout on est tous des hommes'* — when he described one of Napoleon's soldiers who had saved the life of a Russian in the streets of Moscow, which the French were looting. This overwhelming sense of the ultimate tragic fraternity of men is one of the superb characteristics of Russian culture, and it probably predisposed Russians towards idealistic collectivism and the sense of human solidarity. For it is on the same theme, and with the same inspiration that Dostoevsky — and Pasternak and Solzhenitsyn also — wrote most movingly. Here is one example from the *Brothers Karamazov*:

> For every hour and every moment thousands of men leave life on this earth and their souls appear before God. And how many of them depart in solitude, unknown, sad, dejected, that no one mourns for them or even knows whether they have lived or not. And, behold, from the other end of the earth perhaps your prayer for their rest will rise up to God though you knew them not nor they you.

[19]Jean-Paul Sartre: *L'existentialisme est un humanisme*, Paris 1946, pp. 35–36. (My translation.)

During the French Revolution, the Jacobins (see Ch. 4) had called themselves, in their last and most triumphant phase, 'Society of the Friends of Liberty and Equality', deliberately forgetting in their political sagacity the embarrassing third term of the revolutionary triplet: *Liberté, Egalité, Fraternité*. This was inevitable for an anti-Christian revolution. Fraternity too has a Christian connotation, ever since the time of the early Christian martyrs.[20] Greek political philosophy, although motivated by the tragic sense of the fate of man, did not generate the sense of human pity (*pietas*) for the human community as a whole (hence, perhaps its indifference to slavery). The Greeks sublimated the tragic sense of life in the individual, the wise man or the hero. But fraternity embraces all men in all their sorrows, because of their common unhappiness. Men are brothers — and therefore ontologically equal, and ontologically unfree — because they are all bound by the same tragic condition, the same ultimate fate in which all have to share. Hence the major principle of Christian social philosophy 'Thou shalt love thy neighbour as thyself', which extended afterwards into Socialism, into Communism, and into all the variations on other sub-themes. But gradually Socialism and especially Communism separated the principle from its tragic sense, and made of it a worldly, social and revolutionary goal. When thus confused with equality, and separated from its essential tragic sense, fraternity becomes meaningless.

Unamuno's *Tragic Sense of Life* develops the theme of the fraternity of mortals as the basic political conclusion of his work. The premises of his reasoning are stated in two most poignant passages:

> So far as I am concerned I will never willingly yield myself nor entrust my confidence, to any popular leader who is not penetrated with the feeling that he who orders a people orders men, men of flesh and bone, men who are born, suffer and, although they do not wish to die, die; men who are ends in themselves, not merely means; men who must be themselves and not other men, men, in fine, who seek that which we call happiness. It is inhuman, for example to sacrifice one generation of men to the generation which follows, without having any feeling for the destiny of those who are sacrificed, without having any regard, not for their memory, nor for their names, but for themselves.[21]

And in the second passage, he said: 'To love in spirit is to pity and he who pities most loves most. . . A miserere sung in common by a multitude tormented by destiny has as much value as a philosophy.'[22]

Unamuno's interpretation of the commandment on which the organization of society in the Christian philosophy is based, 'Love thy neighbour as thyself', is one of the few in which the entire text is essential to its real meaning. The current collectivistic doctrines and mentality usually lead

---

[20]See also G. Ionescu: 'Reading notes spring 1981' in *Government and Opposition*, Vol. 16, No. 3, Summer 1981.

[21]*Tragic Sense*, p. 34.

[22]Ibid., p. 36.

to the exclusion of the second part, and only the first half of the commandment, 'Love thy neighbour', is repeated by the masses. But Unamuno rightly insists that 'the love or pity for yourself, this intense despair, will lead you to pity, that is to love — all your fellows and brothers in this world, these unhappy shadows who pass from nothing to nothingness. These sparks of consciousness which shine for a moment in the infinite and eternal darkness.' Only if you concentrate on you and on your significance in life, only if you fully comprehend your unhappiness, only then will your instinctive antipathy towards, and jealousy of your peer change into pity — the pity you feel for yourself *qua* man, and therefore for all other men.

This is why the views on life, and on other men, that one obtains from any partial particular perspective (whether social or ethnic, or from the interest, class or national, viewpoint) merely stimulate divisive feelings in the individual. Only when a great humility towards himself as a mortal man, as an ephemeral existence, permeates the conscience of the individual can it be moved by the misery and the humility of all other men. And it is only then especially that the added miseries of inequality and above all poverty, the material misery of other men, become unbearable for the conscience of others. To think first of other human beings in economic, social or political terms is to empty them of their substance and in that sense it runs counter to the essence of the true sentiment of fraternity. Moreover, as Pascal had forewarned, causes can become 'diversions'. Some human beings use causes without knowing it to distract themselves from their own individual agony which they do not want to face. The escapist motivation of such 'causes' varies in proportion with the geographic distance which separates the 'participant' from the events in which he would like to intervene, and with their topicality. Herbert Butterfield has issued a warning against such diversions. He wrote in *History and Human Relations*:

> Nothing is more remarkable — to take only one example, than the way in which the precept 'Love thy neighbour' can be carried to its actual inversion through the intervention of a few abstract nouns. And so loose is our common use of words that some men cannot imagine that they have made any difference when they have transformed the precept into something like 'Work for society' or 'Serve the state'. A dangerous conjuring trick is liable to be involved if we even turn 'Love your neighbour' into 'Love mankind'; for it is easy to love the collective noun rather than people, or to reserve one's compassion for strangers at the other end of the world. And some only have charity for the generations to be born in the future; and, once again, it is just the real live human beings, close at hand, who are so apt to be overlooked.[23]

The feeling of tragic fraternity among mortals which is one of the hallmarks of Unamuno's thinking has been expressed as forcefully

[23]Herbert Butterfield: *History and Human Relations*, London 1951, p. 45.

afterwards only by Malraux,[24] notably during his 'communist' period. Their similar attitude towards the fraternity of mortals is in fact the consequence of their similar attitude towards death — the one enemy which both of them explicitly tried to defeat.

This similarity seems almost incredible considering that everything, in their ideological make-up, should have separated the foremost modern Spanish heretical Catholic thinker from the foremost modern French heretical communist thinker. They had been *physically* in opposite camps in the Spanish civil war for the brief period from 20 July 1936, when Malraux entered Spain as a pilot in the Spanish Republican air force, until 1 October 1936 when Unamuno rejoined, until his death four months later, the opposition to Franco. Unamuno most probably did not know of the unexpected presence of this most unlikely disciple of his on the soil of his Spain. Nor is there, to my knowledge, any evidence that Unamuno knew of Malraux or of his work. But Malraux in Chapter XII of *L'Espoir*, [25] his novel on the civil war in Spain, deliberately described Unamuno's end in Franquist territory as symbolic of the tragedy of Spain, and added that 'Fate had prepared Unamuno's funeral as he dreamt it all his life'.

Malraux's philosophy starts like Unamuno's from the revolt against the essential *Human Condition* (the title of his novel on the civil war in China). For the sake of brevity compare only these sentences from both authors: (a) on the anguish of death: 'the eternal anguish, the source of the tragic sense of life, which seeks a habitation in the depths of the eternal and there awakens consolation' (Unamuno, *Tragic Sense*, p. 204); 'Le fond de l'homme est angoisse, la conscience de sa propre fatalité, d'òu naissent toutes les peurs, même celle de l'angoisse' (Malraux, *Condition Humaine*, p. 180); (b) on the supremacy of suffering: 'Suffering is the substance of life and the root of personality, for it is only suffering that makes us persons. And suffering is universal, suffering is that which unites all us living beings together' (Unamuno, ibid.); 'Tous souffrent et chacun souffre parce qui'il pense. Tout au fond, l'esprit ne pense l'homme que dans l'éternel, et la conscience de la vie ne peut être qu'angoisse' (Malraux, ibid., p. 400); and (c) on the ultimate fraternity and love of men: 'For men love one another with a spiritual love only when they have suffered the same sorrows together, when through long days they have ploughed the stony ground beneath the common yoke of a common grief' (Unamuno, ibid., p. 142). 'De sentir qu'ils étaient unis non dans leurs personnes, mais dans leur passion commune l'émouvait d'avantage comme si chacun de leurs pas l'eût rapproché d'une austère et puissante amitié éparse sur la terre' (Malraux, *Temps du mépris*, p. 129), and 'Ils avaient en commun cette communion souterraine qui avait été en effet, la chretienté, et qui était la revolution; ils avaient choisi la même façon de vivre et la même façon de mourir' (Malraux, *L'Espoir*, p. 41).

[24] In André Malraux: *Romans* (Pléiade), Paris 1970.
[25] Ibid., p. 745.

But, in the same book, set in the period when Malraux and Unamuno both lived in Spain, Malraux had already realized that revolution itself, through which he had at first believed that men could achieve the sublimation of their condition into the supreme reality of fraternity, was not the answer to his tragic quest. For in *L'Espoir*, p. 283, he confessed for the first time that: 'Pour un homme qui pense, la révolution est tragique. Et si c'est pour supprimer sa tragédie qu'il compte sur la révolution, il pense de travers, c'est tout.'

This was Malraux's final *'salud'* to Unamuno.

TRANSPOLITICS

Finally *transpolitics*, the fourth and last concept of political philosophy which derives from Unamuno's philosophy — an expression which Niebuhr coined to describe Unamuno's supra-political loyalty to the absolute level of the ultimate human condition. Unamuno was involved in endless, if contradictory, and opposition-oriented political activities and suffered demotions and exiles and died under house arrest because of them; and he also expressed, at a yet higher level, his political creed which, as we have seen from the preceding three concepts, was summed up in an absolute defence of freedom; an absolute pursuit of human compassion, human equality, and human love; and an absolute, agonistic, activism in the service of these causes on the social and political planes.

But absolute as these pursuits might be, they were still *relative* to the ultimate agony of man, the agony of the human condition; and intransigent as his attitudes to human life could be, they were still secondary to his attitude towards death, the great humiliator of men.

At that level his ideas could be expressed only in the language of philosophy, or poetry, in contrast to the trite language of politics and society. Preoccupied above all with the autonomy of the will, the general will was for him a contradiction in terms. For how can such an essentially relative notion as the politics of men (with the collective and plural connotations indelibly attached to it) contain the essentially absolute notion of man's existence? Or how can the essential 'mystery' of the relation between man and God and their supreme quarrel or reconciliation be so debased and encapsulated as to be contained within the 'problems' of men living together? Or, in consequence, how much should men live together when, in any event, each man dies alone?

Here Unamuno's thinking on politics becomes directly translatable into the terms of this enquiry into the involvement of human beings in politics. Because, if the function of politics is by its very nature concerned with the co-existence of human beings, and if that co-existence is only a relative part of the true existence of the individual human being, then to participate in politics as a *divertissement*, endangers the plenitude of human life which can only be reached outside and above the *Polis* — and where the individual remains alone with his self, and facing God.

THE TRAGIC SENSE OF POLITICS

At least four tragic aspects of politics were well known in the past, but have become unfashionable in the period of political happiness. One is that usually associated with Hobbes's theory of the 'brutish' struggle for survival, in which men kill even their own brothers; when linked with the fratricides which lie at the foundation of two oldest cities, it takes on a differently tragic connotation. Secondly, decision itself, namely the choice (the making of the decision) among equally plausible options and among equally 'just' beliefs or views — is tragic, is indeed the substance of tragedy in Hegel's view. This is most characteristic of politics, ever since the conflict between Creon and Antigone, in so far as politics is the realm of choices, of alternatives, of decision-making. It is linked with the third tragic aspect of politics, illustrated by Aristotle's categoric assertion that action prevails over character, namely that both in tragedy and in politics, *action* develops under its own impetus and sweeps along, makes, and unmakes, the characters caught up in its vortex. The fourth tragic aspect of politics is the risk taken by those who dedicate themselves to politics, from Julius Caesar to Gandhi, President Kennedy and Aldo Moro, of paying with their destinies for their aspiration to conduct the destinies of others.

To take Hobbes's assertion first: the origins themselves of human association are stained with fratricidal blood. Cain killed his brother Abel, and went on to build Enoch, the first city, as recounted in Genesis 4: 'The enemies of the state say that Cain, the first fratricide, was the founder of the state', remarks — again — Unamuno. A similar story is recounted by Livy and by Plutarch in connection with the building of Rome and the foundation of the Roman Kingdom. Romulus first killed his brother Remus. Why? Were the two stories true? If so, the analogous circumstances must denote analogous motivations. Or if apocryphal what does the parable mean? Is it the general sense of the struggle for survival, or, more specifically, the stern law of command—obedience, without which no political organization could be established? Plutarch tells the whole story of how Romulus who 'had more wisdom than his brother' and who 'was born to command and to be obeyed' had to quell the oppositon of his brother and erstwhile partner, Remus, by sacrificing him. Remus opposed Romulus's choice of site for the future city of Rome on the spot where, he, Romulus had seen the twelve black eagles (which ever since have been a good omen for all Roman leaders). So Romulus slew his brother and finished building Rome, and 'was elevated to heaven after death as the God Quirinus.'[26] This fundamental aspect of the tragedy implied in the sense of command and responsibility in politics is too well known to be belaboured again here.

The intrinsically tragic character of the act to *decide* (*cidere*, from *caedere*, to kill, as in sui*cide*, homi*cide*, geno*cide*. . .) is also obvious, in so far as decision itself is defined as 'a cut between the past and the future' or a cut in time. It is the irrevocability of human time, its finiteness, which make decisions tragic. Private decisions are to a certain extent revocable. But political decisions are irrevocable. They are made in public and they are promises which must be kept or wagers which must be won. Moreover a political decision is an option, selected from among other options, a course of action based on a belief, accepted from among other beliefs — equally justifiable, equally plausible.

The random character of political decision-making has been described best by Machiavelli and by Shakespeare: 'For men judge of actions by the result', wrote Machiavelli, 'Hence for all the ill that results from an enterprise the man who advised it is blamed and should the result be good, commended; but the reward by no means weighs the same as the loss.'[27] And Shakespeare's Brutus promises to Rome 'the full petition at the hands of Brutus' only 'if the redress will follow'. But it is to Messala that is given the bitter duty to comment on the tragedy of the wrong outcome of the mistaken decision, of error:

> O' hateful error, melancholy's child
> Why dost thou show to the apt thoughts of men
> The things that are not
> O' error soon conceived thou never com'st unto a happy birth
> But kill'st the mother that engendered thee.

It is therefore only in the result — right or mistaken — that the ultimate validity of the political decision lies, of the option chosen from among the other options which could be envisaged within the space-limits and the time-limits (which are also observed in the rules of classic tragedy) in which the situation is contained. Before the decision all possible options were equally plausible; and each one of them equally defended by those who believed that it was right, and that justice was on their side. Both were right and both were wrong, but one of them is wronged by the other. This resoluteness of the *dramatis personae* in making their respective

---

[26]Ronald Syme: *The Roman Revolution*, 1939, p. 306.
[27]Machiavelli: *The Discourses*, Bernard Crick edn, London 1970, Vol. III, 34–35, p. 500.

views or passions triumph over any custom or rule, and at any cost for others, even at the cost of their lives, is only of the elements of tragedy, that which renders a situation tragic.

It was this element of the opposition of different forms of justice, of moral powers, which Hegel took to be, in the context of the dialectic of the Spirit, the *substance* of tragedy. He first demonstrated this with reference to one of the Greek tragedies, indeed with the to him 'supreme and absolute example of tragedy, *Antigone*'. And he explained in his *Philosophy of Religion* that:

> In this case, family love, what is holy, what belongs to the inner life and to inner feelings, and which because of this is also called the law of the nether gods, comes into collision with the law of the State. Creon is not a tyrant but really a moral power; Creon is not in the wrong. . . Each of these two sides [Creon and Antigone] realizes only one of the moral powers. . . this is the element of one-sidedness here and the meaning of eternal justice is shown in this, that both end in injustice just because they are one-sided, though at the same time both obtain Justice too.

But then, Hegel, for whom real life was the manifestation of the Spirit in its own dialectic, explained also the actual trial and death of Socrates as a similar 'tragedy' in the *History of Philosophy*. For whereas Socrates was 'right' in his duties towards his own 'world of thought' he was wrong towards the existing state and religion. Therefore the death sentence pronounced against him 'bears on the one hand the aspect of unimpeachable rectitude — inasmuch as the Athenian people condemns its deadliest foe — but on the other hand that of a deeply tragic character'.

But action, the action which by its own unfolding precipitates the *dramatis personae* towards their unpredictable fate is what Aristotle, unlike Hegel, considered to be the essential element of tragedy.[28]

To make his meaning clear Aristotle explicitly rejected the theory that the seeds of tragedy are to be found in the character of the hero, even if only after the changes produced in him and in the situation by events. 'Without action there cannot be a tragedy; there may be without character.'[29] In tragedy, as in politics, a character must act by necessity, within the explicitly aesthetic rules of unity of space and time and within the alternative options which it offers. Within these limits it is up to the character to decide upon the course of action to be taken. But once the action has started it gathers its own momentum; it develops its own plot and leads to its own end. Not only does action sweep characters forwards to unforeseeable destinations, it changes them. Indeed it makes them what they are and unmakes what they were.

In tragedy as well as in politics a character is born from action. The

---

[28]Thus: 'The end of politics is not knowledge but action' (*Ethics*, I, 12). 'Tragedy is the imitation of an action not of men but of an action and life, and life consists in action and its end is a mode of action' (*Poetics*, VI, 5 and 10).

[29]*Poetics*, VI, 12.

hesitant Prince of Denmark, mysterious even to himself, and the dull maiden sister from Thebes, become Hamlet and Antigone only through the action they have initiated. But at the same time it is the unfolding of his own action which makes Napoleon fall, after all his victories, at Waterloo. And could Sophocles or Shakespeare have invented a situation expressing more dramatically the tragedy of politics than that of Lenin, lying semi-paralysed for the last two years of his life and watching, like a frightened sorcerer's apprentice, the evil spirits he had uncorked, whirling Russia, the revolution and the world about in their own infernal dance?

With this we come to an essentially tragic aspect of politics: its origin.

The tragic sense of the origin of politics was first and most explicitly expressed in Plato's *Statesman* (*Politikos*), which, significantly, is also the first work ever written under the name of politics.

The *Statesman*, for reasons which elude non-classical scholars, is one of the most controversial of Plato's dialogues and yet one of the least known.[30] Happily however scholars have recently stressed anew its importance for political philosophy.[31]

It is true that the text of the dialogue is particularly cryptic, and that therefore its purpose, or subject, has been differently interpreted. Is the dialogue 'primarily an exercise in philosophical method' and is the definition of the Statesman taken as a good test to find out how a definition should be constructed? Or is its object to find out in reality how a 'statesman', and 'statesmanship' can be defined, and what is the meaning of these two concepts?

Two facts probably confirm the opinion that both in Plato's intention and in the overall significance of his work, the object of the dialogue is the investigation into the meaning of politics. The first is the deliberate

---

[30] I am indebted to Professor J.B. Skemp for having checked the textual accuracy of my interpretation of the ideas of the dialogue.

[31] The new interest in the *Statesman* in the English-speaking history of political thought can be dated from 1952 with the appearance of J.B. Skemp's *Plato's Statesman: a translation of the politics of Plato with introductory essay and footnotes* (London 1952) followed by J.G. Gunnell's: *Political Philosophy and Time* (Wesleyan University Press 1968). Both books deal, one exclusively, the other principally, with this particular work by Plato, and both present a new interpretation based on the significance this work attaches to mortality in the origin and *raison d'être* of politics. The attention thus given to the *Statesman* contrasts with the clearly preferential treatment reserved for the *Laws* and especially for the *Republic* by Sir Ernest Barker in his positive presentation of *Plato in Greek Political Philosophy* (Oxford 1938) and by Sir Karl Popper in his presentation of Plato's political philosophy as an 'enemy of the open society' in his: *The Open Society and its Enemies*, Vol. I, *Plato*, London 1945). Here again therefore the insistent and detailed treatment of this particular work of Plato's is, like that of Unamuno in the previous section, rendered necessary by the fact that these works are generally less well known.

choice of the title, for which a new word had to be coined.[32] The second is that in Plato's political philosophy the *Statesman* represents a change of direction in his thought and life, a turning away from at least some of the ideas put forward in the *Republic*, an earlier work, and more in line with the ideas expressed more violently in the almost contemporary *Seventh Letter*. But Plato's last works also mark his detachment from Socrates. He now affirms his own ideas, which are no longer to be attributed to Socrates. In the *Statesman* Socrates is still there, but he is almost silent, and he is accompanied by the '*Young*' Socrates, who seems to be bewildered by the 'Stranger's' flow of new ideas. In the *Laws*, Socrates has disappeared completely. The ideas expressed in these last two political dialogues are Plato's own. He does not want to, or can no longer, put them in Socrates's mouth.[33]

The *Statesman* is distinctly original both in its approach, which is analytic and functional, and in its purpose which is to examine *real* politics, that is the politics which has been and is organized by men on earth as opposed to the *ideal* politics, what politics ought to be, as discussed in the *Republic*.

To take the purpose first: the *Statesman* is an enquiry into the actual possibilities of political organization open to men as mortals, by the *techne* of politics. The discussion on whether the Statesman 'abandons'[34] the immortal King—Philosopher of the Republic is therefore, from this point of view, superfluous since the overt purpose of the Statesman's enquiry is to see what a *mortal* ruler of other mortals, described in the dialogue by a newly coined word, 'the *Statesman*', can achieve, and how.

In its approach the *Statesman* is a functionalist work in the twofold sense of the word functionalist. It is, in a direct sense, a functional analysis of human society: one of the objects of the discussion is to see which functions and crafts are essential to the survival of the community and to

---

[32]'The word "*politikos*" which serves as the title of the dialogue is normally an adjective meaning "concerned with polis or city-state community". Plato is the first surviving author to use it at all freely as a noun. It is only in the *Phaedrus* that we see the word "politikos" becoming capable of a higher meaning than "politician" so that ultimately in our dialogue it can be described as the "true statesman" who is explicitly distinguished from mere politicians.' (Skemp, loc. cit., pp. 19–20.)

[33]This is why one has to reject Popper's thesis that one cannot be sure that Plato always approves of what the Stranger says – and to endorse Skemp's view that the Stranger is Plato's spokesman, is Plato – a Plato who slowly and tenderly puts a final distance between himself and Socrates.

[34]'We have to be careful, therefore, in speaking of an "abandonment" of the ideal state of the *Republic* in the *Politikos* (Statesman)... They each describe a society in detail but the *Politikos* defines a particular function (which is in fact the supreme function) within society. It is still, in a sense, an ideal society... But this ideal society of the Politikos does not seem as unrealizable as the society described in the *Republic* and it does not call for the special conditions laid down for realizing the society described in the *Laws*.' (Skemp, loc. cit., p. 42.) 'Plato had of course described and denounced tyranny in the *Republic*... In the *Politikos* too he regards tyranny as the worst of the perversities of true government'. Ibid., p. 47.

compare the Statesman's function with them. In an indirect sense, it is an attempt to explain *why* human society came to function and *how*, given the conditions of its origins, it could continue to function. This interpretation is confirmed by the division of the dialogue into three interlinked parts, each with an apparently distinct object, but all three having the same theme: the first deals with the best method of defining the Statesman as the regulator of the life in common of mortals; the second part retells the myth of how the world of the mortals, in which the Statesman will have to rule, came into being; and the third part discusses the ways in which the Statesman can fulfil his task given the finiteness and the ephemerality of the inhabitants of that world — 'the featherless bipeds'.

Coming now to the particular relevance of *The Statesman* to our enquiry, it is significant to see why the discussion between 'the Stranger' and the Young Socrates is interrupted abruptly in the very middle of the dialogue and the *Myth* introduced just as abruptly, at the moment when the Stranger and the approving Young Socrates realize that they have taken the wrong road in their exercise in definition. Why have they taken the wrong road? The circumstances are as follows. While trying to find out what is the meaning of the function of the Ruler, the two participants in the dialogue have continued to think and speak, mistakenly, of the Ruler as *though he were the immortal Ruler*, of say, the *Republic*, and they have forgotten that what they were actually trying to discover was *how a mortal could rule other mortals*. The Stranger (274^d)[35] says;

> Now we must use the story to discuss the extent of the mistake we made in our earlier argument in our delineation of the King or Statesman... We are asked to define the King and the Statesman of this present era, and of humanity as we know it, but in fact we took from the contrary cosmic era the Shepherd of the human world as it then was, and described him as the Statesman. *He is a god, not a mortal.* We went as far astray as that'. (My italics.)

It was because they had gone so far astray in not 'setting apart the Divine Ruler and the human tender of man' (276^b) and in describing the Statesman as if he were still, like the King in the Republic, an immortal, that the Stranger had to interrupt the discussion in the very centre of the work, and to re-situate it in its specific reality, which is the reality of the world of mortals, in which mortals must try to organize their own co-existence by themselves.

In order to explain this fundamental difference between the ideal conditions which could be achieved among immortals and the real conditions which face mortals, the Stranger had recourse to an old myth. That myth, which is probably based, as most commentators agree, on

---

[35] This, and all following quotations from the text of the dialogue are from Skemp's translation in Skemp, op. cit., indicating the paragraphs of the text, as marked on the margin of the pages.

Empedocles's system of the alternating cosmic eras, the era of Love and the era of Hatred, reveals that in

> the life of men under the government of Kronos, a god was their Shepherd and had charge of them and fed them even as men now have charge of the other creatures inferior to them — for men are closer to the divine than they are to the animals. When God was Shepherd there were no political constitutions and no taking of wives and begetting of children (271^e).

But then 'the Pilot of the Ship of the Universe. . . let go the handle of its rudder and retired to his conning tower in a place apart. Then Destiny and its own inborn urge took control of the world again and reversed the revolution of it.' (272^e) When the Universe 'must' travel forward without God, things go well enough in the year immediately after He abandoned control, but as time goes on and forgetfulness of God arises, the ancient condition of chaos also begins to assert its sway. But it is at this very moment that the Stranger (and Plato) warns us that 'we have now come to the point which the whole of this story of ours has been seeking to reach'. Announcing that what will be unfolded will be only 'man's story' because it 'is shorter and more relevant to us now' he describes how:

> Bereft of the guardian care of the Daemon who had governed and reared us up, we had become weak and helpless, and we began to be ravaged by wild beasts. . . Men lacked all tools and all crafts in the early years. The earth no longer supplied their food spontaneously and they did not know how to win it for themselves: in the absence of necessity they had never been made to learn this. For all these reasons they were in direst straits. It was to meet this need that the gifts of the gods famous in an ancient story were given, along with such teaching and instructions as were indispensable. Fire was the gift of Prometheus, the secrets of the crafts were made known by Hephaestos and his partner in craftmanship, and seeds and plants were made known by other gods. From these gifts everything has come which has furnished human life since the divine guardianship of men ceased (in the way our story has just described) and men had to manage their lives and fend for themselves in the same way as the whole universe was forced to do. (274^d)

The desolate scene thus described in which mortals find themselves alone in a desert world, compelled, in order to live until they grow snowy-haired and then die, to feed and shelter themselves, and to reproduce themselves, and yet lacking all crafts is similar to the Old Testament's description of the Fall.

Time itself which now rules human beings, as the agent of individual mortality, awakens in them the will to survive. It is the lack of crafts which causes the highest concern, for without crafts, and without the tools required by the crafts, the 'inborn urge' of mortality will soon decimate the entire species. There are several 'productive' crafts which must be made to function together, and inevitably to compete among themselves, if the herd of those 'featherless bipeds', men, is to be 'fed and nurtured' and therefore saved from extinction.

But, although without the 'productive' crafts there would be no need to rule because there would be no men left to rule, the art of ruling is indispensable. This craft, or art of ruling was, before the Fall, the sole competence of the Divine Ruler. But now, *statecraft* must, of necessity, be exercised by one of the mortals, who will be found among the few who possess this supreme gift; and politics is only a second-best craft to substitute for the divine guidance now lacking to men. This principal theme of the *Statesman* had already been formulated by Plato in the *Protagoras*. Thus:

> Once upon a time there were Gods only, and no mortal creatures. . .
> But when the time came that these also should be created, the Gods
> fashioned them out of earth, and where they were about to bring them
> into the light of day they. . . distributed to them severally their proper
> qualities. . .Thus man had the wisdom necessary to the support of life,
> *but political wisdom he had not.*[36]

And with the *Statesman* as we have seen, the myth is completed by the reminder that the further they are removed in time from the Gods, the more men forget the divine eternal laws and, making new laws of their own for themselves, go astray in the wilderness and chaos of their own ungovernability.

In a typically functionalist way the dialogue afterwards selects the crafts without which mankind would perish and shows why and how the supreme craft, that of statesmanship, consists of *weaving* not only all these productive capacities towards the same purpose of providing the community with the goods and services it requires if it is to survive and prosper, but also, and above all, of weaving by education in the men of the future the moral fibres which will give them more strength in their passage through the gates of time and within the finite world they inhabit 'for a time'. Thus the first work ever to be written under the title of 'Politics' is imbued with the tragic sense of politics.

Both tragedy and Greek political philosophy are inspired by the tragic sense of life, that is, to repeat once more, by the constant memory of man's mortality. To live with this permanent realization of man's mortality signifies awareness that the supreme equality of men, however different their lives, whether they be potentates or beggars, is the equality of death.

But the permanent realization of man's mortal condition engenders in man a sense of precariousness, of dependence on the unknown and the unknowable. Who, if anybody, brings upon my life — the very length of which is itself unpredictable — the inexplicable circumstances which change it, from one day to another, from hell into paradise — and vice

---

[36]Plato: *Protagoras*, Jowett edn, 142 ff. (My italics.)

versa? And if my mortal life is, to use Hannah Arendt's word, *rectilinear,* from a beginning to an end, from birth to death; if, as she puts it, 'the individual life is distinguished from all other things by the rectilinear course of its movement, which so to speak, cuts through the circular movement of biological life. This is mortality: to move along a rectilinear line in a universe where everything, if it moves at all, moves in a cyclical order'[37] — then who is either moving, or not moving, in cycles, around and above me? Are there any other forces which, either by their cyclical renewal or by their immovability, that is immortality, not only escape from my rectilinear trajectory between birth and death, but condition and order that trajectory? Am I, as a mortal, subjected to the movements of immortal forces, and who are these immortals? This is a question common to religion, tragedy and political philosophy. But tragedy and political philosophy in Athens stress the inevitable and inconsolable end of the actor — death.

In consequence both Greek tragedy and Greek political philosophy advise men to remember and to observe the laws of the immortals, or of the Gods, to whom they have once been much closer, from whom perhaps they were once indistinguishable. The myth of the Fall is not only the principal theme of Greek political philosophy but also of Greek tragedy. In the *Oresteia,* presented by Aeschylus at the festival of 458 BC, at the very climax of Athens's power and glory, the curse on the house of Atraeus is attributed by Cassandra, as Professor John Jones shows, to a mysterious 'primal sin'.[38] 'Dark is the cloud of pollution hovering over the man, and rumour carried on voices of mourning proclaims that a mist-thick gloom covers his house' intones the chorus; and at the end of the *Eumenides,* the final play of the trilogy, the Furies chant: 'It is the sins of bygone generations that bring him before them for judgement, and destruction strikes him down — silently, in dreadful wrath'.

Greek tragedy and political philosophy also deny that mortal man can ever hope to be or even attempt to be as powerful as the Gods. Nor can he, to put it in political terms, achieve a vision and a sense of justice as clear and pure as can the Immortal Statesman of the *Republic,* which Republic can be attained only in heaven.

It is against hubris, and especially political hubris, that Greek tragedy is directed; and Greek political philosophy advises men not to believe that their power on earth can be absolute or self-sufficient. The *dramatis personae* of Greek tragedy are kings and princes only in order to prove that the most powerful are the most vulnerable. Because the most powerful are imbued with the sense of their own power, they are shown to the spectators as having fallen into greater depths of suffering than the normal God-fearing man-in-the-chorus, or man-in-the-street. Both

---

[37]Hannah Arendt: *The Human Condition*, New York, Chicago 1958, p. 6.
[38]John Jones: *On Aristotle and Greek Tragedy*, London 1967, now paperback, p. 94.

tragedy and political philosophy insist that the will of man is only conditionally free, that it is *free* only if it always takes into consideration the
part the Gods themselves play in the decision which man believes that
he is taking freely. Or as Sophocles puts it in *Antigone*, the decision is
grounded in 'the unwritten and irrefragable ordinance of the Gods', while
Athene, at the end of Aeschylus's *Oresteia*, reminds the citizens of the
reunited city to 'cast away fear and yet cast not all fear. For who that
hath no fear is safe from sin.' Vernant and Vidal-Naquet express this
felicitously when they say 'Chez les tragiques l'action humaine n'a
pas en soi assez de force pour se passer de la force des dieux, pas assez
d'autonomie pour se concevoir pleinement en dehors d'eux.'[39]

Tragedy and political philosophy both advise and counsel man to
observe the mean because man's life as an individual mortal, and particularly his political life, constitutes ambiguous realms in which the
autonomous decision of the human individual is confronted by the superior
decision of the immortal forces. In this context the mean lies between
what man can do on his own initiative and what he must do in the bare
realm of necessity into which he had originally fallen.

THE DAWN OF OPTIMISM

Almost at the same time as politics and economics were emancipated from
the tutelage of religion, and *pace* Weber of the ethics based on religion, the
idea of something now called happiness or in French, *le bonheur*, took
shape.[40] Several factors, not always easy to connect with each other facilitated this process.[41] These included scientific advance and in its wake the
growing confidence in reason; the development of commerce and industry
and in its wake the premonition of progress: the crisis in the Church, its
divisions, persecutions and wars of religion; the replacement of the ideal
of poverty by that of wealth; the gradual diminution of the fear of
Hell within the Christian observances; the advance of the nation-state,
embodiment of a new class of wealth without power, urbanization,

[39]Jean-Pierre Vernant and Pierre Vidal-Naquet: *Mythe et Tragédie en Grèce
Ancienne*, Paris 1973, p. 37.

[40]The intrinsic logicality of French thinking, and even of the French language,
inclines them towards substantial figurations. This is exemplified in the obvious
difference in political philosophy, and subsequently in political mentality, between
the French self-contained noun: *Le Pouvoir*, and the English necessarily qualified
power: the power of government, of the king, of commanding, etc.

[41]Four modern books help to an understanding of this period. They are: Paul
Hazard, *La crise de la conscience européenne au XVIII*^{ème} *siècle*, 1935 and *La
pensée européenne au XVIII*^{ème} *siècle*, Paris 1935 and 1946; Robert Mauzi, *L'idée
du bonheur dans la littérature et la pensée françaises au XVIII*^{ème} *siècle*, Paris 1960,
and John MacManners, *Death and the Enlightenment*, Oxford 1981.

the spread of literacy and publications, a new concept of 'sociability' and of friendship and love, the adoption of Locke's sensationalist epistemology, which according to R.R. Palmer was 'proposition One of the Enlightenment';[42] and an atmosphere of optimism oriented towards the future.

This diffused optimism was indeed the essential factor. Much of the literature of that time assumed that people were born to be happy. Or, as Locke and Montesquieu advised, they could easily find their happiness which was there to hand, were it not for the blindness which still afflicted them. Montesquieu even argued that a man could find happiness itself, not merely the longing for happiness, in his own heart.

Bombarded by these new factors, the consciousness of the ordinary human being in the second half of the eighteenth century reacted by an ever-increasing awareness of his own individuality. Individualism, in this context, meant the freedom of each human being to act, within the limits of 'sociability', according to his or her wishes. And the totality of these wishes was expressed in that new concept of happiness which suddenly burst out everywhere in Europe. In his *La pensée européenne au XVIIIème siécle,* Paul Hazard gives the following selection of titles of contemporary works on the subject of happiness: *Réflexions sur le Bonheur, Epître sur le Bonheur, Sur la vie heureuse, Système du vrai Bonheur, Essai sur le Bonheur, Della felicità, L'arte di essere felice, Discorso sulla fecilità, Die Glückseligkeit, Versuch uber die Kunst stets fröhlich zu sein, Leben die menschliche Glückseligkeit, Of Happiness; Traité de la societé civile du moyen de se rendre heureux en contribuant au bonheur des personnes avec qui on vit, Des causes du bonheur public, De la Felicité publique, Della pubblica felicità, La felicità pubblica, Ragionamenti. . . riguardenti la pubblica felicità, Riflessioni sulla pubblica felicità, Of National Felicity,* etc.

Everywhere in Europe the pursuit of happiness became a new concern of human beings. Yet at this time − the late eighteenth century − the pursuit of happiness had not yet become as aggressive as it became later, under the influence of materialism.[43] The idea of individual happiness, when it timidly emerged, was essentially circumscribed and knew its limitations and contradictions.

From the beginning, for instance, one of the principal, and most anguishing contradictions lay in the question whether the happiness of one human being could be reconciled with the happiness of others. In the prevailing atmosphere of optimism, many a wishful thinker tried to convince himself that since the world now revealing itself to the clear gaze of the free individual was a world of harmonies, so individual happiness was in harmony with that of others. This was the ultimate meaning of the

[42]Quoted in Mauzi, op. cit., p. 131.
[43]I am not dealing at present with the romantic ideal of happiness which is not relevant to my enquiry.

expression 'sociability', for, to quote Mauzi: 'if the nature of man is to be a sociable animal, if his existence is conceivable only within a human group or in the surrounding mankind, all his instincts must play in the sense of the universal harmony. The idea of an antinomy between individual happiness and general happiness becomes absurd.'[44] But as the new world continued to reveal its specific characteristics, as it threw more light on the significance of the inequalities between human beings, which were less glaring when salvation through poverty was more honoured than happiness through wealth, and as it brought people into closer dependence on each other, with all the conflict and competition implicit in interdependence, so the pious hope of the general harmonization of happiness by some 'invisible hand' proved less and less credible.

Rousseau, as we shall see later, is the most strident critic of the reconcilability of individual happiness with general happiness. It could indeed be said that Rousseau did not believe that contemporary man could experience happiness. The man of the past, natural man, alone, could be happy. The citizen of the future will be happy, but it will be a different kind of happiness. But present man, Jean Jacques's contemporary, can only be torn between occasional glimpses of a past happiness, caught in a moment of ecstasy, and the future and different, happiness which he foresees.

A second contradiction arises between happiness and the observance of virtue. Though fear of the flames of Hell might have declined, and the rules of religious behaviour had become more lax, nevertheless man's life was still bounded by the framework maintained by religious dogmas. Moreover reason itself, which is so often regarded as the enemy of faith, was also based on virtues, some of them identical with those propounded by religion though differently motivated, some advanced by reason itself, and observance of which was made even stricter by the imperative of duty. Both in the context of religion and in the context of reason, moral virtues were the guardians of man's integrity. The eighteenth-century concept of happiness is inseparable from virtue and indeed the French Revolution, having changed the emphasis from private virtue to public virtue, was to proclaim 'la vertu' as the supreme quality.

Moreover the eighteenth-century concept of happiness was still enshrined within the tragic sense of life. It was the second Fall, from the sheltered if austere realm of religion to the free but uncharted horizons of reason, which enhanced the note of tragedy in life.

The new rationalism, or secular humanism, first advanced an idea of happiness which reflected the melancholy of this second Fall. If man's life begins and ends on earth, then, during this short span, let him be as happy as he can. This is the bitter introduction to the new happiness Jacob Burckhardt describes so well in his *The Renaissance in Italy*. To be sure, such a reasoning might lead straight to frivolity and hedonism. By

[44]Mauzi, op. cit., p. 141.

1750, Boudier de Villement published his *Apologie de la frivolité* in which he argued that frivolity would be reprehensible only if man had any chance of understanding the meaning of his existence and of solving his ontological dilemmas. By mid-eighteenth century the two meanings of *libertine* as a free thinker in religion and as a dissolute, licentious man were linked in a more vulgar kind of hedonistic reasoning.

But in general individual happiness in the eighteenth century was conceived of as eudaemonistic rather than hedonistic. Writers proclaimed the lasting happiness which is based on the fulfilment of moral obligation rather than the happiness which is based on the enjoyment of the pleasures of the senses. As Elizabeth Telfer puts it, in hedonism 'pleasure and happiness are important because they relate to what *is* wanted; the ingredients of *eudaemonia* are important because whether or not they are wanted, they are worth wanting.'[45]

The eudaemonistic conception of happiness of the eighteenth century was in fact bounded by the assertion that attainable happiness could only be achieved rationally, because reason alone can appease man's ontological anguish. In a particularly apposite phrase, Hazard states: 'if the souls were really to feel absolutely happy, it would be necessary to extirpate the tragic sentiment of existence from men.'[46] But at the same time reason should place a limit on the unbounded imagination of the senses which demand a constant maximization of happiness.

In this sobering perspective, the eudaemonists advised men to administer their real, but precarious, lot wisely. 'Let us be reconciled with ourselves.' 'Let us avoid ambitions, those constant dangers which threaten the peaceful sailing of our humble boat.' What they sought above all was *'le repos'*, repose. Montesquieu urged the 'balancing of satisfactions', and his advice in his own *Essai sur le bonheur* was 'to adjust oneself to life because life would not adjust itself to us'. In his *Letter concerning Enthusiasm*, the Earl of Shaftesbury denounced enthusiasm as that major defect of human nature, whether it is used in the service of religion or in the service of humanism, and recommended in its place 'this plain, homespun philosophy of looking into ourselves, this plain, honest morals'.

Finally a contradiction was beginning to emerge between the incipient materialism (Bayle, d'Holbach, Helvetius) and the idealism which dominated human thinking for so long. During the second half of the eighteenth century the eudaemonistic pursuit of happiness maintained its idealistic mode, and indeed the French Revolution itself was borne along on a wave of idealism. But materialism was already making great strides, and by the nineteenth century it overtook idealism and became the dominant mode of thought. With the help of the ideologies it has now become the foundation of popular thinking. The most popular argument of materialism

[45] Elizabeth Telfer: *Eudaemonism and Hedonism,* London 1978, p. 95.
[46] Paul Hazard: *La crise de la conscience européenne,* op. cit., p. 189. (My translation).

was and still is that only by changes in the material circumstances can the alienation of man be healed. Man who is matter, interacts with the material environment, and find his unity in his action. This separation between matter and spirit, between body and soul, is only an illusion on which idealism and religion have thrived. But while this debate was to culminate in the nineteenth and even the twentieth centuries, in the eighteenth century it had only just begun to be audible. Idealism, or deism, was still linked together with the authoritative voices of such as Locke, Rousseau and Kant. But for Rousseau the problem of the duality of man, and of the impossibility of achieving human happiness because of this duality, was the dominant problem. The way Rousseau set about solving this problem led from an idealistic position to the affirmation of political happiness, which in turn could be achieved only in and by materialistic ideologies.

ROUSSEAU AND THE IMMOLATION OF MAN

The basic conflict in man's consciousness between the goodness which he carries over from his immemorial past and the evil which surrounds him in society lies at the origins of Rousseau's political philosophy and con- stantly reappears as its *leitmotif*. In simple terms, Rousseau tried to sublimate the intense tragic individual anxiety into the chimaera of public happiness. But the reconciliation he offered to all men failed to heal his own internal dichotomy. The two Rousseaus, the Rousseau of the tragic loneliness and the Rousseau immersed in the life of the community never made peace with each other. One cannot even speak chronologically of a young, tragic and lonely Rousseau and of a mature and integrated Rousseau — for both recur in constant opposition to each other, more often than not in writings dating from the same period.

The essence of Rousseau's *tragic* philosophy is the nostalgic longing to return to the state of natural harmony and beatitude in which man had lived in immemorial times and which had been brutally interrupted by the advent of time, the great corrupter, and by the intrusion of social life, or, in other words by the coming of the *others*. On this point Rousseau explicitly opposes Hobbes's belief that man is by nature aggressive, and that it is this instinctive aggressiveness of the individual which turns social life into the struggle for survival imagined by Hobbes. Rousseau believes that the fight of all against all, as imagined by Hobbes, is not inherent in the natural man but that on the contrary 'l'état de guerre naît de l'état social'. Adam is still unchallenged, but already, with Abel and Cain, fratricide appears in its horrible significance as the stuff of human society.

The longing to return to the original happiness of man protected by a Great Being is almost obsessive in Rousseau. The often quoted account of his ecstasy on the island of Saint-Pierre, described in a letter to Malesherbes in 1762[47] (when he was already fifty, the year in which he published *Du Contract Social*) is important not only because of his portrayal of the mystical sensation, the 'étourdissante extase', which overpowered him on encountering, as in a dream, the incomprehensible Being who embraces everything; it is also significant because he opposes this mystical sensation explicitly to even the most complete triumph of Reason for, he says,

> I believe that had I unveiled all the mysteries of nature I would have
> felt a less delicious sensation than this overpowering ecstasy to which
> my mind was abandoning itself unreservedly, and which in the agitation
> of my emotions, allowed me to cry sometimes: 'O! Great Being,
> O! Great Being' without being able to say or think of anything else.

Bertrand de Jouvenel suggests that this longing for a lost Paradise could have originated in Rousseau's early belief in Original Sin. 'As a child' says de Jouvenel, 'Rousseau had learned in the Ostervald catechism that man had been created good but that, because of Adam's sin his heirs were all born sinners and inclined to evil.'[48] And de Jouvenel's interpretation is confirmed by such remarks of Rousseau, as 'Man, do not search further for the perpetrator of evil; you are that "perpetrator",' or 'I do not see why one should search for the origin of moral evil further than in man, once he is free and accomplished, and therefore corrupted.'[49]

Time, the other human name for mortality, is in Rousseau's eyes the agent of the decay of man and of the institutions he tries to build. Like Plato, and for the same deep reasons, Rousseau showed a preference for Sparta, the state with the lasting institutions, or rather the state whose political philosophy attempts to protect its institutions from the clutches of time, and therefore of change, and therefore of decay; and he shows an equal contempt for Athens, the state 'open' to reform, evolution and progress. 'Human nature' he says, in his own examination of himself, *Rousseau juge de Jean Jacques, Troisième Dialogue,*[50] 'never goes back, and it never returns towards the times of innocence and equality once it has gone beyond them. . . Therefore his [Rousseau's] aim was not to bring back the peoples with large populations, or the great states to their original simplicity but only to halt, if possible, the progress of those states which because of their smallness and situations he thought could be protected against the rapid march toward the perfection of the society and the deterioration of the species'. To believe in progress implies acknowledging and bowing to time, and time implies decay and death.

---

[47]Rousseau, *Oeuvres* (Pléiade, Paris, p. 1141). But see on Rousseau's tragic sense Bertrand de Jouvenel: Introduction to *Le Contract Social*, Geneva 1947, paperback, Paris 1978, and an excellent study by Lionel Grossman in *Studies on Voltaire and the XVIIIth century.*

[48]Bertrand de Jouvenel, op. cit., 1978, p. 73.

[49]In 'Profession de foi d'un vicaire savoyard', Pléiade, IV, p. 588 quoted by de Jouvenel, op. cit., p. 72.

[50]Pléiade, p. 935.

It is the problem of man's corruption, as a mortal being which Rousseau proposes to solve through the submersion and the sublimation of the individual will of each and every member of the society into one single, general will, which fuses all individuals' wills into one, transcending them and surviving them. By curbing one's instincts and desires under the severe demands of the community, and by sacrificing one's will on the altar of the general will, the individual transcends his mortal, anguished and at the same time, cupid, ego, and merges into the oneness of the general will of which he is a temporary and humble part.

This has sometimes been compared with the transcendence of one's mortality obtained by the Homeric Tragic Hero through the *Thymos*, or again through the pursuit of honour in the Spanish and French tragedies and indeed in Shakespeare. But these heroes were achieving their immortality as the most unequal among unequals, whereas Rousseau's citizen obtains his share of immortality as the most equal among equals. Moreover this should be done deliberately and with a clear sense of sacrifice.

Rousseau is only too well aware of the anguish in the heart of modern 'private' man, who must needs be broken, mainly by education, turned into a 'citizen' and submerged into the 'general will'. Only at the price of losing his own identity can he share in the new 'public' happiness. This is of course a far cry from Aristotle's view that individuals can choose between either the 'contemplative' or the 'active' way of life. 'Which way of life is more desirable?' he asks in the *Politics* (VII, II, 3–11). 'The way of politics and action? or the way of detachment from all external things — the way let us say, of contemplation, which some regard as the only way that is worthy of a philosopher?'

For Rousseau this is not a question of choice or of predilection. In *Émile*, his pedagogic treatise, and in the *Contract Social*, the political treatise which appeared almost simultaneously, the conflict between private and public man is lucidly stated, but rapidly dismissed. 'Forced to fight either against nature or against the social institutions, one must opt between making either a man or a citizen; for one cannot make both at the same time', wrote Rousseau in *Émile* (I.1). In the *Contract Social* (2nd version 1762), the theme is forcibly expressed early in the argument (Book II, Ch. 7):

> He who dares to form a people must feel that he is able to change, so to speak, human nature; to transform each individual, who is within himself a perfect and lonely whole, into a part of a larger whole from which that individual would receive, to a certain degree, both his life and his being; to change the constitution of a man so as to strengthen it; to substitute a partial and moral existence for the physical and independent existence which we have all received from nature.

In spite of the ambiguities and the qualifications (the individual is a *perfect* whole; he will receive only to a *certain* degree [*en quelque sorte*] his existence and being from the new whole in which he will be immersed;

the existence which will replace the independent existence will be *partial* and *moral*), Rousseau's words are categoric. The principle applies to all. The only exception he makes is the Christians. In the chapter 'On civil religion' (Book IV, Ch. 8) Rousseau states that

> instead of tying the souls of the citizens to the state [the Christian religion] detaches them from all earthly things; I cannot think of anything more opposed to the social spirit. We are told that a people of true Christians would form the most perfect society imaginable. I can see only one great difficulty in this supposition, namely that a society of true Christians would no longer be a society of men.[51] . . . [The Christian] fulfils his duty, it is true but he does so with a profound indifference towards the success or failure of his actions. . . If the state is flourishing, the Christian is reluctant to join in the public happiness. . . if the state is declining, the Christian blesses the hand of God which lies heavily on his people.

In this quotation from the *Contract Social* we first encounter the expression 'public happiness' (the actual words used are 'félicité publique'). But Rousseau explicitly used the words 'bonheur public' in a 'fragment politique' which was written in the same year as *Émile* and the *Contract Social* under the title *Du Bonheur Public*,[52] but which remained unfinished, and unpublished during his lifetime.

The fragment starts with Rousseau's usual *theme* of the contrast between the discontent of the townspeople plagued by human miseries, and the felicity of the naked savage in his forests. 'Our greatest misfortune' Rousseau reminds us not for the first time, 'derives from the care we take to remedy our little misfortunes'. The best government is not always the strongest. Power is only a means, the end is the happiness of the people. But, he continued, the meaning of the word happiness is even more elusive for the people than it is for individuals. The diversity of political principles and theories which are offered to man is the result of the diversity of opinions on what happiness can really mean.

'Where is the happy man, if indeed such a man has ever existed? Who knows?' Rousseau then confirms as his own the classic definition of happiness. 'Happiness is not pleasure; it does not consist of a changing

---

[51] Voltaire, in his *Idées Républicaines par un citoyen de Genève*, noted with reference to this passage of Rousseau's *Contract Social*, 'this statement is very odd. What is the author intimating? That it will be a society of beasts or a society of angels?'

[52] It was written as a memoir, addressed to the Berne *Societè Economique*, in answer to a questionnaire which the society had sent him. The third question in this questionnaire asked which people could be said to have been happiest in history. Rousseau replied enthusiastically that he would give his full attention to question three 'which he liked best'. He then defined the subject of the memoir he was going to write as 'public happiness', and set to work on it at once. But perhaps because he was distracted by some other, more pressing commitment, or perhaps, as the uncertainties and visible hesitations of the manuscript suggest, because he was defeated by the contradictions inherent in the subject, he gave it up.

mood of the soul, but of a permanent and internalized (*tout intérieur*) feeling which nobody else can fathom apart from the man who experiences it.'

But with political societies it is entirely different. Here, content or discontent is fully apparent and visible. The discerning eye should have no difficulty in detecting such emotions. But does it? Because in a later passage, which is very relevant to the present discussion, Rousseau again stresses the irreconcilable contradiction between 'our duties and our inclinations, between nature and the social institutions, between man and citizen'. As long as this division between man and the citizen continues within one individual, happiness will be out of the question. Only 'if you can make man one, can you make him happy'.

Yet the integration within man which Rousseau has in mind is not to be attained by some form of reconciliation of man's dual qualities, of his nature as man and his nature as citizen, or by a fusion between his two selves, or by transcending them. On the contrary, Rousseau sees the solution in the destruction of one or the other of the selves, so that only one remains and forms the unified self. 'Either you give him entirely to the state or you leave him entirely to himself.' *Tertium non datur*, for 'if you divide his heart you tear it apart'.

Moreover this surgical manner of achieving the integration and subsequent happiness of the individual man is even more essential for the state as a whole, for, Rousseau explains, one must not think 'that the state can be happy in which all citizens suffer. *This moral entity which you call public happiness is in itself a chimaera*, for if the feeling of well-being is not experienced by all, it means that it does not exist and the family does not flourish when the children do not prosper.' (My italics.) Rousseau continues:

> Make men consistent with themselves, being what they seem to be, and seeming to be what they are. Once you have placed the social law at the bottom of their hearts, men who are civil by their nature and citizens by their inclinations, will be one, will be good, will be happy and their happiness will be that of the Republic; for since they will be nothing except through the Republic, they will be nothing but for the Republic; the Republic will have all that they have and it will be all that they are. To the power of constraint you would add that of the will. . . When everyone wants to be happy only for himself, there is no happiness for the fatherland.

All this sounds emphatically clear — especially when Rousseau's philosophy is taught in clichés. But there are two crucial points or clichés which badly need clarification.

The first is who is 'you' (*vous*) in such imperative propositions as: 'Only if *you* can make man one, can *you* make him happy' or 'either *you* can give him entirely to the state or *you* leave him entirely to himself'. At first sight this can be taken, and presumably has often been taken, as the generalizing way of speaking in any language; and it is known that in the French argumentative syntax the usage of 'you' (*vous*) and 'one' (*on*) is more customary than in English. But, on reflection, this cannot be possible in Rousseau's propositions which presuppose actions which connect, or ought to connect two nouns, *the* man (or *the* citizen), and *the* society (or *the* state), which are yet separate or indeed opposed. Here we are no longer in the realm of natural interpenetration between the 'volonté particulière', and the 'volonté générale'. Here *you* or *one*, in principle the legislator, does these things because they must be done so that the *volonté générale*, alias the *people*, alias the *souverain* can function.

'You' or 'one' must have in Rousseau's metaphorical, yet meticulous scheme the *authority*. If 'you' is the legislator, where and how does he acquire that authority if the authority already belongs to the sovereign people? Or would the government which Rousseau defines as 'an intermediary body established between the subjects and the sovereign for their mutual communication, entrusted with the execution of the laws, and with the safeguarding of freedom, civil and political freedom' be also part of the *you*? Be that as it may, we are still left in no doubt that the public happiness which may result from the complete integration of all individuals in the general will, or the community, requires the intermediary of action by a political authority, legislative and executive – that therefore public happiness could also be interpreted as political happiness.

The second clarification that is needed is what has happened or is going to happen to the man sacrificed to the citizen, to the human self urged to drown himself in the general will or consciousness? Will he become an equal among equals, a number among numbers? This is what, in our time, political philosophers have tended to impute to Rousseau. Of course, it is true that the idea of political happiness as it has been applied in the representative democracies, and which Tocqueville describes as 'the tyranny of the majority' has led, and is leading further to the standardization of the minds and consciences of individuals; and it is even truer that the communist states, which invoke more closely, via Marx, Rousseau's idea of the unanimity of the general will, have tried and are still trying to crush all individual consciences and minds into one single social and historical collectivity. But this happened only after two post-Rousseauian *materialistic* ideologies, utilitarian materialism and historical materialism, had pressurized the minds and souls of individuals in entirely different ways, in their respective political systems.

As for Rousseau himself – perhaps the indirect conclusion to all these speculations on the relation between the individual and the general will of the community, which his work has stirred up, can be found, even if out of context, in the opening line of the very last book he published, *Les rêveries d'un promeneur solitaire*, which runs: 'Me voici donc seul sur la terre, n'ayant plus de frère, de prochain, d'ami, de société que moi-même'. ('So here am I now, alone on earth, having no more brother, relative, friend, or society, only myself.')

Chapter 3

Enters, allegorically, the pursuit of political happiness accompanied by its systems

Poor Rousseau had done the harm. Like the sorcerer's apprentice he had uncorked one of the most intoxicating ideas in the whole history of ideas — that people can be made happy by politics, while politics can be made by the people. That idea, once out of the bottle, expanded like a gas, penetrating human minds from within and from without, detonating a series of consecutive explosions which have rumbled on from the eighteenth century to the twentieth century. Gradually it replaced the old doctrine of salvation and became what Jacques Ellul rightly called a political soteriology.

Now many extenuating circumstances can be adduced to excuse Rousseau. One is that whatever recommendations or even injunctions he made, they were abstract, in the specific sense of not concrete. Perhaps the one concrete recommendation he made concerned education — that men should be educated in the new spirit of virtue. But education is a lengthy process, the results of which depend more on the quality of the taught than of the teaching, and on whether the teaching itself is coercive or persuasive. Whereas the changes in the organization of the life of human beings in common, which Rousseau had imagined, had that sense of immediacy and compulsion achievable only by practical politics. There is still controversy about what exactly Rousseau intended but the fact that, to take only one example, the first attempt to put his ideas into practice took place in a large country like France, when he had most insistently warned that they were only applicable to small units of rule with a highly developed communal spirit, like for instance a Greek city-state or a Swiss canton, underlines the discrepancy between his theories and the efforts of those who claimed that they were applying them.

A second extenuating circumstance is that Rousseau's political philosophy was full of contradictions. All works of political philosophy are marked by contradictions. Otherwise they would sink to the low level of ideologies, one of the obligations of which is to present their arguments in such an apparently systematic way — even if truth is mutilated in the process — that simple or less attentive minds are instantly convinced. But

Rousseau deserves only praise for leaving the contradictions in his work wide open, like bleeding wounds. And none was less curable than the contradiction between the autonomy of the individual will and the general will. In the *Contract Social* and in *Émile* Rousseau seemed to have decided to sacrifice the individual to the general will. But in most of his other works he exalted the freedom of the individual above all. You may opt for the one or the other, but the two are irreconcilable, and what is more neither of them is attainable in practice — one could conclude that this is Rousseau's message.

Yet these abstract and contradictory thoughts took on a prophetic aspect when they were subsequently projected on to such real historical developments as for instance secularization, the obsolescence of the *ancien régime*, the dawn of the interdependent industrial society, the accentuation of social inequalities, the sense of progress fostered by the advance of science and technology, the advance of materialism and the expectation of happiness for all human beings — which formed what is called in this enquiry the systems of political happiness.

The enquiry will proceed by, first, outlining the constitutive elements of an ideal-type system of political happiness; and then examining three such 'systems', the idealistic Jacobin proto-system, which made a brief appearance before the industrial revolution, and the utilitarian—liberal and communist dictatorial systems of political happiness, both materialistic and emerging after the industrial revolution. The aim is to establish whether all these systems, and these only, bring together the same constitutive elements and thus confirm the ideal type.

CONSTITUTIVE ELEMENTS OF THE SYSTEM OF POLITICAL HAPPINESS

The principal constitutive elements of the system of political happiness are: the promise of political happiness; an existing nation-state in need of modernization; a new legitimacy based on the representation of the people; an ideology and its prerequisite, ideologization; and a political organization or what is called nowadays a political party.

THE PROMISE

The system of political happiness is first, a promissory system, i.e. it makes promises. Most human relations have always been promissory. The promise is the object and the subjects are a promiser and a promisee, or rather, both sides exchange reciprocal promises in order to achieve a mutual advantage. In public promises — economic, social, or political

— where collectivities are involved, the promise is general; but that does not make the public relations less promissory. On the contrary, one form of public relationship, the political relationship, is the most promissory of all, since it is proved by deeds and is assessed only by its results.

In the context of social relations Rousseau thought that social organization itself was a contract — that all units of rule were founded on a mutual collective promise. But the logical difficulty in Rousseau's proposition was that it merged both elements, the promiser and the promisee, into one single actor: the people. Rousseau's explicit rejection of representation made things worse, and has led to the confusion from which the exercise of democracy has suffered ever since.[1]

Hobbes's model of the promissory political relationship was more plausible, because it was bilateral. In Hobbes's relationship the promise was political peace (and not political happiness); the subjects, or the people, were the promisees and the promiser was the sovereign, 'the one person, of whose acts a great multitude, by mutual covenants with one another, have made themselves everyone the author, to the end he may use the strength and the means of them all, as he shall think expedient, for their peace and common defence.'[2] The goal in Hobbes's promise was protection, and the promissory relationship was seen as necessarily stable.

But in the system of political happiness the promissory relationship is bound to escalate or, to put it differently, the higher the promise of the political promiser, the greater the commitment of the promisees to follow him politically.

THE NATION-STATE

The second constitutive element of the system of political happiness, *the framework of a nation-state*, also pre-dates the system, or indeed the system needed it in order to be set up. The nation-state arose as a result of the break-up of the universal Empire and the universal Church of Western Europe; the victory of the principle *Cujus regio, ejus religio*; and the end of regional feudalism. Sovereignty, the basic concept of the nation-state, and in itself a political promise, required central control of

---

[1]Or, as explained by Reinhart Koselleck: 'The one and unconditional will from which was drawn the sovereign decision of the absolute sovereign, was claimed by Rousseau for society. The result is the law to be implemented by itself. He dethrones the visible sovereign who, because he holds the power, is doomed to be corrupted, but keeps the sovereign will as the principle of decision. Instead he attributes it to the society, which because it is a society, cannot have a sovereign will. . . Rousseau's paradox in which the nation had a general will which makes it a nation cannot be achieved in a direct political way. He liberates a will which, initially has no executor. Because it cannot be either represented or delegated (*Contract Social*, II, 1, 2) the will as such evaporates in its transparence.' Reinhart Koselleck: *Le règne de la critique*, Paris 1979, p. 156. (My translation.)

[2]Hobbes: *Leviathan* (Oakeshott edn), Oxford 1960, p. 112.

that part of the earthly surface which the single sovereign could defend against the foe from without and disorder from within. This forms the state. Such a surface is populated more often than not by people speaking mainly the same language, as in France for instance. This forms the nation-state. Later the introduction of a representative political system transformed the nation-state into the people's state: representation facilitated centralization. But centralization is also brought about by industrialization, as we shall see later in this enquiry.[3] Moreover as industrial society develops and the surfaces of the units of rule become larger, the decision-making centre, which in the nation-state is national, moves further away to federal, or transnational centres.

The nation-state becomes the people-nation-state. The two concepts, people and nation, are considered to be interchangeable. This is a modern conception of legitimacy. But it gave rise to one of the most serious confusions which has bedevilled modern politics, and it is aggravated by the fact that the concept of people has, as we shall see, many meanings — the two most important of which are the *national* meaning, and the *social* meaning. Indeed, it is only because of this permanent confusion that the current phase of the history of politics has seen the emergence of a doctrine of 'socialism in one country' and of a 'national-socialist state'.

IDEOLOGY AND IDEOLOGIZATION

Two main ideologies emerged fully fledged at the end of the nineteenth century: Liberal—Utilitarianism and Communism. Both ideologies were foreshadowed in the French Revolution, in an amalgam of contradictions, doomed to be self-destructive.

Nationalism is not an ideology in the sense given to this word in our enquiry (see above pp. 23—26). For in its original meaning of the sentiment or consciousness of kinship (that is of the evident community, indeed family, of language, customs and more often than not territory) it is immemorial, and did not merely come to the surface in the nineteenth century. Now nationalism is the common denominator of all ideologies because since each ideology has to be propagated within the framework of national politics, that is of a nation-state, it has to be presented in national terms and with a nationalistic motivation, even if only secondary. This also explains why in moments of crisis the nationalistic motivation can triumph over other motivations (as, for instance, before the First World War when the powerful Socialist parties in France and Germany voted for war between their peoples). Or why it can be re-born in a National-Socialist form (which was the ambiguous name chosen by Hitler for its Fascist brand) or in a National—Communist form as the Soviet form and all current forms of Marxism—Leninism have been since Stalin came to power. But, as this point we cannot anticipate too much.

[3] See for a different view E. Gellner, *Nations and Nationalism,* Oxford 1983.

There are at least two major differences between socialism and utilitarianism and communism which render it inappropriate to describe socialism as 'a fully fledged ideology of the nineteenth century'. One is the absence of any single work of ideological philosophy — and of any single author — from which the ideology proceeds and to which it must conform. The intellectual origins of socialism are so multiple and so diverse that they become lost in folklore. Its main tenet, the pursuit of equality, is immemorial and instinctive, almost like the tenets of nationalism. The two *original* authors to whom socialism can refer are Christ and Marx — the ideologist. Indeed at the end of the nineteenth century, when in Germany, or even in England socialism became more ideological (through William Morris, Hyndman and the Hampstead Marxist Club) it also became formally Marxist. Conversely, in spite of the efforts of German revisionism at the end of the nineteenth century, the Swedish and German socialist parties later, in the twentieth century, explicitly proclaimed that their programmes were incompatible with Marxist ideology.

The second major difference, which will become clearer in Chapter 5, is the ultimate incompatibility between socialism and materialism. Because of its Christian origins, socialism is essentially idealistic; and in spite of its collectivism, socialism or Social Democracy defends the institutions guaranteeing political freedom, that is to say the freedom of action and belief of individuals. This is also why, like utilitarianism, and unlike Marxism or Marxism—Leninism, socialism is more evolutionist than revolutionary.

POLITICAL PARTY

This, like ideology, is a modern political phenomenon. It is, though, an expression applied as early as the seventeenth century to such intra-parliamentary formations as the English Whigs and Tories and in the eighteenth century to the Swedish Caps and Hats. Anachronistically it is also applied to Guelfs and Ghibelines in Florence, to Blues and Greens in Byzantium and even *pace* Roland Syme, to 'Caesar's party.'[4] But the really modern concept is that of a 'representative political party' functioning within a Parliament and legitimated by some form of electoral process. The broader and more essential the element of representativeness becomes within the framework of the nation-state, the more indispensable the political parties become as the intermediaries in the process of representation, with the side effect of centralization. Often originally regional or social in origin, the representative political parties necessarily become, or try to become, national, and when the moment arises, federal or international. The representative political party was and is the middle-man of political business.

But with the advent of ideologies, the date of birth of which is actually

[4]Roland Syme: *The Roman Revolution*, Oxford.

almost coincidental with that of the representative political parties, they became gradually interlocked with ideology. The major new representative political parties in the twentieth century were in reality ideological parties – and the previously established parties had to colour their initial pragmatism with some counter-ideologization.

On the other hand, ideologies and the operations of ideologization could not achieve their final purpose without giving birth to ideological political organizations, which afterwards became their indispensable instrument. Without political action and experiment, the ideology remains a Utopia; without leading to action and to organization, ideologization remains a futile exercise in preaching. In Marxist terms, if the role of philosophy is henceforwards to transform the world, obviously what is needed is to set up an 'organization', Lenin's key-concept, which would take it upon itself to do the transforming according to the precepts of the ideology.

In this context, *organization*, or indeed political organization must be understood in two senses, one functional, the other social.

In the functional sense the party organization or apparat is the national, sometimes international, network of cells and agencies, which fulfil the tasks of the political party under the ideological and administrative command and discipline of the 'centre'. The second meaning is social: the party organization is the group of dedicated or indeed professionalized people who see their party as an enterprise which might produce far more prestigious and more substantial rewards than commerce, industry and finance, and to the success of which they consequently dedicate their lives – as activists, agents or apparatchiks. Indeed, the stake in this gamble is a winner-take-all stake. The political party, although etymologically only a 'part', has a functional propensity to absorb the 'whole'. (Lenin's monolithic revolutionary party manifestly proclaimed its aim of exclusive domination.) And behind both the competitive and the revolutionary political parties the driving force is the 'organization', in the sense of apparat, the socio-professional group as well as the institutional entity, which functions as an anonymous machine and imposes its own momentum on the men who form, it. Indeed it is becoming more and more evident that in modern political systems, the party-organization has become a force in itself, emancipated from and dominating its membership and sometimes even its leadership. But here again we cannot anticipate too much.

Chapter 4

The Jacobin proto-system of political happiness

Le bonheur est une idée neuve en Europe
Saint-Just

The French Revolution must be seen[1] in some respects as the crisis point of multiple national and transnational historical trends, which were influenced and precipitated by it, but which would have developed even if the revolution had not occurred.

In other respects, the French Revolution is unique — unique in its original features and unique in its consequences for the history of the world. One must combine both these views of the French Revolution if one wants to place this particularly complex phenomenon in its right context.

---

[1] Most of the ideas in this chapter were discussed in a weekly seminar held between 7 January and 4 May 1981, at the Institut de Hautes Etudes Sociales in Paris, under the joint presidency of Professor François Furet and myself, under the title of: *Peut-on conceptualiser le Jacobinisme? ou les ambivalences de la démocratie.* The contributions which, I hope will be published in a volume, were as follows: G. Ionescu: 'Peut-on conceptualiser le Jacobinisme? Aux origines des ambivalences de la démocratie'; F. Furet: 'Le concept du Jacobinisme dans la philosophie politique française'; F. Furet–Edad Halévy: 'Les sociétés de pensée et l'ambivalence opinion politique – propagande'; Pierre Manent: 'L'ambivalence homme-citoyen'; P. Birnbaum: 'L'ambivalence levée en masse–participation'; A.I. Forrest: 'Les comités revolutionaires, l'ambivalence spontanéité-organisation'; Norman Hampson: 'Le comité du Salut public et l'ambivalence parlement-parti'; Edad Halévy: 'Les élections de 1789 et l'ambivalence répresentation–manipulation'; F. Dreyfus: 'Le centralisme français avant et après le Jacobinisme'; V. Wright: 'Le Jacobinisme dans la Commune de 1871; M. Merle: 'Etat National–Fédéralisme'; G. Ionescu: 'Conclusions'.

I must thank the Social Science Research Council for a grant which allowed me to undertake the research in France during the academic year 1980–81, and the University of Manchester, Department of Government, where I worked.

References are henceforward made in the form: Seminar: Furet, Birnbaum, Forrest (etc.) and must be checked with the above list of contributors.

To take some examples of the first view; old-fashioned Marxism used to reduce the French Revolution to the triumph of the capitalist bourgeoisie over the *ancien régime.* But in the view of the French historian, François Furet:

> the Marxist popular interpretation of the French Revolution turns the world upside down: it situates the revolutionary break on the economic and social level, while nothing more resembles French society under Louis XVI than that same society under Louis Philippe. . . For neither capitalism nor the bourgeoisie had any need for revolutions in order to appear in, and to dominate, the history of the major European countries in the nineteenth century.[2]

Similarly, on the sociological plane, the more detailed and more precise analyses made by modern historians of the fluctuating relations at the dawn of industrial society, between royal officials, bourgeoisie, nobility, peasants, craftsmen, merchants, industrialists, entrepreneurs and last but not least workers, which are often described in Marxist sociological interpretations as only three homogeneous classes, have cast serious doubts on many previous oversimplifications.[3]

More to the point in this respect is Saint-Simon's view that the French Revolution had been a check, indeed an obstacle, to the advance of industrial society in France.[4] He argued that the revolution failed to achieve its historical mission of accomplishing the transition from feudal society to industrial society, from the politics of centralized government to the politics of power diffused among all producers and industrialists, and from the politics of narrow 'patriotism', to the transnational politics required by the modern economy of the industrial society.

Another example of the transnational causes of the French Revolution is the scientific, intellectual and cultural movement of the eighteenth century. The revolution was greatly assisted by the systematic activity of official, semi-official, and even clandestine, cultural associations in which 'new' ideas were exchanged and propagated. The role played by these organizations has been illustrated in A. Cochin's[5] investigation of the activities of pre-revolutionary *sociétés de pensées* and more specifically of the Masonic lodges. More recently, and with greater subtlety R. Koselleck[6] and Robert Darnton[7] have studied the phenomenon of ideological transmission, or what is presented here as ideologization, before and during the revolution.

[2]François Furet: 'The French Revolution revisited'.

[3]See for an up-to-date survey, William Doyle: *The Origins of the French Revolution*, Oxford 1981.

[4]See G. Ionescu: *The Political Thought of Saint-Simon*, Oxford 1970.

[5]Auguste Cochin: *L'Esprit du jacobinisme*, Paris 1979.

[6]Reinhart Koselleck: *Le Règne de la critique*, Paris 1979.

[7]Robert Darnton: *Mesmerism and the End of the Enlightenment in France*, Cambridge 1968.

Finally, the revolution only temporarily deflected the consolidation of the nation-state which had been undertaken by the centralizing policies of the French monarchy, as Tocqueville has stressed in his classic work. Jacques Godechot's *Les institutions de la France sous la Révolution et l'Empire* has contributed a great deal to the understanding of the process of institutionalization during the period of the 'constitutional government' of the revolution. But like Soboul[8] and Cobb,[9] Godechot believes that the Jacobin-manipulated 'revolutionary government' (August 1792 to October 1794) produced, by a *sui generis* process of spontaneous generation, only 'transitional' institutions; so transitional indeed that even the names, or rather nicknames, they were given at the time were *ad hoc*, such as 'armées révolutionnaires' or 'armée des sans culottes'. According to Godechot and to Cobb these non-institutionalized organizations, born by spontaneous (revolutionary) generation, were the by-products of the escalation of the action of mobs unleashing irrevocable political events.

If we turn now to what made the French Revolution *unique* we find that it was marked by four principles which had not appeared together in the English and American Revolutions. They were:

1. *The anti-Christian principle* The English, the American and the French Revolutions can be regarded as three historical stages in the consummation of the sovereignty of the people. But while the two first stages were effected within a Christian political conception, the French Revolution is in its very essence anti-Christian. 'I see on the stage only two facts, two principles, two actors and two persons: Christianity and the Revolution' exclaimed the radical Michelet in the opening sentences of his *Histoire de la Révolution Française* – agreeing only on this one fundamental point with all the Right-wing historians of the revolution. And Tocqueville, in *L'Ancien Régime et la Révolution*, explained that in all great revolutions which had preceded the French, either the laws had been attacked and the beliefs respected, or those who had attacked religion had not challenged the civil constitution. 'But in the French Revolution' he added 'the religious laws having been abolished together with the civil laws, the human mind lost its balance entirely'. Philosophically the anti-Christian stand prevents the hopes of men from rising beyond their existence on earth.[10] But politically the

---

[8]Albert Soboul: *Précis d'histoire de la Révolution française*, 2 vols, Paris 1962, and *Les Sans-culottes parisiens en l'an II*, Paris 1958.

[9]Richard Cobb: *Les Armées révolutionnaires*, Paris 1956.

[10]In her very profound and thought-provoking book, Mona Ozouf described the difficulties experienced by local leaders of the revolution in educating the 'people' in the new secular spirit. She quoted for instance this almost epigrammatic sentence from a report of the Commissaire des Ardennes to his superior: 'Le mal d'être ici-bas reporte souvent les âmes des habitants des campagnes vers d'autres espérances'. Or, in an impoverishing English translation: 'The sorrows of life on earth often take the souls of the inhabitants of the countryside back to other hopes'. Mona Ozouf, *La Fête Révolutionnaire*, Paris, pp. 322–23.

anti-Christian stand also signifies the affirmation of the autonomy and the supremacy of politics. In an ultimate logic, the 'people' cannot be sovereign if the people is not the sole master of its destiny.

2. *The Republican principle*   Whereas the English Revolution ultimately rejected Republicanism and culminated in the constitutional enmeshment of the sovereignty of the people with that of the King (the King-in-Parliament), the French Revolution, like the American Revolution took the principle of the sovereignty of the people to its ultimate conclusion; the Republic.

3. *The principle of the representation of the sovereign people*   The French Revolution needed a form of representation in theory equivalent to universal manhood suffrage: The National Assembly based its legitimacy on the assumed will of the 'sovereign people', and the political parties or groups formed within the National Assembly claimed to be electorally mandated by the sovereign people.

4. *The principle of the abolition of the interests*   The fourth principle is particularly significant as only the French Revolution banned the functioning and denied the legitimacy of organized socio-economic 'interests'. It established instead, in accordance with the Rousseauist conception of the general will, a strictly bipolar relation between the French citizen[11] (erstwhile man) and the French state. The French Revolution abolished by law most functional intermediary socio-economic bodies. The intermediary bodies which it created were the political factions and parties formed within the representative assemblies and identified by membership of the clubs. But the 'interests' were soon re-established in and by the industrial society, whose imperatives proved more lasting than those of the revolutionary political will.

It is in the unique character of the French Revolution that the original contribution of the Jacobins must be sought. In order to do so we must first retrace as briefly as possible the history of the Jacobins, and then examine how the constitutive elements of what was going to become the system of political happiness were first pre-figured in the Jacobin proto-system.

A BRIEF SUMMARY OF THE HISTORY OF THE JACOBINS

The States General of France, elected in March–April 1789, held their first sessions in June in Versailles. Since the newly elected deputies did not know each other, regional affinities brought them together and the Club Breton was founded by the deputies of Brittany. Although the Club bore

[11]Seminar: Pierre Manent.

a regional name it nevertheless soon became the meeting place of the deputies of the third estate, intellectuals (see pp. 90–2) of all kinds, lawyers, professionals, officials and *abbés*, who were imbued with the ideas of Rousseau or Mably (Condorcet and Siéyès were among them) already widely spread by the *sociétés de pensée.*

On 17 June 1789, the deputies of the Third Estate unilaterally declared themselves to constitute the French National Assembly, a decision finalized three days later by oath of the Tennis Court and by the deputies of the clergy and the nobility joining the assembly of the Third Estate. The new Assembly described itself as the Constituent Assembly, the function of which was to draw up a constitution for France. It was the first of the three assemblies of the French Revolution.

On 5 October 1789, the King and the Assembly were forced by the Paris crowds to move from Versailles to Paris. The Breton Club, by then already much radicalized, also moved to the capital and established itself in the former convent of the Jacobins in the rue St. Honoré, a few yards from the Assembly. It took the name of *Société des Amis de la Constitution.* At first the Club was open only to carefully selected members, but soon its debates became public and were attended by large crowds. Its main objects were to provide an arena for debates; to enable 'friends of the constitution' to co-ordinate their views before debates in the Assembly; and to establish and maintain contacts with the affiliated societies in the provinces which soon sprang up in large numbers, 152 in 1789, 2,000 by 1793. The Jacobin Club organized 'bureaux de correspondence' with the affiliated societies from which, according to the Statute of 1789, it 'received instructions' and to which 'it transmitted the sense of the decrees of the National Assembly, to the implementation of which all these societies were especially dedicated'. The membership was scrutinized by three committees: of administration, presentation and verification. Expulsion from the society could amount to political death.

The Jacobin Club was not the only political club in Paris nor was it the most revolutionary. On the contrary, in comparison with the Club des Cordeliers, another former convent,[12] which was frequented especially by Danton, Marat, and Camille Desmoulins, and in which political personalities and the crowds mingled freely, the attitude of the Jacobin *Société des Amis de la Constitution* was both more positive and more élitist. But only the Jacobins succeeded in setting up the network of 'correspondence' or communication with affiliated societies throughout France, and a disciplined membership. However, in the Assembly itself, members of all these democratic clubs formed an amorphous group, known later as the Mountain, because they occupied the upper benches in the hemicycle of the Assembly.

[12]Voltaire in his *Dictionnaire Philosophique* reminds us that the religious schools of thought of the two convents had been engaged in ferocious theological quarrels. He would have been amused by the continuation of the quarrel, in political terms, between the two convents-clubs. Voltaire: *Dictionnaire Philosophique*, Pommeau edn, Paris 1964, p. 253.

The attitude of the members of the Jacobin Club varied on the great issues of the revolution. The events of 14 July 1790 marked a turning point with the emergence of the Commune of Paris as a powerful representative organ of the people of Paris. The proclamation by the *fédérés* of the federation of France, at the instigation of the people of Paris, is rightly considered to symbolize the birth of the new sovereign nation of France. But this change in the conception of sovereignty crystallized two of the main issues facing the revolutionaries: kingdom versus republic and federation versus unitary state.

The failure of the attempted escape of the King and the royal family on 20 June 1791 further sharpened the conflict of attitudes. In spite of a declaration by the Constituent Assembly that the King was inviolable, a petition to depose him, originating in confused debates in the Jacobin Club, was taken by the people of Paris to the meeting place in the Champs de Mars. On their return to the centre of Paris the demonstrators were stopped by troops who eventually fired on them, killing a number. The so-called massacre of the Champs de Mars was yet another major turning point in the revolution.

The Jacobin Club was itself by now split on many of these issues. Three hundred deputies, who were members of the Club, refused to adopt the plainly republican motion to 'replace the King by any constitutional means'. Led by Barnave (its first president), Barrère, Siéyès and Talleyrand all left the premises of the Club, taking with them the archives and records, and moved to the Convent of the Feuillants on the opposite side of the street. They announced that they were forming a *'Société des amis de la constitution, séant aux Feuillants'*,[13] and wrote to the various affiliated societies to inform them of the move. Of the well-known Jacobins only Robespierre and Pétion remained in the Jacobin Club. But the Club was already so solidly established as a political and organizational entity, so customary had it become for the people of Paris to resort to it, to listen to, and to try to influence, its debates that the move to the Feuillants soon proved to be a failure. Possibly also Robespierre's reputation as the one 'incorruptible' friend of the people and as the real leader of the democratic movement, was already a decisive factor. By the autumn of 1791, out of 630 or so affiliated societies, some 552 had remained staunchly Jacobin and only 83 had followed the Feuillants.

Robespierre, at the head of a small group of radical Jacobins, now decided in favour of an infusion of new blood into the old Club, purging those who had deviated and recruiting only sound revolutionary members in Paris and throughout the country. This was especially important because the electoral campaign for a new assembly, the future Legislative Assembly, was being prepared and the Club needed many loyal deputies. At its last session, the Constituent Assembly passed a decree forbidding

[13]Gérard Maintenant, 'Les Jacobins à l'épreuve: la scission des Feuillants', in *Les Jacobins*, special issue of *Cahiers d'histoire de l'institut Maurice Thorez*, Nos 32–33, Paris 1979, p. 97.

the popular societies to obstruct the implementation of any legal measure, to submit collective petitions or to send deputations in the name of the society. This marked the first conflict between the representative assembly and the factions or parties.

The decree remained void, as on 1 October 1791 the new assembly, elected on the basis of a new, qualified, but very wide suffrage, began its sessions. The 'affiliated societies' had campaigned very vigorously for Jacobin candidates. Robespierre himself was unable to stand, since on his own motion members of the Constituent Assembly were barred from standing in the next elections. But he had already made his mark as one of the most influential orators of the Jacobin Club, in which he exercised great influence. In October and November he went on a long propaganda tour of his native Artois, and it was during these months that the 'societies' reached the unprecedented number of 2,000. One of Robespierre's principal themes was universal suffrage. He was at this time also elected to the Paris Commune, the government of the city.

Meanwhile, in April 1792, the government of France, in the hands of the deputies known as the Girondins (many came from that area of France), had declared war on Austria and Prussia and their allies. The advance of the Prussians in summer 1792 exacerbated fears of a reactionary plot, and on 10 August 1792 a popular insurrection led by the Commune of Paris attacked the Tuileries, and resulted in the suspension of the constitution and the arrest and deposition of the King.

The next day elections to a new national Convention were decreed. Robespierre was also now editing a newspaper, *La défense de la Constitution*, which was distributed to all the societies and associated libraries in the land. His defence of the supremacy of Paris over the territory of France was opposed by Brissot and other deputies of the Gironde. In the meantime the Jacobins, who had at first opposed the war, changed their tack. They now directed their criticism against the generals appointed by the Girondins, and condemned the lack of centralization necessary in their view for the achievement of victory.

The new Convention was elected on a suffrage that was almost universal and began its sessions on 21 September 1792, against a background of mounting indiscriminate terror. On 22 September the society changed its name to *Société des Jacobins, amis de la liberté et de l'égalité*. It still included such opposing factions as the Girondins (partisans of the war and of a federal decentralized France); Hébertists (partisans of egalitarianism and of the working people of Paris as against the bourgeoisie); Dantonists and Robespierrists, the 'indulgents' and the 'hardliners'. From now on the nature of Jacobinism changed. While the trial of the King proceeded, Robespierre stepped up his attack on the members of the Gironde, urged on by the increasingly revolutionary Commune of Paris. On 20 January 1793, after a rousing maiden speech by the young Armand de Saint-Just, the Convention sentenced the King to death, and he was executed the next day. Shortly afterwards France also declared war on England.

On 6 April 1793 the existing Committee of General Defence was replaced by the Committee of Public Safety which for all intents and purposes was to be the government of France for the next fifteen months. The first government was led by Danton and his friends. By June 1793, the Girondin faction had been expelled from the Convention (they were to be executed on 10 October 1793). On 10 July it was the turn of Danton, who was expelled from the Committee of Public Safety to which Robespierre was appointed on 27 July. On 10 October, the 'constitutional' government was declared to be a 'revolutionary government' until the end of the war.

The principles of the new *revolutionary government* of France were expounded by Robespierre in a speech on 25 December 1793, and the Jacobins in Paris and throughout the country intensified the measures of 'public safety', in other words systematically and legally organized terror.[14] The new rulers of France turned first on the Hébertists, accusing them of anarchist conspiracies against the state. Arrested and tried on 21 March 1794, the friends of egalitarianism and the working people were executed on 24 March 1794. Then came the turn of Danton and his followers who were dispatched in April. The committee of Public Safety succeeded in imposing an increasingly centralized administration on the country by means of which it organized the war effort and intensified the terror, using the network of Jacobin societies throughout France and its own special agents 'en mission'. But even the remaining Jacobins were no longer united. Robespierre's proposals to establish the cult of the Supreme Being alienated many of those who wished to intensify the measures of de-Christianization. Reaction against the Paris-led terror was spreading in the provinces, and in the capital itself revolutionary fervour was being suppressed by the Jacobin dictatorship, while the indiscriminate appetite of the guillotine struck terror in the breasts of members of the Convention. On 9 Thermidor (27 July), Robespierre was overthrown by a joint vote of all his enemies. He was executed together with Saint-Just and a total of 105 Robespierrists the next day. On 23 Brumaire (13 November) the Convention decreed that the Jacobin Club should be closed.

---

[14] At this point it is worth quoting for its retrospective tragicomic effect, Trotsky's comparison between Bolsheviks and Jacobins: 'They were idealists. . . We are materialists. . . They were rationalists. . . we are materialists. . . *They chopped off heads, we enlighten them with class-consciousness*'. Quoted in Christopher Hampson: *Socialism in a Crippled World*, London 1981, p. 89. (Italics in the text.) Poor Trotsky!

THE CONSTITUTIVE ELEMENTS

This brief summary of the history of the way in which the Jacobins accelerated the pace of the French Revolution and precipitated its final disaster, should provide us with sufficient evidence of their conception of the revolution as a proto-system of public happiness. For in spite of the fact that they did not have enough time even to begin to establish such a system, and that the prerequisites of a functioning industrial society were still in embryo, all the constitutive elements of such a system can already be detected.

THE PROMISE OF HAPPINESS

In the Jacobin vocabulary political happiness is still called public happiness as in the language of Rousseau. But it is now activated by a political will and by a political organization. 'The goal of society is common happiness' asserted the first line of article I of the Declaration of the Rights of Man (but significantly it added to the title the words 'and of the Citizen' on 2 October 1789). But in the mouths of such political leaders, as Robespierre and Saint-Just,[15] this assertion becomes an impulse to action, because it has a political finality. 'Your only concern must be the happiness of a great people and of mankind' Robespierre enjoined the deputies to the Convention on 25 September 1792.

In his 'correspondence' with the provincial Jacobin Clubs Robespierre writes: 'Brothers and friends, we are now able to begin again this correspondence with you, the link of which is patriotism and the object of which is public happiness.'[16] In other speeches he expounded the same idea:

> in a word what we want is to fulfil the wishes of nature, achieve the destinies of mankind, keep the promises of philosophy, absolve providence of the crimes of the long reign of terror. [What we want is] that France. . . should become the model for the other nations. . . and that by sanctifying our work with our blood, we should see at least the first light of the dawn of universal felicity. This is our ambition, this is our goal.[17]

[15]According to the calculations undertaken at the *Centre de lexicologie politique* of Saint-Cloud on the political vocabulary of Robespierre and Saint-Just, the expression 'bonheur' especially 'bonheur public' reaches with them one of its highest frequencies. See Françoise Theuriot 'La conception Robespierrienne du bonheur' in *Annales Historiques de la Revolution Française*, 1970, pp. 207–27.

[16]Letter of Robespierre to the 'affiliated societies' of 1 August 1791, published in the *Journal des debats des Amis de la Constitution*, No. 36, 1791.

[17]Robespierre's speech on the principles of the ethics of politics. Report submitted on behalf of the Committee of Public Safety, 18 Pluviôse Year II, 5 February 1794.

Or: 'Yes, this delightful country [France] where we live, on which nature has bestowed most especially its gifts, is made to be the realm of freedom and of happiness. . . O sublime people, accept the sacrifice of my entire being, happy is he who is born in your midst! even happier he who can die for your happiness.'[18] And in his very last speech, before his execution, he exclaimed: 'We had left France in a profound impression of calm and of happiness. Looking at this sublime reminder of the first people of the world, who could have believed that crime could still exist on earth?'[19]

Saint-Just expressed the same ideas. To him belongs the famous exclamation 'Happiness is a new idea in Europe,'[20] (which was not true; 'le Bonheur' was an idea current in France in the seventeenth century. What was new was the idea of *political* happiness). He also gave the almost equally famous warning; 'You will perish, you who run after wealth and who try to find a happiness other than that of the people.'[21] Saint-Just's constant concern with public happiness was how to keep it public, how to prevent it from being eaten away by the human instincts and the greed of individuals or groups. Thus while he insisted that 'Our goal is to establish a sincere government which would make the people happy' and that 'you have given us the task of guarding the happiness of the fatherland' he constantly saw that 'everybody sacrifices public happiness to his own.'[22]

It is also Saint-Just who provided a more precise description of what public happiness actually meant:

We have promised you the happiness of Sparta and that of Athens in their heyday; we have promised happiness of virtue and mediocrity, the happiness which springs from the enjoyment of what one needs, and without excesses; we have promised you a happiness made of the hatred of tyranny, of the delights of a cottage and of a fertile field tilled by your own hands. We promised to the people the happiness of being free and undisturbed so as to enjoy in peace the fruits and the customs of the Revolution; that of going back to nature, to morality and to found the Republic.[23]

Material belongings, ownership and exploitation enter only indirectly into this reasoning. Both Robespierre and Saint-Just considered ownership

[18]Robespierre: Speech on religious and moral ideas. Report submitted on behalf of the Committee of Public Safety, 18 floréal Year II, 7 May 1794.

[19]Speech of 8 Thermidor Year II, 26 July 1794.

[20]The entire text runs as follows: 'Europe should learn that you do not want to have henceforward either an unhappy man or an oppressor on French territory, that this example should fructify the whole world, that it should spread the love of virtues and of happiness. Happiness is a new idea in Europe.' 13 Ventôse, 3 March 1794.

[21]'Vous périrez, vous qui courrez à la fortune, et qui cherchez un bonheur à part de celui du peuple'. Report submitted on behalf of the Committee of Public Safety, 23 Ventôse Year II, 13 March 1794.

[22]Speech on arrested persons, Report presented on behalf of the Committee of Public Safety and of General Security, 8 Ventôse Year II, 26 February 1794.

[23]Saint-Just: Report presented on behalf of the Committee of Public Safety, 23 Ventôse Year II, 13 March 1794.

or private property to be one of the prerequisites of the society they wanted to found. To be sure, their kind of private ownership had to be a just ownership, 'the ownership of the goods which is guaranteed by the law'; or in its constitutional formulation, it must be ownership 'limited by the obligation to respect anyone else's rights'. And they were also egalitarian. But their conception of equality was moral and political rather than material and economic. 'Robespierre is anti-socialist' Michelet explicitly says. Economic equality was for them the consequence of the civic morality of the new society, of the transformation of men into citizens. Their attitude was illustrated by the struggle the Jacobins waged in the Convention against the opposition of the Hébertists, until they succeeded in sending these economic levellers to the guillotine.

Behind that bucolic description of happiness, which Saint-Just had in mind, lies the system of public happiness as he had described it in his *Fragments sur les Institution Républicaines* (posthumously published in 1800).

> If the people loves virtue and frugality; if arrogance is erased from human faces, if decency comes back into the city, and the counter-revolutionaries, the moderates and the rascals crumble into dust; if we are terrible to the foes of Revolution, and kind and loving towards a patriot; if the officials go into their offices so as to do the good work without seeking to win reputation, and having only their hearts as witnesses; if you give land to the poor people; and if you take it away from the scoundrels; then I recognize that you have made a revolution. But if the contrary happens, if there is no revolution, then, there is no hope whatsoever of achieving virtue and happiness on earth.

Saint-Just does not make the connection between virtue and 'happiness on earth' accidentally; it lies, on the contrary, at the very heart of the theory of public and, in consequence, political happiness. Virtue, 'la vertu', is the key concept of Jacobin public morality. Norman Hampson rightly defines it as: 'Vertu, in the classical sense of the subordination of the individual to the citizen'; and he adds that *vertu* 'took precedence over all other human values, even over democracy itself'.[24]

The concept of virtue understood as the 'subordination of the individual to the citizen' transformed *individual* happiness into *public* happiness. The citizen is the public side of man — of the individual; it follows that public happiness is the happiness which the citizen alone can enjoy as a reward for his absorption in the *public* sphere of life, regardless of how the private, authentic, and unique self feels about this absorption, if this self still exists. As we have seen, in the discussion of Rousseau's abstract theory of the immersion of the 'volontés particulières' in the 'volonté générale', such an immersion must be effected by someone — by the mysterious 'on' or 'vous'.

But in the mouths of *political* leaders like Robespierre and Saint-Just that 'on', 'one' can be unmistakably identified with 'we' — with the

---

[24]Norman Hampson: *The First European Revolution*, London 1969, p. 108.

promiser who makes the promise to the promisee that if he will do something — in this case practise the virtues of a citizen — he will in exchange obtain as a reward, something which otherwise he would be unable to achieve — in this case public happiness — happiness being the ultimate purpose of life on earth. When Saint-Just says 'We have promised you. . . the happiness of virtue' he explicitly makes the political promise of happiness, or, pleonastically, the promise of political happiness: I can and shall give you happiness provided you join me in my action to form a new society, ruled by me on behalf of the people. Moreover, the consequent, symmetrical threat is pronounced in the same breath: you will not be able to be happy if you do not follow my guidance and immerse yourself in the people led by me; and you will perish if you do not.

'*Vertu* takes precedence over democracy', public happiness takes precedence over individual happiness, and the duty of the political leaders is to see that these precedences are observed. These were the principles which bridged, in the eyes of the Jacobins, the change of political means, when they passed in theory as in practice, from *constitutional* to *revolutionary* government. The change of means was brusque and total but the fundamental justification remained the same. For, at the beginning of constitutional government in the first issue of his new journal, *Defense de la Constitution* (19 May 1792) Robespierre published an 'Exposition of my views', in which he stressed, as Aulard remarks, in the very first line,[25] that 'It is the constitution as it is that he is defending' [which then meant monarchy]. But once in power, Robespierre soon stressed the differences between what he himself called constitutional government and what he called 'revolutionary government.'[26] 'Constitutional government' he argued in December 1792, 'is concerned principally with the civil society; and the revolutionary government with public freedom. Under the constitutional regime it is almost enough to protect individuals against public power; under a revolutionary regime the public power itself is constrained to defend itself against all the factions which attack it.' 'What is then to be done?' he continued: 'To indict those who invent perfidious systems, to protect patriotism even in its mistakes; to enlighten the patriots and incessantly to raise the people to the height of its rights and of its destinies'. The speech culminated with a contrasting description of vices and virtues: 'Virtues are simple, modest, poor, often ignorant, sometimes rude; they are the quality of the poor, and the patrimony of the people. Vices are surrounded by wealth, armed with all the attractions of voluptuousness. . .', etc., and with the supreme invocation: 'O virtues! are you less needed for founding a republic than for governing a peace?'

To sum up these remarks on the first element in the Jacobin system of

---

[25] A. Aulard: *Histoire Politique de la Revolution Française*, Paris 1901, p. 182.
[26] Speech on the principles of revolutionary government, 25 December 1792, 5 Nivôse Year II.

public happiness, the promise of happiness, we shall turn once again to Tocqueville who first noted that: 'It was the vision of a perfect state that fired the imagination of the masses and little by little estranged them from the here and now. Turning away from the real world around them, they indulged in dreams of a far better one and ended up by living, spiritually, in the ideal world thought up by the writers.' Then Tocqueville shows how the revolutionaries imagined that their kind of ideal world could be brought about:

> When we closely study the French Revolution we find that it was conducted in precisely the same spirit as that which gave rise to so many books expounding theories of government in the abstract. Our revolutionaries had the same fondness for broad generalizations, cut-and-dried legislative systems and a pedantic symmetry; the same contempt for hard facts; the same taste for reshaping institutions on novel, ingenious, original lines; the same desire to reconstruct the entire constitution according to the rules of logic and a preconceived *system* instead of trying to rectify its faulty parts.[27]

I italicized the word *system* because it is the key-word. For what emerged in the minds of men who thought about politics in that age, when the epistemology of science was undergoing major change, was the pursuit of a scientific system for society as a whole. Society could be organized as a system — provided that, like any system, it had a central impulse for its input and output processes. Political happiness had 'fired the imagination of the masses'. What was needed was a system of political happiness which was workable both in theory and in practice.

We now come to the second constitutive element of the Jacobin system of public happiness, namely the prerequisite of a structured nation-state in which the system can be constructed.

THE NATION-STATE

This is a modern phenomenon — but its component parts, the concept of the state and the concept of the nation, appeared at least as early as the seventeenth century. Both concepts are particularistic since they were born in opposition to the universal principle. As Dante had sensed in the fourteenth century, the divine right of kings was 'in its origin an assertion of the right of the lay against the ecclesiastical supremacy.'[28] Indeed in the conflict between popes and emperors the problem of sovereignty was fought over in direct territorial and political terms. Nation is a much older idea than state as it is interchangeable with 'people' and with the emotional connotation of kinship. It was only in the eighteenth century and notably in the French Revolution that *nation* became the pivot of the new

---

[27] A. de Tocqueville, *L'ancien régime et la révolution*, p. 240.

[28] J.N. Figgis: *From Gerson to Grotius*, Cambridge 1931, p. 63.

motivation of the organization of sovereignty, and of the new *state*. So stunning was its appearance that Immanuel Kant one day prolonged his daily walk round his house to go to meet the coach from France which bore the news of the 'spiritual unity' which had been achieved on the fateful 14 July 1790.[29]

But in order to assess the role played by the revolution in the formation of the French state one has to recognize first that great progress towards the administrative unification of the kingdom had been achieved by the absolute monarchy. In the second half of the eighteenth century, Estates survived only in three great provinces: Burgundy, Brittany and Languedoc. The administration of the towns, the economy, the corporations were all regulated by the state and all major manufacturing industries depended on the state.[30] Gallicanism furthered the subordination of the Church to the King; Jansenism was destroyed in the seventeenth century and the Jesuits were expelled in the eighteenth century by royal decision. Most significant of all, the militia set up in 1699 became a permanent national army in the eighteenth century. The King stated the number of men and of regiments he required — and the local authorities provided them, by hook or by crook.

After the summoning of the States General in 1789 and its transformation into the Constituent Assembly the work of centralization was continued. Aulard, a less excitable historian than Michelet, asserted that 14 July 1790, the feast of the Federation at the Champs de Mars, was the day on which the 'unification of France was achieved and its fatherland was founded [patrie]'. This statement is however very controversial. The *fédérés*, who had flocked to Paris from all corners of France under the auspices of the Commune of Paris, represented regions and communes, i.e., local units seeking rather for decentralization. Yet this time, as Aulard pointedly observes, these centrifugal units were animated by a 'kind of centripetal force of national unification.'[31] What had created this new and centralistic French 'nationalism'? (An expression invented pejoratively by the Abbé Barruel in 1789.)

One answer to Aulard's question is that the urge to national unification was greatly forwarded by the war. War was the *deus ex machina* of the French Revolution, which by stepping up popular emotions gave a welcome opportunity to its leaders to operate the transition from constitutional to revolutionary government (as in the Russian Revolution

---

[29]'To see Kant. . . running in the streets, like a woman, to get the news, was not that a surprising prodigious change? In fact there was no change at all. That great mind was only following its own way. What he had failed to find so far in science, spiritual unity, he could now see being established by itself by the heart and the 'instinct'. Jules Michelet, *Histoire de la Révolution Française*, Pléide, Paris, vol. I, pp. 415–16. (Italics in the text.)

[30]See especially Jacques Ellul: *Histoire des Institutions, de l'époque Française à la Revolution*, Paris 1962, 'Mainmise de l'état sur la Nation', pp. 460–534 and Seminar: F. Dreyfus.

[31]A. Aulard: *Histoire Politique de la Révolution Française*, Paris 1901.

war—communism gave its leaders the pretext to forget the promise to abolish the state and nationalism and to set up the most centralized and most nationalist—imperialist state). Even in the history of British democracy war is an experience which, especially in an industrial society, always pushes the state towards further centralization.

In the case of France, war created a new sense of kinship, 'patriotism', across the whole land; and it imposed the *ad hoc* intensive centralization of means of production, resources, labour, transport, etc., which the 'army' required. This gave a new impetus to the control of society and its activities by the state. The Robespierrist Jacobins had initially opposed the war, fearing that it would concentrate opinion behind the King. But they soon realized its uses in furthering their own centralizing policies.

War had in fact been at first a popular policy and the Girondins as well as the representatives of the opposition of the provinces to the capital, Paris, realized more promptly than the Jacobins the strength of popular feeling. Moreover once begun, war acquired its own impetus. The first, almost unimaginable successes, notably the victory of Valmy on 20 September 1792, were won by the 30,000 national recruits of the people's army to the cry of '*Vive la nation*'. Rightly Michelet noted that this was 'already the ARMY OF THE REPUBLIC'. Victory at Valmy gave birth to this army and its formation was decreed on 21 September by the Convention.[32] The concept of 'nation' inspired the people at the beginning of the war in the midst of unprecedented 'national' effort.

Later, however, when the nation was torn apart, and the provinces were looking towards Paris with resentment, the Robespierrist Jacobin Committee of Public Safety used other means of unification for the conduct of the war effort with a new political intensity. The old administrative machine as rejuvenated by the revolution and the new political machines of the Jacobin clubs or societies were used to establish with the help of the call to patriotism ('*La Patrie en danger*') a much more centralized state-machine than the monarchy could ever have achieved.

It was at this historical junction between war and revolution that the Jacobin political organization proved its effectiveness. For the Jacobins were themselves a Paris-based centralistic organization, using the methods of political representation to spread their own ideas and influence over the territory of France. Moreover, since the Jacobins were a 'society' (taken here as a proto-political party), and since they had a catechistic set of principles and theories to bestow upon their followers (taken here as ideologization), they were acting, as all national parties act nowadays,

---

[32] J. Michelet: *Histoire de la Révolution Française*, Pléiade, I, Paris 1952, p. 1132. (Capitals in the text.)

as a second circle of democratic centralization. Roederer[33] allegedly stated in a report of August 1791 that the organization was 'a transmission-belt — in both directions — between the National Assembly and the legal population of the country: the Jacobin organization is a means of pressure over the public powers. . . The society is a school of civic education for the young citizens. . . It is a haven of patriotism for all.'[34]

THE LEGITIMACY OF THE WILL OF THE PEOPLE

In the vocabulary of the French Revolution *peuple* had many meanings. *Le Peuple* was first the abstract collectivity of Frenchmen living within the territory of the Kingdom of France and speaking — or forced to speak — the French language. It was also the French *peuple* which was re-invested in the Revolution with the absolute right of sovereignty, previously incarnated by the Monarch. And it was this same *peuple* which was represented in the National Assembly.

Yet a distinction was simultaneously drawn between '*le peuple français*' and '*le peuple de Paris*'. Soon after the revolution the contradiction between these two fundamentally opposed 'peoples' led to political conflict between the Assembly and the Commune, between France and Paris. This was one of the causes of the collapse of the revolution. For '*le peuple de Paris*' was used in yet another symbolically frightening sense as 'le peuple en marche', 'people' as a crowd, assembled or marching, or rioting in the streets of the capital, or even capturing its centres of power. Indeed, the supreme advantage of the 'peuple de Paris' during the revolution, was its capacity to be present and to act on the spot, to be the maker of events.

The concentration in towns and especially in a capital, of a discontented population, vulnerable to ideological contagion and easily mobilized into demonstrative action has become, since 1789, a prerequisite of modern revolutions. *Le peuple*, or in particular *le peuple de Paris* was in reality the insurrectional motor of the French Revolution. In contrast with the Russian Revolution and those which followed it, in which pre-revolutionary and revolutionary parties played a leading part, the spontaneous action and the impetus of 'the people' in action dominated the development of events in the French Revolution. Political 'organizations' emerged in the French Revolution only *after* the 'people' had already triggered off the action of the drama. On at least four occasions in the first 'constitutional' period of the revolution, namely the storming of the

---

[33] Jean-Pierre Roederer (1754–1835) — former Counsellor of the Metz parlement under the *ancien régime*, deputy of the Third Estate, member of the Jacobins where he was in charge of problems of organization and administration — but from which he parted company to re-surface only after Robespierre's fall and make a brilliant career under the Empire.

[34] Gérard Maintenant: 'Les Jacobins à l'épreuve', p. 98.

Bastille on 14 July 1789, the return to Paris of the King and the Assembly on 6 October 1789, the storming of the Tuileries and the suspension of the King on 10 August 1792, and the day of the Federation on 20 September 1792, the intervention of the 'people' gave to events their major twists and turns, and the 'leaders' and the 'organizations' only followed.

Moreover in the particular critical period between the flight of the King in July 1791 and September 1791 when the new Constitution modelled by Condorcet, was voted in, that anonymous entity 'the people' was pushing developments from outside. Away from Paris, the peasants had taken the law into their own hands, denounced feudal rights, destroyed archives and title deeds, burnt chateaux and ceased to pay dues. But, after feudal rights and taxes were abolished together with the *ancien régime* on 4 August 1789 the peasants were again soon forgotten; and their resentment against the urban centres, and Paris especially, was soon to be directed against the to them, new, centralizing atheistic—revolutionary regime in Paris. For it was in Paris that the revolution was actually happening and it was from Paris that it radiated over the whole of France.

Political representation is by itself a series of concentric circles through which the periphery is linked to the centre and the centre acts upon the periphery. When Siéyès asked the question 'What is a nation?' and gave the answer: 'A nation is a body of associates living under one common law and represented by the same legislature', the novelty of his definition resided in the second part. From the city-states to the Roman Empire, to the Empire of Charlemagne, to the absolute monarchies, all units of rule recorded in history had lived under a common form of government — good or bad. But never before had there been a government whose legitimacy was explicitly stated to derive from *all* human beings dwelling within it, regardless of their social rank, legal status, profession or dwelling place — as the revolutionaries claimed was the case in the French Revolution.

Political representation, ideally through universal suffrage, is the hyphen between nation-state and people. The concept of the sovereignty of the people was the dual concept which asserted this dual power.

In the new constitutional doctrine of the new sovereign state of France, or rather the French people, the whole people had become the sovereign, hence the importance attached to a suffrage as universal as possible. It was this change too, from divine or royal, to popular or national sovereignty which fostered the new nationalism.[35] But the irony here lay in the fact that this was not what the *fédérés* of 1790 had in mind when they had come to Paris to proclaim the unity of France. What they had in mind was

[35]'The Revolution meant that if the citizens of a state no longer approved of the political arrangements of their society they had the right and the power to replace them by others more satisfactory. Here, then, is one prerequisite without which a doctrine such as nationalism is not conceivable.' Elie Kedourie: *Nationalism*, London 1960, pp. 12–18.

a Federation of Communes, with Paris as the principal Commune. Most of them thought that together with the Commune of Paris they would form a France of the Communes, a federation of provinces.

Here lay the great misunderstanding, the misunderstanding between those who wanted a federal French democratic nation-state and those who wanted a unitary French democratic nation-state; and here also arose the parallel misunderstanding between those who wanted a free association of all French Communes with the Commune of Paris and the Commune of Paris which, once freed from its subordination to the monarchy, wanted to subordinate all other Communes to itself.[36]

So, for several clear reasons, and a lot more obscure ones, there occurred that extraordinary historical paradox whereby the Commune of Paris — by definition a decentralized unit — became one of the most influential factors in the centralization of France. The 'Commune of Paris' was more 'Paris' than a 'Commune'. What it wanted was the restoration of Paris to its role of capital, but this time the capital of a democratic France. And it was able to achieve its ambitions because in the revolutionary vacuum of authority the Commune, which itself was formed of little Communes,[37] possessed the functional authority of a Commune. It exercised a direct local executive power as against the indirect national powers of the Assembly. Or as Mathiez shows, 'The [Paris] commune possessed executive powers. It was through their agency that the departments and districts executed the laws and that the taxes were fixed and collected. They had the right to call out the National Guard and the troops. These two rights and especially the latter were to be operative in the storm of the revolution.'[38]

IDEOLOGY AND IDEOLOGIZATION

The intellectual movements in late eighteenth-century France, notably the cultural atmosphere of democratic sociability, the assertion by intellectuals of the possibility, indeed of the obligation, to transform the misery of man into public happiness led to open ideologization during the Revolution. It is from their technical gift for ideologization, or what Tocqueville called 'proselytism', that the Jacobins derived their force.

'*Association* and *Predication* were the weapons of the Jacobins' exclaims

---

[36] Cf. on the federation of Communes, Rousseau: '*Considérations sur le gouvernement de Pologne*', III, p. 971.

[37] The Paris Commune was divided, since the Municipal Law of 1789, into forty-eight sections; each of them with an Assemblée Générale. . . These Communal General Assemblies were the primary Assemblies for the national elections. Each section had also many other organs, Commissaires de Police and Revolutionary Committees. All the Paris Communes formed a Conseil General, where, as their individual attitudes varied from issue to issue, a majority of twenty-five was necessary.

[38] Albert Mathiez: *La Révolution Française*, Paris 1922–26, p. 238.

Michelet categorically. (For the definition of *intellectuals* and of *democratic sociability* see below pp. 90–2). He adds that they based their preaching in their regular meetings only on Rousseau: 'Ils n'avaient qu'un livre, une bible, Rousseau; . . . mais Rousseau varie sur ce point . . .'.[39] For his philosophy had no avowed purpose of indoctrination and he himself had no system to offer, no disciples to form, no school of thought to organize and no political action to recommend. And if the Jacobins did appeal to his authority there is no evidence in the speeches of Robespierre or Saint-Just, the authentic Jacobin doctrinaires, that they understood Rousseau's philosophy properly, or that even if they understood it, they intended to transmit his ideas as they were. Thus the degradation was double: from Rousseau to the Jacobins, and from the Jacobins to the people. For there was no resemblance between his abstract speculations and the opportunistic interpretations which the various factions made of these speculations, when they were in opposition, as against when they were in terroristic power. Yet the process of ideologization soon proved uniquely effective. In Paris more and more rooms were opened in the Jacobin convent, including of course the chapel, and more galleries were built so as to let the crowds follow the debates – and frequently impose their own conclusions. In the country at large more and more societies were affiliated. The Jacobin press and publications, and notably Robespierre's own journals, 3,000 printed copies of his speeches, and his public 'letters' were circulated to all affiliated societies as well as to the front where they were prescribed reading for the soldiers. In the premises of the *sociétés* themselves, *cabinets de lecture* (reading rooms) were opened twelve hours a day and the 'letters' sent by the correspondence bureau from Paris were earnestly discussed in official meetings.

Tocqueville had sensed that behind the *facts* of the French Revolution, behind the *palpable* economic, sociological, historical and political causes, there persisted the mystery of the instant formation and spread (communication) of the feelings which united the men who made these facts. His admission comes in a letter written almost at the end of his life when he was still, however, working on the second part of *L'Ancien Régime et la Révolution*. 'Independently of all that can be explained in the French Revolution, there is something which remains unexplained in its spirit and in its actions. I can sense where that hidden object is, but do what I will, I cannot lift the veil.' But then Tocqueville added, in this footnote, which reads rather like a note for some future investigation of the matter: 'To dig further into this idea and show that the Revolution consisted of *that* more than of the facts; that it was impossible that ideas being what they were, the facts would not be very much like the facts we have seen'. (My italics.)

---

[39] J. Michelet: *Histoire de la Révolution Française,* Pléiade, II, Paris 1952, pp. 39 (n.) and p. 196. (Italics in the text.)

Commenting on Tocqueville's recognition that 'philosophy' and the philosophical ideas of the French Revolution were not its only cause, François Furet[40] remarks: 'There was therefore another force at work than that of the books or of the ideas, a force upon which Tocqueville had long pondered without ever being able to define it'.

There are innumerable explanations of this mysterious transformation of the mentality of Frenchmen in a couple of decades — ranging, to take only two extremes, from the low-Marxist socio-economic deterministic theories to the high allegoric theory of Foucault, who argues the existence of a seventeenth-century break in European epistemology followed by the 'appearance of man' in that epistemology. Most of these theories are only too well known. But two might well be re-examined here. They both have the advantage among others of being centred around contemporary concepts — by which I mean concepts formulated, indeed actually given their names in pre-revolutionary France. The two concepts of *intellect* and *intellectuals*, on the one hand, and of *democratic sociability* on the other, were both coined and in circulation in the pre-revolutionary era.

The intellect is the assertion of the human spirit that it can elevate itself, by its own power, to the highest spheres of knowledge (hence also the limited meaning which Kant gave to the re-born word within his philosophical terminology). As opposed to rationalism (*ratio-rationalis*) or humanism (*homo-humanum*) intellect has not produced an explicit attitude, or a formulated school of thought (*intellectualism* was a feeble and ephemeral doctrine). But intellect produced instead a new professional vocation, and a new social group: the intellectuals — or rather the French expression: *les intellectuels*. In France the expression has enjoyed since its birth, and has retained until now, a positive meaning if compared with the slightly pejorative sense it had and still sometimes has in English. 'Les intellectuels', were those people who believed that they themselves could scrutinize the spheres of knowledge previously considered inscrutable, that they could have only one purpose: to find and serve the 'truth', and therefore that they should be treated by society with respect. They were of all kinds: scientists, philosophers,[41] teachers, lawyers, novelists,[42] playwrights, journalists, artists, actors, painters, publicists and soon politicians. They saw themselves as performing a new function in society; they had to function for the benefit of society, to which they alone could

---

[40]A. de Tocqueville, letter to the Kergorlay, 16 May 1858 in *Egalité sociale et liberté politique*, Pierre Gilbert (ed.), Aubier-Montagne Paris 1977, p. 248, François Furet, *Penser la Révolution Française*, Paris 1978, pp. 250–51.

[41]It will be noted that Pascal and Descartes are the last two great minds in France to be both philosophers and scientists (and equally good at both). Already with Condorcet the philosopher distinguishes himself from the scientist, whose work he interprets.

[42]Choderlos de Laclos is one of the most intriguing of the Jacobins. That the author of *Les Liaisons Dangereuses* should afterwards become an influential member of the Jacobins and later even a censor of publications under the Jacobins, is a particularly piquant detail of the revolution.

bring the new knowledge it required: as the physicists can pronounce on the laws of the universe, and physicians on the laws of the human body, so the physiocrats tried to analyse the laws of the production of wealth. New sciences were devised of which political science and political economy were among the most popular. Some ministers of the *ancien régime*, like Turgot, were already 'un intellectuel'.

The intellectuals also believed that they should be free to function for the benefit of the people. If it is true that, once emancipated and instructed, the 'intellect' of men can act by itself, then those whose intellect had been so aroused, those who had found the truth through their knowledge, must 'go' to the people, to those who have not yet been aroused, who are still unable to dare to know, and who still cling to the old tabus. As the *ancien régime* did not provide sufficiently open avenues of influence and promotion for them and as the contact with the people was difficult, the 'intellectuals' began to feel a need to consider together their role in what they knew to be a new era in the history of the culture of France. For, within the culture of religion and faith, confidence in science and reason had by then consolidated itself.

Within the rich cultural activity of France this confidence can already be distinguished by the second half of the eighteenth century. Those whom one can now call intellectuals, those who rejected the dominant, basically religious mentality of the epoch, began to form their own groups, more or less secret. Seeking meeting places for the exchange of ideas between like-minded men, they congregated in reading rooms, cafés, museums, clubs, salons, or indeed academies of learning, while the Masonic lodges provided an even more secret undercurrent. The members of the 'sociétés de pensée', to use the phrase aptly coined by Auguste Cochin, were mainly scientists, lawyers, philosophers, abbés, political theorists; but they welcomed educated people of all ways of life, regardless of their social origin, or officials such as the *officiers du roi* (local officials, who had usually purchased their offices).

Auguste Cochin's book on these 'sociétés de pensée', which was first published in 1921[43] might seem on the surface to be inspired by the same sentiments as the anti-Jacobin propaganda during the revolution. These outpourings described the revolution as the result of a conspiracy fomented in the depths of such societies, mainly Masonic lodges, which had undermined traditional French society by propagating revolutionary ideas, and which, at the dawn of the revolution emerged into the light of day, grouped and disciplined, as the Society of Jacobins. According to the anti-Jacobins, the alleged aim of this society was to put the whole nation into the power of a handful of adventurers. But Cochin was an authentic historian. His emphasis is on the research still to be carried out in order to explore the origins of the revolution. Since he died young, immediately

---

[43]A. Cochin, *Les Sociétés de Pensée et la démocratie*, Paris 1921, republished Paris 1979 as *L'Esprit du Jacobinisme*.

after the First World War, his work remained unfinished. He succeeded however in demonstrating that the election of deputies to the States General in 1789 in Brittany and in Dijon had been 'manipulated'. Intellectuals in the various societies and lodges had prepared lists of candidates known beforehand for their radical views and had taken advantage of the ignorance or the indifference of the electors to secure their election. Cochin was also able to show that some of the societies later turned into political 'clubs', notably Jacobin clubs — and that their most important members became the leading spirits in these 'clubs'. Cochin's research is now being continued and whatever light it may throw on propaganda and electoral manipulations before and during the revolution will be of enormous benefit to its study in depth.

Similar conclusions on the manipulation of the revolution are drawn, albeit on entirely opposite premises, by the school of thought most opposed to that of Auguste Cochin: that of Professor Soboul's neo-Marxist interpretation of the French Revolution. In the Soboul school, although the background is the deterministic birth of the new socio-economic structures, of capitalism and of the bourgeoisie, and although the working classes are described as acting spontaneously as the agent of, and inspired by, their historically determined role, yet the part played by 'organizations', from the intellectual associations and societies, to the Jacobin clubs, is duly emphasized. The reproach directed at the Jacobins, that they had fallen victim to their bourgeois heritage instead of fighting for the cause of the proletariat, as did for instance Jacques Roux (one of the obscure heroes of Marxist historiography), is one of the major themes of the Marxist interpretation of the French Revolution.

The other expression which was fashionable in those pre-revolutionary days, but which unlike that of 'intellectuals' soon disappeared, was 'democratic sociability'. This somewhat ephemeral and elusive concept has two meanings. ' "Democratic sociability" was an expression applied to all *sociétés de pensée* and any other semi-clandestine meeting places of intellectuals', suggests Eddad Halévy;[44] but, he adds,

> seen from the year 1730 this democratic phenomenon is surprisingly new for under the monarchy of the *ancien régime* there were no legal associations apart from those which had been authorized by the monarchy and were related to the corporate society. What distinguished these societies from the traditional forms of organization is the fact that they had no other apparent motive for their activities than the 'exchange of friendship'.

It is this phrase, 'exchange of friendship', which is relevant to the second sense in which the term 'sociabilité démocratique' was used. For there is a

---

[44]Seminar: Eddad Halévy, 27 January 1981.

linkage between the 'sociétés de pensée' and 'sociabilité démocratique'. The former term was coined by Cochin to cover all intellectual meeting places, whether official or secret. 'Sociabilité démocratique' was the name contemporaries themselves gave to the trend developing *within* the *sociétés* towards a widespread 'exchange of friendship', a desire for contact and communication among intellectual equals (regardless of social inequalities).

'Sociability', then as now, signified the propensity of men to live in friendship with each other — a well-known sentiment, identified already, according to the Encyclopedists, in Seneca's philosophy. (D'Alembert went further when he asserted that sociability was part of national character and contrasted French sociability with English reserve — a country 'where one had to be *invited* by one's friends for supper!')[45] Why then the need for a new, pleonastic expression, 'democratic' sociability? If sociability is the quality of being friendly with people, and if the *demos* is the people, why this tautological insistence? The reason can only be found in the urge of intellectuals to share their newly acquired knowledge and interests, ideas, and aspirations as widely as possible, with the people in general, with the nation as a whole. Hence the tendency of the societies and lodges to multiply, so as to penetrate further and more deeply into the layers of that '*grand inconnu, le peuple*', to establish contact, to make friends and to *organize* them.

THE JACOBIN PROTO-PARTY

The question whether the Jacobin organization can properly be called a political party, has divided historians and political theorists alike for a century and a half. Let us first take the classical historians, Michelet and Aulard, and then examine the views of a few prominent modern French historians.

Michelet describes the Jacobins from the point of view of organization, political technique and doctrinal inspiration, in exactly the same way as we would describe a modern political party. But Michelet does not call the organization he describes a party except incidentally or metaphorically. He does not regard it as the same kind of institution as those which already existed in France in his time. Thus he writes:

> If one recognizes the decomposition, the impotence of the Girondins, as well as the symptoms of disorganization shown by society as a whole, one must recognize the necessity of the Jacobins. A political machine was needed, a new force of action, a powerful level of energy. The situation required a force which while not dominating the

---

[45] 'La sociabilité fait le principal caractère d'une nation'; D'Alembert in his preface to his *Eloges Académiques.*

Assembly entirely, would lead it, would remove the obstacles from its path, would select, purge in advance the men and the ideas, keeping the Assembly on the narrow, inflexible line of 'principles'.

And after showing that the Jacobins had not until then (1792) directly influenced either the starting point — or the turning points — of the history of the revolution Michelet adds:

The stiffness of the attitude, the postured inflexibility was even more necessary for them, because in reality their own creeds were far from being clear. But, in spite of that whatever changes there occurred in the situation, whatever deviations the changing situations imposed on their doctrines, they expressed unity. This apparent unity, this firmness in some formulation, this intolerance towards those who, while animated by the same spirit were not expressing it in the same words, helped the Revolution more than once, but often had fatal effects on it.[46]

Thus while Michelet clearly describes the Jacobins as a fully fledged political party, he does not actually use the word party. Aulard, on the contrary, speaks constantly of *partis* in the French Assemblies. But Aulard does not attach the same importance to organization as does Michelet, nor does he mention the Jacobins explicitly as one of those parties. For him the principal parties are the Girondins and the Montagne, or as he calls it *le parti montagnard*. Yet when he reaches September 1793, he so often calls the Jacobins Montagnards and the Montagnards Jacobins that, having himself noticed this change in nomenclature, he remarks in an aside that 'Jacobins or Montagnards (these two terms are then synonymous)'.[47]

With the modern French historians the same hesitation prevails. Albert Soboul, in his socio-economic interpretation of developments, states that 'The central Jacobin club became the lynchpin of revolutionary organization and gradually curtailed the autonomy of the popular revolutionary societies. The Jacobins came from the middle ranks of the bourgeoisie.'[48] Thus for Soboul the Jacobins were a political organization comparable to a political party, so comparable that even its class-origin can be identified; it is a bourgeois party, and this is why it finally impeded the popular revolution. Jean Poperen makes the analogy with modern parties even clearer by detecting the existence of an 'apparat' within the Jacobins: 'At this stage of the Revolution the influence of the masses is no longer exerted independently but through the organized classes, that it to say the Jacobin apparat.'[49] In François Furet's global vision the Jacobins are

[46] J. Michelet: *Histoire de la Révolution Française*, Paris 1850, Vol. V, pp. 46—47 and 51—52. (Author's translation.)

[47] A. Aulard: *Histoire Politique de la Révolution Française*, Paris 1901, p. 417.

[48] Albert Soboul: *A Short History of the French Revolution 1789—1799*, University of California 1965, p. 106.

[49] Jean Poperen: 'Introduction' to *Robespierre, textes choisis*, Paris 1974, Vol. III, p. 17. (My translation.)

a cause as well as an effect of the 'democratic' amalgam which is the revolution.[50] The whole vision is best summed up by Furet as follows: 'The originality of contemporary France is not that it passed from an absolute monarchy to a representative regime or from the world of the nobility to bourgeois society. Europe took the same path without revolution and without Jacobins — even though events in France were able here and there to escalate the evolution and to provide the model for its imitators.'[51] So much for the historians.

The political theorists are similarly divided. Moisei Ostrogorski published his seminal book on competitive political parties: *La démocratie et les partis politiques* in 1902 (the year when another Russian, Lenin, published his seminal book, *What is to be done?*, on Communism and the monolithic political party). Ostrogorski was the first to put forward the theory that the bureaucratic organization of the political party would influence, corrupt and finally obstruct the functioning of true representative institutions in democratic regimes. It is a theory which has since been taken up by Weber, Michels, Mosca and many others. But Ostrogorski, whose principal case-studies were the American and especially the British political parties, because they provided him with a nominal historical continuity, explicitly excluded French democracy and its political parties from his historical examination because of their alleged lack of historical continuity. He says in his introduction:

Of all countries of democratic regimes, France included, it is England which offers greater scope for this work. In the French democracy as it emerged from the Revolution, the new order had been challenged and violently interrupted several times, so that the evolution of a new society does not always offer the direct and distinct filiation of causes and effects required by the investigation.[52]

Maurice Duverger however, spoke overtly in his pioneer work on modern political parties of 'the birth of the parties in the French Constituent Assembly of 1789' and stressed that 'the example of the Jacobins deserves to be mentioned because it is characteristic of an entire phase of the pre-history of political parties'.[53]

The most categoric interpretation of the Jacobins as a party is that of A. Gramsci who linked together, in a lightning explanation of the need of the modern state for centralized conduct, Machiavelli's *Prince*, the Jacobin party and the Communist party.[54] In his *Little notes on Machiavelli's Politics* he states: 'The *modern* "Prince" [his book] must

---

[50] François Furet: 'The French Revolution Revisited' in *Government and Opposition*, Vol. 16, No. 2, 1981, pp. 200–19.
[51] François Furet: *Penser la Révolution Française*, Paris 1978 and Seminar.
[52] Moisei Ostrogorski: *La démocratie et les partis politiques*, Rosanvallon edn, Paris 1979, p. 38. (My translation.)
[53] Maurice Duverger: *Les Partis politiques*, Paris 1959, p. 3.
[54] Antonio Gramsci: *The Modern Prince and Other Writings*, New York 1957.

contain a part devoted to Jacobinism'; and in the *Quaderni* (19, 1934–35)
he develops the idea thus:

> Speaking of Jacobinism and of the Action-Party, one factor which must
> be stressed is the following: the Jacobins conquered the function of
> leading party through their own struggles. . . This trait characteristic
> of Jacobinism (but it was also that of Cromwell and of the Roundheads)
> and therefore of the great revolution, consists in forcing the situation
> (seemingly) and creating irreparable faits accomplis. . . The third
> Estate would have fallen into all these successive 'traps' had it not been
> for the energetic action of the Jacobins. The Jacobins were therefore
> the only party of the revolution in action. Against a certain tendentious,
> and anti-historic, view we must insist on the fact that the Jacobins were
> realistic like Machiavelli and not makers of abstractions. . .[55]

In order to stress the revolutionary character of the Jacobins, so as to
point up its analogies with the Communist party in the 1920s, Gramsci
concentrated on years 1 and 2 of the revolution; and he also assumed that
the Jacobin party always 'led' the masses, in the sense that life created
faits accomplis. Both these assumptions are questionable. The Jacobins
had existed since October 1789, and indeed called themselves Jacobins
officially since September 1792. And from October 1789 to October 1793
there were many occasions when the Jacobin deputies, or the decisions
taken at the Jacobin Club, lagged behind or ran counter to the wishes of
the 'masses'.

But there are some permanent traits, some continuities in the history
of the 'Jacobins' which, when brought to light, characterize them as a
party, or to be precise as a proto-party.

One of these continuities was their uninterrupted co-existence with and
dependence on the National Assembly. Like a modern political party the
'Jacobins' acted within the orbit of the National Assembly. As in any
modern constitution, the National Assembly, as the seat of the representation of the 'people', was the centre around which the political
parties gravitated. In theory in the monolithic states, in reality in the
constitutional–pluralistic states, the function of the political parties is to
select and procure the election of a sufficient number of their candidates in the National Assembly to form the government; and after the
government is formed, to inform the voters of the intentions of the
government and the government of the reactions of the voters. The same
tasks are also accomplished in opposition (when the party is in a minority
in the Assembly) but in the opposite direction. The political party is a
sub-agency of the agency of representation which is the National Assembly.
The two are linked by an institutional umbilical cord.

The metaphor is more apposite in the case of the Jacobins who were
born with and within the Constituent Assembly and were not elected
beforehand as a homogeneous group of deputies. Once they had been

---

[55] Quoted from Jacques Guilhaumon: 'Gramsci et le Jacobinisme historique' in
Les Jacobins, op. cit., pp. 160 and 182–84.

brought together in that body by the 1789 elections of the Third Estate, the heterogeneous individual deputies sought each other out by doctrinal elective affinities. Admittedly the 1789 elections had been, as Cochin has shown, manipulated to a certain extent by the 'sociétés de pensée' — and radical affinities were therefore expected to predominate. And admittedly the Third Estate itself committed an arbitrary act when it proclaimed itself to be the National Assembly, thus unilaterally assuming the representation of all Frenchmen, without having received a national mandate for that purpose. Finally, under different overall names, the most durable of which was *La Montagne*, the deputies who were discussing their common attitudes at the club des Jacobins not only formed different and opposing groups, but their own attitudes fluctuated according to the issues. Only after the split with the Feuillants and later still after the successive purges of the Girondins, the Hébertists and the Dantonists, did the hard core of the Robespierrist Jacobins finally emerge in its ultimate unity.

But these historical circumstances, which to a great extent blur the lines of development do not in essence alter the reciprocal, functional, relation between the proto-party and the proto-assembly. The Montagne, influenced by and finally taken over by the Jacobins, was during the 'constitutional government' a part of the National Assembly.

But when they reached the height of their power, that is when they had unilaterally proclaimed *the passage from the constitutional to the revolutionary government*, then the hard core of the Robespierrist Jacobins, closely allied now with the Commune of Paris, did try to muzzle the Convention. It is at this point that the contrasts between the pluralistic (constitutional) parties and the monolithic revolutionary party can best be detected. Robespierre and his party did not dissolve the Convention, and in the end they were overthrown by it. In the Russian Revolution Lenin, who had learnt the lesson, dissolved the Constituent Assembly so as to ensure the continuation of the government of the monolithic party.

Since both Assembly and party are agencies of the representation of the people, the elected Assembly being the principal and constitutional one, and the party or parties the subsidiary and extra-constitutional[56] ones, conflicts of representation between these two institutions, like the conflicts of two series of concentric circles on the surface of a pool, might become possible when the party wants to dominate the Assembly. Functionally the political party has a propensity to enlarge its mandate. Originating either as a regional representation (Breton, in the Jacobin case) or as a social representation (industrial working class in the Bolshevik case), and acting as a party, and especially a party with revolutionary propensities, it is inherently propelled to consider itself, and to become, a national party, to represent the whole and not a part — as a 'party' is etymologically bound to remain. Theoretically this is done on Rousseau's assumption that the 'people' is the whole — or on Marx's assumption

---

[56] In the Leninist Soviet Constitutions (1919 and 1923) the party was not mentioned. It was mentioned for the first time in Stalin's Constitution of 1936.

97

(or Saint-Simon's for that matter) that the people, being composed of those who work, the workers are the people. In practice this is effected through the recruitment in and by the organization of people from all regions and classes provided they share in the ideology and serve in the organization.

The next stage of this process of representative monopolization is reached when the party, acting now as a national representation, is unable to impose the measures it would wish to enact on the other and superior agency of national representation. It either accepts the rules of the majority/minority game, or it challenges the National Assembly, combining parliamentary and extra-parliamentary action, and revealing in the process its essentially anti-parliamentary nature.

This is the moment when the Jacobins changed their definition from 'constitutional government' to 'revolutionary government' — and the moment when they tried to neutralize the Assembly by exerting two pressures upon it: the pressure of the government from above and the extra-parliamentary pressure of the 'Commune', 'the people' or 'the masses', from below.

This is also why the Jacobin proto-party in its brief existence, embodied both types of political parties which were afterwards to dominate the politics of both kinds of democracies in industrial society. It had been the prototype of a constitutional—pluralistic party, and then became the prototype of a monolithic—dictatorial party.

Inside the political party itself there is another continuity: the continuity of organization.

Now, did the Jacobins have such an 'organization'? Can one say that the Jacobins were the precursors of this phenomenon? Here a certain element of elusiveness creeps in. For while it is undeniable that the Jacobins had an organization, that they *were* an organization, it is also undeniable that their organization differed considerably from that of the modern political party. It can be argued that the Jacobins did *not* have an organization because:

— many of the affiliated 'clubs' were formerly 'learned societies' transformed overnight into political agencies by the events of the revolution;
— in spite of the discipline which the self-proclaimed 'mother' society would have liked to impose from Paris, the local societies or clubs acted very much on their own, in the heat of the moment and according to their own interpretation of the instructions from Paris;
— the membership of the Jacobin Club or Clubs was composed of progressive citizens who accepted and recognized the general revolutionary principles and expressed their willingness to fight for them, regardless of whether they were of Cordelier, Hébertist, Girondin, Dantonist, or Robespierrist inclinations. The purges by Robespierre started only in 1793.

- in the Assembly and in the government — that is in the principal executive committees of the Assembly — the political orientations of the members were as indistinguishable as in the above list. Only by negative means, like 'purges' could a faction be identified. Otherwise groups and attitudes were so interchangeable, according to issues, personalities and circumstances, that one could not speak, in the modern sense, of party unity;
- finally, the Jacobin organization did not always 'lead'; the Jacobins often followed the impulse of the revolutionary Commune, and were faced with historical *faits accomplis* by the people, to which they had to adapt their own positions and strategy. Here again the difference with the pre-revolutionary, carefully organized, and insurrectionally prepared, Bolshevik party is characteristic.

Conversely it can be argued that the Jacobins *did* have an organization in so far as they had the only centrally supervised national network of agencies — the 'affiliated' or 'sister' societies in at least 2,000 localities — (and some, often merely symbolic, international 'Jacobin' associations: Italian,[57] Polish,[58] Austrian,[59] and even English[60]). The 'mother' organization in Paris was in constant 'correspondence', through its 'correspondence bureau' with the 'sister associations' [*sic*], distributing the main speeches and pamphlets, and writing letters and addresses to the 'sisters' so as to help them to interpret events — and indicating the lines of action to be adopted at the local levels. In turn the local agencies oriented the conduct of the centre through their feedback reporting on the evolution of events, conditions and states of mind in their constituencies. Visits and counter-visits were made by representatives of both sides. Of all the 'clubs' of the French Revolution only the Jacobins had set up this well-defined organizational network. The Cordeliers who had a much wider influence in the press, or the Girondins who numbered a great number of philosophers, writers and journalists in their ranks — both of whom were therefore in closer contact with what one might anachronistically call the 'media' — had no nationwide organization. And, when the Feuillants tried to win over the Jacobin organization they failed miserably, the 'societies' remaining faithful to their real 'mother'.

Secondly, within the 'mother' and 'sister' organizations a strict ideological and moral discipline prevailed. Membership was granted after examination by two special committees and was certified by a 'card' which members had to present when asked to do so, within the precincts of the club.

Membership in the 'mother' (Paris) society as well as in the affiliated societies in the provinces was granted by means of a special procedure.

[57] Indro Montanelli: *L'Italia Giacobina e Carbonara*, Milano 1972.
[58] B. Lesnodorski: *Les Jacobins polonais,* Paris 1965.
[59] Denis Silago: *Jakobiner in der Habsburger Monarchie*, Vienna 1962.
[60] E. P. Thompson: *The Making of the English Working Class*, London 1966.

Old members 'presented' the candidates to a special Committee of Presentation of the *société*, and this was followed by verification, made by the special Committee for Verification of the club. Membership could be refused on the grounds of ideological or moral defects — but not on social grounds: Dukes, marquesses and bishops were among the founding members. Membership could be suspended or withdrawn from members who had deviated ideologically. Such purges happened often. They became even more frequent once the factional struggle started in earnest on issues of political decision and ideological orientation. Elimination from the club amounted then to a political death sentence.[61]

The counter-procedure was, in the early stages of the club, for a great number of members, or indeed an entire 'faction' to 'leave' the premises of the club and install themselves in the premises of another club (usually also situated in a secularized convent), with the overt aim of reducing the effectiveness of the Jacobin Club. The most famous of these attempts was the secession of the Feuillants.[62] Complaints or denunciations for mis-behaviour were made in public sessions and if the accused was present he could in most cases present his or her own defence, and call on counter-witnesses.[63] Accusations were either against the political or ideological statements made by the person denounced, or against his or her behaviour in the revolutionary society. Michelet describes how 'the fear of Jacobin excommunication' was the beginning of the terror. By punishing their own members they could frighten all the deputies of the Convention. The first man to be 'purged' from the Society was Fauchet[64] on 19 September 1792, the second, already much more important was Brissot, the leader of France during the earliest and most difficult part of the war — the war which he had wanted so much. Brissot was elimi-nated from the Jacobins on 10 October 1792. The most important purge of all, that of Danton, was prepared by these same means and was to follow in March 1794.

As the revolution escalated and as the Jacobins, allied with the Commune, became the most influential factor in that escalation, and, on the other hand, as the executive power of the Assembly was taken over by the Committees of Public Safety and General Security, which had to conduct and implement all the measures required by the war and by the revolution, the disciplined 'organization' assumed another role. It became

[61]See for instance report on the extraordinary meeting of 2 June 1791, when a man was denounced for having taken part in the discussion with the help of a card he had borrowed from a real member. He asked to be taken home by two candidates to show them his own card. The members would not let him leave the precincts. The President had to remind members that 'the temple in which they sat is a temple of liberty; if somebody wants to get out he should be free to do so'. The members still protested. Aulard, *La Société des Jacobins*, Vol. II, Paris 1891, pp. 469–71.

[62] See above, p. 76.

[63]Aulard, op. cit., p. 472.

[64]Ibid., p. 493.

the backbone of the revolutionary administration. This is what a modern political party also does in some other countries: in the United States, to a relative degree and with a different purpose during the system of patronage of General Jackson's presidency and still, though much less, now; and directly in Soviet Russia and in other communist regimes, since the VIIIth and Xth Party Congresses of the Bolshevik party decided to place the administration of the state under the control of the party. Michelet, again, noted the procedure most clearly. He says, narrating the events of April 1793:

> The Jacobin Society entered as a whole in the administration. In April it had occupied 10,000 jobs, through its own members or its creatures. . . The rising force which had irresistibly taken the members of the Jacobin Society to all posts at once, effaced the Girondin influence. The Girondins were still strong in the Convention, honoured by it, chairmen, secretaries, members of all its committees. But they no longer had agents at the base. They remained at the highest levels, isolated; they were like a head which could be cut off with one blow. Of all the public powers, the one the Jacobins seized most avidly was that of justice. The dangerous, terrible, functions of the revolutionary tribunals, which everyone also hesitated to accept, were solicited by the Jacobins.[65]

Having taken over the essential sectors, the nerves of the government of France, it was easy for the 'pure' Jacobins, the Robespierrists, to get rid of Danton, who had until then exerted the most direct influence on the Committee of Public Safety. Historians have rightly differentiated between the first Dantonist Committee of Public Safety, and the Second Robespierrist Committee of Public Safety. But in point of fact Robespierre was not acting as a prime minister, and had no direct responsibility. He was acting through his men, through his influence, through his complete absorption in the direction of events, but without supreme official authority or recognition.

But then by this fusion of state and party power in their hands, the Jacobins became the predecessors of those ideological political parties which assert that public happiness can be provided by the people, for the people, through the intermediary of the central agency of the party-state.

Finally, the continuity of leadership is also characteristic of a political party. It is generally assumed that the Jacobins had no one particular leader. At least three personalities seem to have achieved an equal degree of popularity: Marat, Danton and Robespierre — until the assassination of Marat and the elimination of Danton by Robespierre left the latter alone.

---

[65]See also Aulard, *La Société des Jacobins*, Vol. V, p. 475. At the meeting of 27 September 1793, the member Gauthier declared: 'The salvation of France depends on the choice which will be made for the organization of the revolutionary tribunals. Almost all have been chosen from among the Jacobins, and we can be sure of their zeal and of their purity.'

Hence the interpretation by some historians of the internecine struggles within the Montagne as the dramatic gestation of Robespierre, and hence the equation of Jacobinism with Robespierre.[66]

Robespierre's career runs parallel with the entire tragedy of the Jacobins. A young unknown lawyer of bourgeois origins from Arras, Robespierre came to Paris as a deputy of the Third Estate in 1789. He was, at the beginning, largely unaware of how the revolution would develop. He was not an extremist, an insurrectionist, not even initially a republican. But he was a Rousseauist, and consequently a founding member of the Jacobin Club. He believed in the 'general will' and in the autonomy of politics. Like Rousseau, he was anti-Christian, but he believed in God as a Supreme Being. He thought that he was the servant of what he called law — so much so that when he was defeated by his united adversaries, not only did he refuse to hide, he desperately sought to be lawfully arrested.

At the Jacobin Club his speeches, which were the dress rehearsals for the speeches he was to deliver the same or the next day in the Assembly, were a mixture of rigorous legalistic thinking and of revolutionary mysticism which electrified both audiences. His rhetoric lacked the visceral power of Danton's oratory, or the inflammatory vulgarity of that of Marat, or the transcendental cruelty of that of Saint-Just. But although in the escalating revolutionary circumstances the word 'statesmanship' does not make very much sense, his oratory impressed by its semblance of statesmanship. From a politically central position in the whirlwind of the revolution he was able to defeat the Right-wing, the Girondins and the Left-wing of the revolution, the Hébertists, thus paving the way for the triumph of the Jacobins, and his own.

His personal position was central because he exerted his influence in the three centres of power; he was a leader in the Assembly, in the Commune and last but not least in the Jacobin Club; yet dominating — as he did — the Jacobin Club through his rhetorical genius, Robespierre was none the less not in control of its 'organization', until after the split between the Feuillants and the Jacobins. The Jacobin Club seemed then to

[66]None of the modern social historians, Soboul, Godechot or Cobb denies the continuity through the revolutionary government of the Jacobin leader, Robespierre. Godechot wrote: 'But the true theoretician of the revolutionary movement was, in reality Robespierre, who had in any event inspired the acts of the insurrectional Commune of Paris from 10 August to 21 September 1792'. And Cobb — whose analyses of the crowds and of such acephalous popular groupings as the *sans-culottes* or the *armées révolutionnaires* has thrown new light on the making of a revolution — confirms this continuity at the very beginning of his massive study of *Les Armées révolutionnaires* when he says 'in the texts the expression *armées révolutionnaires* appeared for the first time in April 1793. . . On 3 April Robespierre declared at the Jacobins: 'We must raise an armée révolutionnaire; that force will have to be formed by all patriots, all *sans culottes*; the faubourgs must be the power and the hard core of this army'. And so they were. Jacques Godechot: *Les institutions de la France sous la Revolution et l'Empire*, p. 257; Richard Cobb, *Les Armées révolutionnaires*, Paris 1956, p. 34.

reach its lowest ebb. And it was at the very moment that Robespierre almost alone (only Pétion helped him) proceeded with its reorganization.

But, in the end, his action was inspired by a much more profound cause, *the* most profound cause: faith. Rousseau's idea of a 'civil religion' had failed to convince, during the revolution, both those who had preserved their Catholic religion, and those who, once launched on the path of atheism, rejected any kind of religion. Only Robespierre always professed his belief in Rousseau's Supreme Being, and therefore always tried to moderate the de-Christianization campaign. Once he had achieved power, Robespierre turned his long-contained anger against the militant atheists. These were the anarchists and the Hébertists for whom the denial of religion, the desecration of churches and the persecution of the clergy and worshippers, was the essence of the Revolution itself. Robespierre had them sent to the guillotine on 24 March 1794. And then having reached the apex of his power, the tyrant, as he was already called, proceeded to establish a state religion. In his famous report of 18 Floréal on the 'relations between moral and religious ideas and republican principles', he decreed 'a civil profession of faith'. He denounced atheism *on political grounds* as anti-republican for 'in the eyes of the legislators everything that is useful in the world and good to practise on earth is the truth. The idea of the Supreme Being and of the immortality of the soul is a constant reminder of justice: as such this idea is both social and republican.'

On the same day the decree was presented to the National Assembly, and it was unanimously adopted, amidst cries of feigned enthusiasm from the deputies, none of whom approved of it. Its text is still astonishing, as evidence of sheer human aberration. The oddest is the first article, which states that 'the French people acknowledge (*reconnait*) the existence of the Supreme Being and the immortality of the soul' — an incoherent attempt to preserve both sovereignties, that of the people who 'acknowledge' or 'recognize' as in a diplomatic relation or a concordat, the existence of the Supreme Being, and that of the Supreme Being who because he is Supreme is necessarily the sovereign. Which of the two sovereigns, treated on equal terms, in this impossible way, was the ultimate sovereign?

And what made Robespierre, when, after a long struggle, he had at last achieved complete control of the state, put his utmost energies into securing the passing of this aberrant, divisive and useless decree by the Assembly? Was it because, at the apotheosis of his career, he wanted to be both the ruler and the arch-priest of the newly shaped French community? Or was it a new search for the immortality of the soul, thus saluting the innumerable men whom he had sent to death, and the prescience of his own death?

Robespierre was guillotined before he could answer any of these questions; indeed he seemed strangely detached, aloof, even indifferent, in the days of Thermidor. His death in the extraordinary conditions which he himself had created marked the end of the Jacobins — and of the Jacobin system of public happiness.

As we now close this examination of the significant features of the history of the Jacobins — one more ought to be mentioned, which is particularly relevant to the main argument of this book: its significance as a tragedy.

The whole history of the Jacobins has in it all the making of a tragedy. Like a tragedy, its 'plot' observes the unity of time: five years only for all those history-packed developments; and the unity of space: the one and indivisible France. Like a tragedy it has had and will always have a characteristically cathartic effect on the people and peoples to whom the tale is told. And as in a Greek tragedy — indeed as if a Greek tragedian had purposefully planned its plot so as to ensure that the spectators would draw from it the eternal moral that Hubris must lead to Nemesis — all those who acted in it, men and institutions alike, blind with hubristic passion, fought each other until they all lay dead on the stage, while from behind the scenes the martial fanfares of the victor could already be heard.

Chapter 5

Materialistic politics

The nineteenth century inaugurated the age of materialism which, in two different meanings, came to dominate both industrializing and industrial societies. Materialism in the first sense refers to the increased wealth and rapidly spreading physical comfort attributable to the achievements of commerce and industry, which encouraged people to concentrate on the enjoyment of material goods. But it was also in the nineteenth century that a new note sounded from those quarters which had in the past preached the observance of spiritual values and taught people wisdom: this was the doctrine that only matter exists in the world. Intoxicated by scientific advance, the new materialistic philosophers taught people, already predisposed to exchange their spiritual values for glittering material temptations (or to believe, as Marx put it, 'that the miracles of the Gods were rendered superfluous by the miracles of industry'), that spirit and human consciousness had no life of their own but were determined by, and dependent on material circumstances. Spirit was replaced in materialistic or ideological philosophies by such worldly notions as interest or class consciousness. Caught up in this double materialistic pincer movement, most human activities were from now on orientated towards the pursuit of material happiness — or what was understood generally as progress.

Politics, which in the wake of the secularization and the industrialization of society, had acquired increasing prominence, benefited most from this materialistic climate of opinion, since the mechanism of political action itself is, as we know, essentially promissory. The promise of materialistic happiness, meaning happiness to be achieved on earth by material means, was best adapted to the purposes of popular, and later mass-politics, because of its specific worldly character. For the materialistic promises were indeed soon transformed into ideologies, which are inherently worldly; and ideologies gave birth to ideological political parties.

Two ideological philosophies made the greatest impact on the culture of industrial societies, and succeeded through effective ideologization and the organization of ideological parties in becoming the models for systems of political happiness. These were utilitarian liberalism as founded on hedonistic materialism; and Communism as founded on historical materialism.

It may seem surprising to juxtapose in one analysis two political philosophies which have opposed each other for the last 130 years,[1] since the revolutions of 1848 and the publication in that same year of the Communist Manifesto. And indeed there are many differences between Bentham's utilitarian hedonism and the communist political philosophy, originating in Marx's historical materialism. In the first place, Bentham (1748–1832) belongs to the pre-industrial age, while Marxism is post-industrial (Marx was born in 1818 and died in 1883). Hedonistic materialism is practical reformism, while historical materialism is a revolutionary Messianism; the former is concerned with man's present enjoyment of life, the latter with the ultimate transformation of man; the former sees the solution in individual interest, the latter in collective equality; the former favours and the latter opposes both private property in the economy and representation in politics; Benthamism declares that the identity of interests is the sum total of all private interests, which can be ascertained through 'felicific calculuses', whereas Marxism maintains that all institutions, processes and beliefs are inherently class-determined and class-vitiated, and are bound therefore to create a mounting conflict which can only be solved by the advent of a classless society.

Nevertheless, from the general point of view adopted in this enquiry Benthamism and Marxism have many features in common. First of all the two ideologies both gave rise to systems of political happiness which, though they were formulated in the nineteenth century, have achieved their full maturity and their domination over the minds and the lives of people in industrial societies only in the twentieth century. No other ideology has ever enjoyed such a long continuity or such a universal impact as these two. Fascism and National-Socialism were *counter-ideologies* and *counter-systems*, born after and moulded on them, notably on Marxism—Leninism, in the hope of combating them with their own weapons; but as they lacked true intellectual foundations these two counter-systems produced only destruction. And although anarchism showed a vigorous intellectual continuity and indeed consolidation from Proudhon and Bakunin to Kropotkin, it is inherently unable to produce any kind of 'system'. Nor did any of the exponents of modern social theories like Saint-Simon, Auguste Comte, Spencer, Durkheim or Pareto succeed, even if some of them wanted to, in capturing the popular imagination. And if Darwin's zoological and Freud's psychological theories did capture it, the impact of their works on the general public was only indirectly political. Whereas Benthamism and Marxism had immediate

---

[1]Although many authors, and notably Talcott Parsons consider Marxism as a 'bridge between German idealism and English utilitarianism'. (Cf. article in the *Encyclopaedia of Social Sciences*.)

political consequences, partly also because they were intended by their founders to become political systems.

The influence of the ideas of the French Revolution on the works of both Bentham and Marx was fundamental. But given the different periods in which they lived, this influence was exercised in a different manner, and with different results. Bentham actually lived through the excitement of the revolution itself. From an initially anti-Jacobin stand he gradually, under the influence of James Mill and then of the whole group of English radicals who shared many of the Jacobin attitudes, became a radical himself (see below, pp. 121–2 for the transformation of ethical utilitarianism into political radicalism and afterwards into liberalism).[2] The generation of philosophers to which Marx belonged had no direct experience of the revolution. They assimilated it either through the rationalistic interpretation of Kant or especially through the dialectic interpretation of Hegel. It was this latter interpretation which reached Marx, even if he later turned Hegel's idealistic dialectics 'on its head' into dialectical materialism.[3] Both Bentham and Marx saw the French Revolution as the first practical experience of the new 'social sciences' or indeed of the social mathematics as proposed by Condorcet.[4] But as distinct from the French revolutionaries, who within their vague Rousseauianism remained idealistic, if not fideistic, the philosophies of Bentham and Marx were scientifically materialistic. This materialsim was also of French origin, going back to pre-revolutionary days, as it derived from Helvétius.[5] Here again however the difference in generations made itself felt. Bentham regarded Helvétius as a genius from whom he borrowed his two main principles, that of 'pain and pleasure' as the two sovereign masters of human life, and that of 'interest'. Marx, at a greater distance in time, had measured the mediocrity of Helvétius's philosophy, but was linked to Helvétius's militant atheism — since atheism via Feuerbach, was also at the root of Marx's philosophy.

Unlike the Jacobin ideology which remained idealistic, the Benthamist and Marxist ideological philosophies relativized, under the influence of materialism, the concepts of virtue, virtues and values. It was under the impact of such ideas that the absoluteness of moral principles began to dissolve. For if in a world imbued with materialism and atheism or

[2]'Bentham had arrived at the last stage. For a long time he had been indifferent or even hostile to democratic ideas, but now he found himself, under the pressure of a number of circumstances, insensibly led to profess the same doctrine as Cartwright, though basing himself on different principles... Bentham, along with Cartwright, "the father of reform" became the philosopher of the party, "the chief thinker of Radicalism".' Elie Halévy, *The Growth of Philosophic Radicalism*, Oxford 1972, pp. 263–64.

[3]As regards relations with Jacobins in his own lifetime, Marx proved very critical of their attitude during the Paris Commune of 1871.

[4]On Condorcet, see also K.M. Barker's *Condorcet. From Natural Philosophy to Social Mathematics*, Chicago 1975.

[5]Helvétius, 1717–71.

agnosticism the independence of the human spirit is denied on the grounds that it is dependent on exterior conditions, measurable through such yardsticks as interest or class-consciousness, then no absolute value can subsist, least of all absolute justice. 'Once having reached this point', wrote Helvétius, 'I easily discovered the source of human virtues; I saw that without sensitivity to physical pain and pleasure, man, without desires, without passions, equally indifferent to everything, would not have experienced personal interest, and that physical sensitivity and personal interest have been the authors of all kinds of justice.'[6]

Greek philosophy must have been thoroughly forgotten by the new materialists, or they would not have failed to note the similarity between Helvétius's arguments and those of Callicles in Plato's *Gorgias*.[7] This estrangement from the Greek philosophers explains Bentham's indignation when he observed that 'in Aristotle's catalogue the virtue of benevolence — effective benevolence — is forgotten and there is nothing in its stead but *justice*, which is but a portion of benevolence in disguise' (italics in the text, supposedly to mark indignation), or his explicit preference for happiness rather than justice: 'be the meaning of the word justice what it will, what regard is it entitled to otherwise than as a means of happiness?' Similarly Marx rejected absolute justice, and affirmed that 'right can never be higher than the economic structure of society and its cultural development conditioned thereby'.

The fundamental values of right and justice were thus relativized according to the way man's conscience was determined by material circumstances or according to the kind of happiness which materialist doctrines recommended him to pursue. If we compare this position with Kant's assertion that absolute values have priority over the 'empirical ends which people call happiness', it comes as no surprise that minds already seduced by the promises of materialism should reject that assertion as old fashioned and Utopian.[8] The dominant principle now was how to maximize the individual and total sum of material happiness, or of exterior goods so as to enable 'all' or 'the greatest number' to share in it. For both materialisms, hedonistic and historical, accepted that one way or the other, human happiness can only be achieved on earth, if only for the obvious reason that there was nothing beyond human existence; and both asserted that man would extract from nature all that he required (Sartre's

[6]Helvétius: *De l'Esprit*, Third discourse. (My translation.)
[7]'Callicles: I tell you frankly that natural good and right consist in this, that the man who is going to live as a man ought to encourage his appetites to be as strong as possible instead of repressing them and be able by means of his courage and intelligence to satisfy them in all their intensity by providing them with whatever they happen to desire.' Plato, *The Gorgias*, in I. Dilhan: *Morality and the Inner Life*, *A Study in Plato's Gorgias*, London 1979, p. 88.
[8]'Such is the requirement of pure reason which legislates *a priori* regardless of all empirical ends (which can all be summed up under the general heading of happiness).' Quoted in Kant's *Political Writings*, H. Reiss (ed.) p. 73.

'anti-nature dream') once his energies had been intensified, multiplied and sharpened by the technical revolution he had himself pioneered.

It was in the light of these considerations that both Bentham and Marx made their promises of happiness. Bentham promised that 'we shall never make the world the abode of perfect happiness: when we shall have accomplished all that can be done, this paradise will yet be, according to the Asiatic idea, only a garden, but this garden will be a most delightful abode, compared with the savage forest in which men have so long wandered'. Marx in turn promised that 'the positive abolition of private property and thus of human self-alienation and therefore the real reappropriation of the human essence by and for men' would be achieved in communist society; and that such a balance between production and consumption would be reached that each would receive 'according to his needs'.

What should be noted in the materialist ideological philosophies is above all their prescriptive character, their activation of the human will towards human happiness, and as the means to achieve the 'goal'. Bentham speaks wistfully of the paradisiac moment 'when we shall have accomplished all that can be done'. He thus implies that human beings should engage in a constant operation by means of which the greatest number would share in as much happiness as can be provided by their own 'accomplishment'; and Marx describes economic and legal operations like the abolition of private property and of all institutions which protect it, as the condition for the advent of Communism with all its moral and philosophical consequences of happiness. In other words, what distinguishes these philosophies from others is not only that they make obvious promises of material happiness, but that they link the promises with — and indeed condition these promises by — the *action* which human beings must undertake in order to enable the ideologies to fulfil their promises. Or, in Marx's well-known words: 'The philosophers have only interpreted the world in various ways; the point is to change it'.

Now, as we know (see pp. 23–6), this is what distinguishes an ideological philosophy from a philosophy; and this is what leads to its transformation through ideologization into an ideology — a set of beliefs shared by groups and multitudes — and then through organization into the political activity necessary to fulfil the material promise. In their different, indeed opposed ways, with all their politically contradictory ends and means, both materialistic ideological philosophies have followed the path of all ideology — from ideological philosophy to political party and political system. There are reasons for their exceptional success, some particular, one more general. One of the particular reasons is that both Bentham and Marx were born ideologists. Both conceived their entire doctrinal corpus as a guide for action, as a lever for reforming or transforming man and his society, as the gospel of a militant faith. The will of militancy was manifest in their work and action. Their purpose was to arouse around their ideas and principles the enthusiasm of men who, converted themselves, would be ready to convert others in order to build together the organization which would undermine and attack the old structures so as to open the way for the new ones, theirs. Both had wanted their ideological philosophies to undergo ideologization.

Other more general reasons were that:

— they condensed, indeed encapsulated their complex arguments which subsequently became slogans to be learned and repeated;
— they appealed implicitly and explicitly to low common denominators, sensuous desires and hedonistic appetites in the case of Bentham, social jealousy, envy and class hatred in the case of Marx;
— they published tracts, brochures, and in the case of Marx even manifestos, parallel with their scholarly treatises, with an exclusively propagandistic and inflammatory character. Bentham contributed to these in a particularly sententious and pedantic style, hammering oversimplified ideas in repetitious and catechistic formulations. His brief sentences are reminiscent of articles in a legal code, presumably because of his early legal training. Marx, a choleric and bitter man, was a born polemicist, more often than not linking together the man and the work in vitriolic attacks on his enemies;
— finally they both gathered disciples around them. Each had at first a 'spouse' or disciple—collaborator and co-author, James Mill in the case of Bentham, Friedrich Engels in the case of Marx. Together with these ideological spouses they drew together the novices and proselytes around their respective faiths. They indoctrinated and catechized them with the utmost intransigence, rewarding and punishing them according to how well they had learned their lessons and lauded their masters. The style in which James Mill, Peronet Thomson, George Grote, Romilly, and John Browning wrote about Bentham was positively idolatrous. And John Stuart Mill claims in his *Autobiography* that the 'Benthamic or Utilitarian propagandism' emanated from his father, James Mill, and describes how it was directed in three channels, the first conducted by himself.

Marx and Engels also recruited disciples: Liebknecht, Kautsky, Plekhanov. But there were differences between the Benthamite and the Marxist methods of ideologization. One lay in the exegesis itself which was much less adulatory of the leader and more concentrated on the doctrine in the Marxist than in the Benthamite family. The other had to do again with the chronological gap between the two theoreticians. By Marx's time, conditions had ripened for mass political action in the politically enfranchised industrial societies. Therefore Marx needed and sought political acolytes rather ,than ideological disciples. And finally there was the difference in nature between the principal disciples themselves. Bentham's disciple, John Stuart Mill avowedly failed to reconcile the open contradictions within utilitarian liberalism. Lenin, Marx's principal disciple, exacerbated the internal contradictions in historical materialism by putting Marx's theories into practice in an unwarranted way. This will be dealt with in more detail in the chapters dealing specifically with each of the two systems.

The more general reason for the success of the two materialistic ideologies and subsequently for that of the political systems which they engendered lay in the coincidental conformity of materialist philosophy with the materialist aspirations of people in industrial societies. The ideologies gave materialist answers to materialist questions in a materialist *Zeitgeist*. Bentham's hedonistic utilitarianism corresponded with the enthusiastic mentality of the dawn of science, industry, capitalism and the enjoyment of life. It exhales the arrogant confidence in the future achievements of rational man typical of the first half of the century of materialism; it exalts the practice of hedonism, indeed of indulgence in all pleasures, especially the pleasures of the senses, playing shove halfpenny ranking equally in terms of psychological hedonism with reading poetry; it recommended money-making and usury; but in order to absolve these and other hedonistic activities from moral doubts or public opprobrium, it provided people with a consequentialist ethical system with the help of which they could measure and legitimize the ultimate utility of their action.

Marx's historical materialism is even more suffused than Bentham's with the ambitions of rational man, indeed, according to him, the time had come in the 1850s to 'transform' the world, most particularly because in the meantime capitalism had shown clearly that the foundations of industrial society were badly in need of transformation, notably the relations of production from which classes and the class struggle derived. Marxism prophesied a millenary happiness for the entire human species, once the bad economic structure should have been replaced. Its general tonality was ascetic, but it promised a total liberation of man's capacity to enjoy life when capitalism, together with hypocritical bourgeois ethics, should have been overthrown.

So each of the two founders of systems of political happiness responded differently, each in his own half of the first materialistic century, to the changing trends of the *Zeitgeist*. One exalted the unbounded confidence in the material triumph of man through the harmony of interests which were the motor of the ever-progressing human society; the other the unbounded confidence in the material triumph of man through the abolition of the conflict-generating institutions of the capitalist system, and its replacement by the system of Communism in which the human species would be freed from alienation. In this sense it is true that if Bentham sought primarily for the adherence of the individual bourgeois to his ideology, Marx sought above all that of the collective working class which had by this time appeared on the socio-economic stage. But it is equally true that both addressed their audiences in materialist terms exhorting them on how best to achieve material happiness. Both audiences have survived to this day, contrary to Marx's expectations, and they have intermingled in the course of the evolution of society.

As a result both discourses are still continuing in the guise of a polemic between ideologies, or worse still, of a confrontation between two world systems.

But between the two, whenever the polarization of the extreme ideologies and ideological attitudes was not pulling too strongly, successive generations have succeeded in achieving theoretical and empirical compromises. Socialism crystallized as a modern creed in the nineteenth century, as a reaction against the materialistic tenets ('interest' or 'profit') of utilitarianism. By the twentieth century it had also become a reaction against the revolutionary and dictatorial tenets of Marxism—Leninism. Socialism, as has already been shown (p. 70) cannot easily be reconciled with materialism.

The intrinsically functional industrial society led socialism increasingly to shed its ideological overtones. In its new, empirical, guise it accepted along with the other 'central' parties (Liberal, Conservative or Christian Democrat, Agrarian, etc.) the principles of the welfare society and the mixed economy. It thus kept the role of the state as the instrument of distributive justice and equality within the limits in which it must be confined if it is not to become totalitarian, as in the Marxist—Leninist systems; and it maintained intact its respect for the freedom of the individual and for the moral values, or rather for the aspirations towards moral principles of human conduct.

Moreover, in some of its numerous theoretical formulations (for socialism does not have one single original ideological philosophy to which it dogmatically adheres) new socialist theories were able to reconcile the realities of industrial society with the ideals of socialism. Thus, in British socialism, R.H. Tawney, by slightly playing with words, but also as a result of a genuine modern inspiration, reconciled the concept of functionalism, essential to the understanding of industrial society (but considered by contemporary Marxist and neo-Marxist theorists as an American, specifically Parsonian 'capitalist' euphemism), with socialist aspirations. 'A society which aimed at making the acquisition of wealth contingent upon the discharge of social obligations, which sought to proportion remuneration to service and denied it to those by whom no service was performed, which inquired first not what men possess but what they can make or create or achieve, might be called a functional society, because in such a society the main subject of social emphasis would be the performance of functions' wrote Tawney in 1920.[9]

It is the moral sense of the functioning of an industrial society which has brought liberal and socialist thinkers closer together in the twentieth century. And it is in the ultimate reconciliation between modern liberalism, modern conservatism, and socialism that the new, political solutions of co-existence in industrial society might still be found, thus avoiding the domination of materialist ideologies.

[9]R.H. Tawney, *The Sickness of an Acquisitive Society*, Fabian pamphlet, 1920.

Chapter 6

The utilitarian–liberal system of political happiness

The 'principle of utility' understood as Bentham understood it . . . gave unity to my conceptions of things. I now had opinions; a creed, a doctrine, a philosophy; in one among the best senses of the word, a religion; the inculcation and diffusion of which could be made the principal outward purpose of a life. And I had a grand conception laid before me of changes to be effected in the condition of mankind through that doctrine.

J.S. Mill.

The epigraph shows that we are concerned here with the ideological aspect of the works of Bentham and J.S. Mill, with their impact on the minds and souls of modern men after the process of ideologization, which both authors had so assiduously pursued, had reduced and denatured their ideas into popular slogans. Complete studies on Bentham and J.S. Mill are legion and, understandably, some of the most recent, because they are more detached, are among the best.[1]

The proposition that Benthamist utilitarian hedonism contains a promise of happiness is a tautology. Bentham's whole philosophy is nothing if not a promise of happiness, 'the greatest happiness for the greatest number'. Equally there is no doubt about the hedonistic character of Benthamist philosophy (which Carlyle called a 'pig philosophy'). For in his first major book, *An Introduction to the Principles of Morals and Legislation,* Bentham inserted the 'catalogue of motives corresponding to that of Pleasures and Pains'[2] which substantiates its hedonism. Some thirty years later, at the height of the campaign for the ideologization of

---

[1] Ross Harrisson: *Bentham,* London 1983; Alan Ryan: *J.S. Mill,* London 1974.
[2] *The Works of Jeremy Bentham,* ed. John Bowring, Edinburgh 1843, Vol. I, Ch. X.

utilitarianism he completed and confirmed this catalogue for *popular use* in the widely distributed tract 'A table of the springs of action: showing the several species of pleasures and pains, of which man's nature is susceptible'[3] (of which, to his credit, J.S. Mill was highly critical). In the 'table' the first five pleasures and pains of the fourteen listed are as follows:

No. I — of the Taste — the Palate — the Alimentary canal — of intoxication; corresponding Interest — Interest of the Palate — Interest of the Bottle:
No. II — of the Sexual Appetite, or of the Sixth Sense; corresponding Interest — Sexual Interest;
No. III — of Sense, of the senses; viz. generically or collectively considered, corresponding interest; interest of sense — of the sense — Sensual Interest;
No. IV — derived from the matter of wealth . . . Corresponding Interest Pecuniary interest. Interest of the Purse;
No. V — of curiosity. Corresponding Interest, Interest of the Spying Glass:

Thus the first 'pleasures' which human beings were primarily to pursue were the elementary instincts and the epicurean refinements. Bentham described himself as being situated 'twixt an Epicurean and a cynic'.

In the Benthamite doctrine the concept of 'the greatest happiness for the greatest number' is linked with a second main concept, that of 'interest' — taken directly from Helvétius. 'A thing is said to promote the interest, or to be for the interest, of the individual when it tends to add to the sum total of his pleasures', states Bentham in the same work. But he corrects and completes this principle by adding that 'the interest of the Community then is what? — the sum of the interests of the several members who compose it'. This is the principle of 'the identity of interests'.

But 'interest', or the materialist 'self-interest' was a controversial concept. Rousseau used it but only Helvétius gave it a place of honour. A.O. Hirschmann, in his elegant essay, *The Passions and the Interests,*[4] has reminded us that 'the infatuation with interest as a key to the understanding of human action, carried over into the eighteenth century when Helvétius proclaimed . . .: "As the physical world is ruled by the laws of movement so is the moral universe ruled by laws of interest"'. But Hirschmann himself greets the appearance of the concept of interest in history as a 'new paradigm', 'called upon to counteract the passions', and believes that 'when the term "interest" in the sense of concerns, aspirations and advantages gained in currency in Western Europe in the late sixteenth century its meaning was by no means limited to the material aspects of a person's welfare'. This is undoubtedly how the word 'interest' came to regain respectability, after the Christian era during which

---

[3] Ibid., pp. 195–219.
[4] Albert O. Hirschmann: *The Passions and the Interests*, Princeton 1977, p. 43.

its most current, popular, meaning had been the odious one of 'usury'.[5]

But *pace* Hirschmann, this was a materialistic respectability, which emerged at the beginning of financial capitalism. It is significant that Bentham's very first work was a *Defence of Usury showing the impolicy of the present legal restraints on the terms of pecuniary bargains* (London 1787). Usury, even the charging of interest, was condemned on moral grounds by Christian ethics in the Middle Ages. Yet it was on this morally doubtful ground that Bentham launched his liberalizing offensive against 'restraints' of all kinds, which might obstruct the free affirmation of the human personality. On the other hand, in so far as usury is at the roots of financial capitalism, Bentham's initially revolutionary defence of it shows his innate ability to perceive and follow the trends of the economy in his time.

And it is also significant that only one year after the publication of Bentham's *Defence of Usury*, Saint-Just, then aged twenty, wrote, in *Organt*, a poem of twenty cantos — which was published in 1789 as a book, these illuminating verses on the moral concept of interest:

Jaloux de voir son oeuvre trop parfait
Dieu sur la terre envoya l'intérêt:
L'indépendance avec l'Egalité
Gouvernaient l'homme, enfant de la Nature
Et destiné par son essence pure
A la vertu comme à la liberté.

Mais dans le monde arrive l'Intérêt
L'Egalité tout à coup disparait,
L'Ambition dresse sa tête immonde
L'Amour en pleurs abandonne le monde,
La Tyrannie invente les serments:
Le Désespoir égare les amants;
L'Or fait des lois, et l'Intérêt amène,
Le Déshonneur, les forfaits et la Haine.[6]

Nothing could symbolize better the essential difference between the Jacobin proto-system of political happiness, and the materialistic systems of political happiness which were to follow it, than this original divergence between the Jacobin concept of 'vertu' and the concept of interest as defined by Helvétius and taken over by Bentham.

---

[5] Etymologically, in Latin, interest, was initially the third person of the present *inter*-esse (*intersum, interest*) meaning therefore: intermediary.

[6] Which in a free translation means: 'Vexed by the perfection of his work/ God sent Interest down to earth./ Until then, Independence and Equality/ had governed man, child of nature/ destined by his pure essence/ to virtue and liberty. But when Interest arrived on earth/ Equality disappeared at once/ Ambition raised its ugly head/ Love left the world in tears/ Tyranny invented its oaths/ Despair led lovers astray/ Gold imposed its laws, and Interest, brought with it/ Dishonour, infamies and hatred'.

Interest is a materialistic concept because it reduces human cognition and human inquisitiveness to mere worldliness, that is, to the world of matter which, according to materialism, contains, conditions and confines within its own limits the world of spirit as well. The human being who moves only within the palpable world, where needs and wants prevail, reacts to it, and acts in it according to his *interestedness* (whence, as we shall see, the concept of interest was born). 'What's in it for me?' is the basic question asked by interestedness — implying that if there is nothing explicit to be obtained from a circumstance, a contact or a problem there can be no interest, and the human being need not feel concerned; but by the same token interestedness implies that if there is something to be had for this individual, then the process of obtaining it should be unlimitedly maximized and all moral or spiritual considerations should be subordinated to this aim.

Thus by situating 'interest' at the centre of human life, and making of it the mainspring of human actions within the sphere of worldliness, Benthamism, implicitly and explicitly, subordinated the whole of human nature, all human thought and action to it. Moreover by making interest into the pivot of human comprehension and by relating all moral values to it, thus relativizing those values which are nothing if they are not absolute — Benthamism tore human nature away from its spiritual centre.

For, although interest presents itself as a moral principle, or in other words as a precept with the help of which men (that is, the new men thrown out of the haven of traditional moral values into the stormy seas of modern economics and politics) protect their consciousness against the impulses of their instincts, it is in reality a justification of the instincts and of their satisfaction. And although hedonistic utilitarianism presents itself as the method for the application of reason to man's behaviour, it only provides, through the essentially relative criterion of utility, a means to express in rational terms the impulses of instinct as listed in Jeremy Bentham's original 'table of the springs of action'. This is why in spite of the efforts made by John Stuart Mill and Sidgwick to dehedonize utilitarianism, it was the simplistic hedonistic formulation, the equation between interest and the instinctive pursuit of pleasure, which, after having been ideologized, permeated the thinking and the behaviour of people in liberal industrial, societies, educated, as they are, to pursue above all the maximization of their interest and pleasure in life. And this simplistic formulation is correct; for while it is true that in the consequentialist calculus the moral costs of obtaining a pleasure count as pains, to be deducted from the ultimate pleasure, it is even truer that the real purpose of the calculation itself and of the action it might justify, is and remains the achievement of worldly contentment in a worldly environment.[7]

[7]Tocqueville's positive interpretation of the concept of interest nevertheless confirms this view: L'interêt bien entendu est une doctrine peu haute mais claire et sure. Elle ne cherche pas à atteindre de grands objets; mais elle atteint sans trop d'efforts tous ceux auquels elle vise. Comme elle est à la portée de toutes les intel-

In the light of the above, A.O. Hirschmann's theory that the eighteenth-century pre-Benthamite concept of interest, and specifically of the interest of money-making, was the necessary and welcome conceptual antidote against passions, is in itself unconvincing (and also avoids the confrontation with the utilitarian concept of interest). Hirschmann would like us to believe not only that 'the money-making activities were approved in themselves because . . . they kept the men engaged in them "out of mis-chief" — like princely caprice, adventurous foreign policies, etc. — but also that these activities were the result of a desperate search for avoiding society's ruin'.[8] Passions, and notably the three 'lusts' described by St Augustine, lust for money, lust for power and sexual lust, were the danger. But in Hirschmann's view, interest is, on the contrary, inherently controlled by reason, and limited by reason to practical purposes. Implicit in this way of thinking is the assumption that passions were exacerbated and expressed in excessive and violent forms presumably because of the exaltation and intransigence characteristic of the ages of faith, when purity could only be white like a dove and passions red like blood, or indeed black as Hell. Every action or even intention could only be good or evil, with purgatory as a post-factum intermediary. According to the same assumption, therefore, reason introduces into human judgement a sense of proportion in the assessment of man's life in this world, which engenders the quest for impartiality, and in turn breeds the attitudes of toleration and co-operation.

In this reasoning, whereas the lust for power is an essentially selfish passion, the activity of money-making is an altruistic interest. To make this point crystal clear Hirschmann refers directly to Weber's argument that money-making was 'the result of a desperate search for individual salvation'. Hirschmann argues, on the contrary, that money-making or indeed 'the diffusion of capitalism' was the presumably collective search by men of reason 'for a way of avoiding society's ruin, permanently threatening at the time because of precarious arrangements for internal and external order'.[9]

It is strange that Hirschmann does not even allude in his polemic against Weber to Bentham, to hedonism or to utilitarianism, for Weber, also without mentioning Bentham by name, had stressed that although '[Benjamin] Franklin's moral attitudes are coloured with utilitarianism', nevertheless, 'the *Summum bonum* of this ethic, the earning of more and more money, combined with the strict avoidance of all spontaneous enjoyment of life, is above all completely devoid of any eudaemonistic,

---

ligences, chacun la saisit aisément et la retient sans peine. S'accomodant merveil-leusement aux faiblesses des hommes, elle obtient facilement un grand empire, et il ne lui est point difficile de le conserver, parce qu'elle retourne l'intérêt personnel contre lui-même et se sert pour diriger les passions, de l'aiguillon qui les excite . . .' See *De la Démocratie en Amérique,* Vol. II, pp. 128—9.

[8] A.O. Hirschmann: *The Passions and the Interests,* Princeton, 1977, p. 130.

[9] Max Weber: *The Protestant Ethic,* p. 132.

not to say hedonistic admixture'.[10] Indeed, in Bentham's case, money-making, was associated from the outset with the obtaining of pleasure. This is maybe another reason for Bentham's tenacious hatred of asceticism. For, as Max Weber reminds us, it was the latter-day ascetic monks in the Catholic Church, and the ascetic Calvin in the Protestant religion, who continued to treat usury as *turpitudo* and as a sinful practice against the precepts of the Gospel.[11]

THE LEGALISTIC MIND IN ETHICS AND POLITICS

The origin of Bentham's ideas has been often and very well retraced. But we should always remember that his mind was that of a lawyer, that his logic was legal logic. At the root of his reform of ethics one finds his initial ambition as a student of law to reform the penal and penitentiary systems.[12] The very principle of utility was derived from his early research on penal law and systems of punishment, and explicitly from the treatise *Delle delitte e delle pene* (1764) of the Italian penal reformer Cesare Beccaria, himself influenced by Helvétius. What both Beccaria and Bentham sought was a scientific *procedure* based on an almost mathematical system whereby the utility of the punishment would be calculated in terms of the intensity of the pain inflicted.

> [Bentham] was the disciple of Beccaria as well as of Helvétius. On the one hand he carried the application of the principle of utility to the solution of legal problems further than it had been taken by Beccaria. On the other hand he made use of the various observations scattered throughout Beccaria's little treatise to endow the utilitarian philosophy with a mathematical precision, and he found there, rather more explicitly than in Helvétius, the formula of 'the greatest happiness of the greatest number', 'la massima felicità nel maggior numero'.[13]

A precise reconstitution of the history of Bentham's ideas is particularly useful for two reasons. First it allows us to see where the basic inadequacy

[10] Ibid., pp. 57 and 58.
[11] See especially the long footnote 29 in Chapter II, in Max Weber's *The Protestant Ethic*, pp. 200–2.
[12] Bentham's main concern in the 1770s was to write a work of critical jurisprudence, explaining and justifying the correct principle of legislation, together with the production of a fully rational and justified criminal code. R. Harrison: *Bentham*, London 1983, p. 47.
[13] Halévy also quotes this hymn by Bentham to Beccaria: 'Oh my master, first evangelist of reason, you who have raised your Italy so far above England and I would add above France, were it not that Helvétius, without writing on the subject of laws, had already assisted you and had provided you with your fundamental ideas . . .' Elie Halévy: *The Growth of Philosophic Radicalism*, Oxford 1972, p. 21.

in the theory of utility *as applied to the sharing of happiness* has originated. For in the beginning that theory was applied to the avoidance, or
the reduction, or the justice of the *pain* inflicted by society or by the
legislator as a punishment on the criminal for the misdeeds he had committed. The evaluation of the relation between the pain inflicted by the
legislator, or by society, on the perpetrator and the deed which he had
perpetrated, is conceivable on two practical grounds: because it entails an
objective and even arithmetical calculation by the legislator, or by society,
of how much pain or how intense or prolonged should be applied to the
range of crimes and misdemeanours normally committed by men in different circumstances; and because in any event the punishment can be
applied 'despotically and methodically' by the legislator to the guilty
individual, since the law, which is objective (in the sense that it is general
and that it existed before the particular offence was committed) authorizes
the judge to order the public authorities to inflict a given amount of pain
upon an individual as the punishment corresponding to his offence. What
both Beccaria and Bentham sought was a means of cleansing punishment
from subjective reactions — whether of society or of the judge — hence the
attempt to calculate the amount of pain to be inflicted in all cases to make
sure that it was regarded in terms of its utility.

But when Beccaria, and especially Bentham, moving on to the pursuit
of happiness, tried to apply the utilitarian method to the measurement
of happiness, two essential factors were turned upside down, thus rendering the proposition incongruous. Objectivity, especially if defined as
legal objectivity, is missing: for if an individual contemplates embarking
on an action inducing happiness or pleasure, there is no written law and,
moreover it is that same individual who performs and judges the pros and
cons of that action. It is he who will decide whether the pleasure he
derives from it will outweigh in the utilitarian calculus the pains he will
inflict on others or on society as a whole, and whether in those circumstances the happiness he will derive will still yield a marginal utility. As
A.J. Ayer put it, 'the right action for Bentham is that which produces the
greatest aggregate of happiness no matter how few enjoy the pleasure or
how many suffer the comparative pains'.[14]

Also lacking from the future pleasure-inducing action under consideration is the *certainty* that the action will be carried out, as distinct from
an action which has already been perpetrated and which is afterwards
submitted to judgement and the subsequent evaluation of punishment.
A future, pleasure-inducing action is one possibility among other possibilities, whereas a verdict and the ensuing punishment are *ex post facto*
actions: all its circumstances can be reconstituted, and its consequences
are there to be seen. Now modern interpreters of utilitarianism are mostly
critical of the assumption that experts, relying on the objective help
of computers, can assess the consequences of a public action objectively.

[14] Quoted in J. Lively and J. Rees: *Utilitarian Logics and Politics*,
Oxford 1978, p. 41.

How much more uncertain therefore is the subjective assessment, made by a human being, likely to be, who is considering an action which he presumes will entail some happiness for himself, since otherwise he would not consider it? Moreover in Bentham's catalogue of pleasures the most outstanding are related to the most powerful instincts of man: hunger, thirst, sexual desire. This confirms that the very idea of a pleasure-inducing action must be prompted by an instinctive urge which cannot but trouble from the beginning the objectivity of the consequentialist calculus.

The relevance of the theory of utility to the field of ethics aroused doubts in the end even in its own author, Bentham. At the end of his life — *Deontology*[15] is a posthumous work — Bentham tried to reintroduce some of the basic principles into utilitarianism, notably that of duty. He recognized that the 'word utility . . . has not been found applicable to all the cases' and is 'too weak to express the force of the obligation . . . The mind will not be satisfied with such phrases as "It is useless to commit murder" or "it would be useful to prevent it"; and so of incendiarism and of acts of great magnitude of mischief'.[16]

But the fact that Bentham's moral theories on the proper enjoyment of happiness were a misapplication of his legalistic cast of mind, was to some extent compensated by the fact that those theories sounded more at home in the context of public and especially governmental action or political decision-making. Bernard Williams writes:

> The notion of a *minimum* commitment is an important element in the rationale of utilitarianism and, if I am right, it particularly applies at the public level. Utilitarianism does in certain respects live up to this promise, in the sense that certainly it rests its judgement on a strictly secular and unmysterious basis, and derives (or at least hopes to derive) its substantial input from what people as a matter of fact want, taking its citizenry as it finds them.[17]

But although Bentham and his disciples were doing their utmost to popularize his ideas, or what is called here to ideologize them, by means of his moral treatises such as *A Fragment on Government (1786), An Introduction to the Principles of Morals and Legislation (1780),* they took some time to make a political impact. Nor did Bentham himself show any interest in direct political action. His contempt for the English political circles which had ignored his attempts at penal reform, and disregarded his project for an ideal prison, the *Panopticon,* which he submitted to all European monarchs, including Catherine II of Russia, grew with his advancing years. It was James Mill who linked together the ethical theories

[15] Jeremy Bentham: *Deontology; or the Science of Morality.* In which harmony and co-incidence of duty and self-interest, virtue and felicity, prudence and benevolence are exemplified. From the MSS of Jeremy Bentham, arranged and edited by John Bowring, London, Edinburgh 1834.
[16] Ibid. pp. 34—35.
[17] H.C. Smart and B. Williams: *Utilitarianism For and Against,* Cambridge 1973, p. 136.

of utilitarianism with radical politics, thus giving a new and lasting foundation to liberalism.

THE BIRTH OF UTILITARIAN LIBERALISM

Bentham's first approach to the political applicability of his philosophy was neutral in the sense that, as Halévy puts it, 'during the whole of the first period of his existence Bentham does not seem to have been concerned with problems relative to the improvement of the constitution of the state: he considered happy those countries which had a despot — a Frederick, a Catherine — to execute the wishes of the philosopher promptly, without deliberation and without obstacles'. 'Then' he continues, 'the upheaval brought about by the French Revolution embroiled the princes and the philosophers. Bentham became the great man of the liberals of the continent. In England, he suffered from the indifference and insolence of ministers and their agents. He joined the Westminster Radicals, became converted to their opinions, and provided them with a theory'.[18]

Grosso modo Halévy's account is convincing. But Bentham's conversion to radical politics (and for that matter the adaptation of his rigid *legal* mind to the imagination required for the understanding of those politics) happened late in his life. The *Catechism of Parliamentary Reform,* Bentham's first work in defence of democratic principles, was published only in 1809 when he was sixty-one; and as Jack Lively and John Rees describe in greater detail, the change was brought about under the direct influence of James Mill.[19]

When James Mill published his *Essay on Government,* in 1819, he was mostly concerned with electoral reform, then the subject of intense public debate. As a radical he was putting forward the belief of the English radicals that the establishment of universal male suffrage was the key to the free expression of the consciousness of men, or at least of all Englishmen. This belief was now denounced, not only by the Tories but also by the Whigs, as being of Jacobin origin, and to a certain extent it was true that the French Revolution had precipitated the ideas of the English radicals. But the way James Mill linked the allegedly Jacobin theory of universal male suffrage with Bentham's theory of the greatest happiness made Bentham's conversion to radicalism irresistible.

James Mill's *Essay on Government* was one long cry of discovery. Mill had discovered that the legal and philosophical method of 'the greatest happiness of the greatest number' corresponded in politics to the method

---

[18] E. Halévy: *The Growth of Philosophic Radicalism,* Oxford 1972, pp. 490–92.
[19] Jack Lively and John Rees: *Utilitarian Logics and Politics,* containing the text of the 'Essay'.

of representation based on universal suffrage. The way in which he revealed this 'identity' of purposes was almost syllogistic. He took as his first premise the proposition that in so far as 'the lot of every human being is determined by his pains and pleasures . . . its [the government's] business is to increase to the utmost the pleasures, and diminish to the utmost the pains which men derive from one another' (a sentence which he reproduced almost exactly from Bentham): and his second premise was that 'good government appears to be impossible. The people, as a body, cannot perform the business of government for themselves. If the powers of government are entrusted to one man, or a few men, and a monarchy, or governing aristocracy, is formed, the results are fatal.' Thus he came in the end to the great conclusion which reconciled these two antagonistic premises, his Eureka: 'In the grand discovery of modern times, the system of representation, the solution of all the difficulties, both speculative and practical, will perhaps be found.'[20]

James Mill was right, and on this score John Stuart Mill was also right to consider his father as more effective than Bentham in the final formulation of utilitarianism. The utilitarian vision of the interest of the individual does match with, and is politically dependent on, the electoral representation of the individual. Moreover, if utilitarianism could not be made to open up into politics, that is into the sphere of practical experimentation, it would have remained a pious ethical recommendation. But for James Mill the ethical utilitarian theory of the 'identity of interests' was applicable in politics under the guise of the theory of 'democratic representation'. The belief that the fusion between Bentham's prescription of aggregate happiness and James Mill's theory of popular representation could provide *the* best method of government, indeed the real science of government, was almost reminiscent of Condorcet, who combined belief in the total progress of science with belief in the mathematics of political representation as the overall solution for the regulation of human affairs.[21]

In the polemic which ensued between James Mill and the Benthamites and the Whigs, in the columns of the *Westminster Review* and the Whig *Edinburgh Review*, the most characteristic description of the fusion between Bentham's science of happiness and Mill's science of politics is to be found in an article by Perronet Thompson, in which he replied to Macaulay's criticisms. Here the synthesis is formulated in the most abstract way. Beginning in the idolatrous style typical of Bentham's disciples, the author describes how 'Mr. Bentham, at Oxford . . . he being at that time not quite twenty-one years of age . . . Like Archimedes on the discovery of the principles of hydrostatics . . . exclaimed Eureka . . .' when he discovered in a pamphlet by Dr Priestly the phrase [borrowed from Helvétius] 'the greatest happiness of the greatest number'. For then it appeared to him

[20] In Lively and Rees, op. cit., pp. 56 and 73.
[21] See K.M. Barker: *Condorcet. From Natural Philosophy to Social Mathematics*, Chicago 1975.

'that the object of good government might possibly be the carrying the diminution of evil, or the increase of happiness, to its *maximum*. This was the vision of which the prophet caught a glance from his Pisgah, and straightway girded himself to enter on the promised land. . . .'[22] In that vision *'Justice* stood forth as the rule of appropriation which produced the greatest happiness . . . *Equality* meant equality in the safety of such rights as the rule of the greatest happiness assigned . . . *The sovereignty of the people* meant the acknowledgement of the essential right of the community to obtain its own happiness in its own way.'

Significantly though, the concept of 'interests' as socio-economic groups was simply ignored by Bentham and Mill. Yet the term, in that same sense, was already in circulation in the vocabulary of political economy in English, since the time of Hobbes, Adam Smith, Burke and Madison. And a similar notion, under the name of 'producers', had been used by Saint-Simon as one of his key concepts in the interpretation of industrial society. But Bentham and Mill failed to link the concept of socio-economic groups with their own theory of interest.

This failure cuts right across the logic of James Mill. For while as a utilitarian he based his theory on 'interest', as a radical he stood against the representation of interests. Lively and Rees make this point very clearly: 'The Utilitarian Radicals stood outside this consensus [between the Tories and the Whigs on the necessity of the representation of social pluralism]. James Mill attacked the idea of functional representation directly in the *Essay*, significantly choosing as the object of his attack a defence of it by a Tory, Lord Liverpool.'

Lively and Rees also introduce most usefully at this juncture the argument against the representation of interests put forward by George Grote, another utilitarian. He argued, they say, that,

> There could be only three species of interest in a society: 'first the interest of any one man: that of a group: that of the whole community'. Since it is impossible to construct a governing body which secures at the same time the interests of more than one group, it is clear that these three types of interest are mutually exclusive, and that a governing body which would promote the universal interest must inevitably discard all inclination to the separate interst of any class whatever.[23]

This was according to Lively and Rees 'the crux of the disagreement' between the utilitarian and the other parties. For whereas both Tories and Whigs saw the general interest as an amalgam of group interests, participating by means of the representative system in the processes of decision-making and policy-making, the utilitarians saw the general interest as 'an objective criterion of government policy and legislation, definable through the utility principle; and the achievement of a representative democracy would

---

[22] For all texts see Lively and Rees, op. cit. and in particular, pp. 139–40, 142. (Italics in the original).

[23] Ibid., p. 38.

be to ensure that it became the actual standard of legislation and government policy'.[24]

Regardless of these contradictions, utilitarian radical philosophy was rapidly achieving political success. The few radical MPs, who had formed its first parliamentary representation, were joined by a number of dissenting Whigs. Meanwhile in continental Europe, the partisans of the basic liberties of speech, faith, association and the press, as against the restoration of monarchical absolutism, had come to be known by the name of *liberales*, first given currency in the Spanish Cortes of Cadiz in 1812, summoned to lead the opposition to the Napoleonic invasion of Spain. 'It was a time, as is known, of rapidly rising Liberalism', noted John Stuart Mill. The name was extended to continental radicals and to French doctrinaires, whence it made its way to England and was adopted in mid-century by the new Liberal party. A natural collaboration was established between the new parliamentary organization and the influential but politically ineffective Radicals. When, as he recognizes in his *Autobiography*, John Stuart Mill was elected to Parliament in 1865, he considered it to be his duty 'to come to the front in defence of advanced Liberalism on occasions when the obloquy to be encountered was such as most of the advanced Liberals in the House preferred not to incur'.

The Liberal party was the first in the history of British political parties to provide itself with an organization the purpose of which was to capture the attention, and ultimately the votes, of an electorate progressively enlarged by the Reform Acts. From the first 'caucuses' of Joseph Chamberlain and Schnadhorst, the Liberal Associations and the Federation of Liberal Associations, there grew, between 1857 and 1868 a most powerful political machine called the Liberal party.[25] In spite of frequent difficulties and splits, the Liberal party, because of its organizational homogeneousness succeeded in keeping together a heterogeneous 'coalition' of at least three major attitudes: utilitarianism, constitutionalism, and radicalism; and in concealing under the cloak of general programmes the contradictions at the heart of the ideology itself. Like the Jacobin clubs, the Liberal caucuses and local organizations and communities fulfilled the function of introducing co-operation and discipline into the many factions and groups, however disparate their original attitudes.

Indeed, even if the task of the Liberal party had only been to reconcile the difference between the radical revolutionary wing and the utilitarian constitutional wing of its following, or the individualist with the socially oriented, or the centralistic with the decentralizing trend, the process of ideologization would have been difficult enough. But what proved even more difficult, however, as the new party and the industrial society advanced together on the same front, was to reconcile the social and

---

[24] Ibid.
[25] Moisei Ostrogorski: *La démocratie et les partis politiques,* Paris 1903. Reads even more topically today than when it was first published.

economic problems of that industrial society with the eminently moral and political approaches of the Benthamist ideological philosophy.

Yet it seemed that society in Western Europe was so confidently pursuing human happiness that the idea of procuring it by progressive permissiveness was sufficient in itself to arouse popular enthusiasm. If, in retrospect, one were to single out one common denominator to express the popular success of the tenets of liberalism, the most comprehensive might well prove to be progressive permissiveness. What precisely does this formula imply?

To be sure, economic *'laissez-faire'*, political 'freedom', social 'emancipation' and moral and religious 'toleration', each of these is, in its field, a permissive attitude. Permissiveness as a whole amounts to the conception according to which if human beings were allowed to do all that they wished to do, they would each and all be happy. But in a consequentialist way utilitarianism 'put into scientific form the application of the happiness principle to the morality actions' as John Stuart Mill stresses. Hence the reformism of the utilitarians — the idea that the laws of society should be changed to enlarge the legal morality. Unlike anarchic permissiveness, progressive permissiveness implies that *society itself* should allow people legally to experiment with all kinds of behaviour and to profess all kinds of creeds. Society would benefit from the continuous lubrication of its institutions provided by the change in moral conception, and by the 'progress' made toward further permissiveness. For progress cannot be achieved unless man can experience all forms of knowledge and behaviour, which only permissiveness will allow him to do. Progress breeds permissiveness, and permissiveness breeds progress.

Progressive permissiveness is essentially a materialist doctrine. Its origin lies in Helvétius; it is opposed to Rousseau's concept of public virtue, and even more so to Kant's moral imperative. It has become increasingly materialistic in the generally hedonistic atmosphere of the industrial society. As we shall shortly see, Bentham's successors, from John Stuart Mill to Sidgwick did their utmost to eliminate their master's emphatic hedonism from the conception of utilitarianism. But they never succeeded in eliminating it from the theory, and it was too late to eliminate it from the practice.

THE DILEMMAS OF UTILITARIAN LIBERALISM

John Stuart Mill, whom his father and his father's master had not succeeded in transforming into a utilitarian robot, inherited the difficult legacy of their doctrine. It was a difficult legacy for him, because his own mind had been imbued from earliest infancy with the utilitarian doctrine, and he was never able to free himself from its influence. It was also a difficult legacy because the contradictions in the doctrine were to a great extent irreconcilable. I will limit myself here to the three dilemmas that faced him which come nearest to the subject of this enquiry.

As A.D. Lindsay shows in his introduction to Mill's *Utilitarianism* Mill had first tried to separate Bentham's obvious hedonism from utilitarian theory and to give the theory a different ethical basis. He did not succeed either in practice or in theory. In practice, because utilitarian ideologization had by then proved far more effective in awakening the public to the idea of the pursuit of happiness than to its consequentialist condition. And he failed in theory because, to quote Lindsay: 'Had Mill possessed Bentham's saving irreverence he would have broken away from Benthamism altogether, and tried to construct a system to the facts which he recognized'. But did he break away? The evidence all goes to show that he held to the ideas of his forerunners. As he deliberately proclaimed in the final paragraphs of the conclusions to his monumental *System of Logic,* 'the general principle to which all rules of practice ought to conform is that conductive to the happiness of mankind, or rather of all sentient beings'. The main suggestion he made for reducing the element of hedonistic materialism in Bentham's utilitarianism was to divide pleasures into 'higher' and 'lower' categories: the 'higher' pleasures should be more commendable; and to accept that 'when secondary principles conflict', the principle of utility must be appealed to. But as Sir Isaiah Berlin remarks, 'as he gives no indication how this notion *drained of its old materialistic* but intelligible content is to be applied . . . that leads one to ask what, in fact, was Mill's real scale of values'?[26] If I italicized the reference to materialism it is because here lies the real cause of John Stuart Mill's failure to reform Benthamism, as we shall see.

The second utilitarian dilemma Mill failed to solve arose from the analysis of the interrelation between the legal, moral and political planes of the society he interpreted in utilitarian terms, and its changing social and economic planes. Yet, unlike his predecessors, by 1861 when he produced his very important *Representative Government*, he had had ample opportunity to observe the functioning of industrial society and the enlargement of the sphere of politics which that functioning had produced. His own economic analyses, in his *Principles of Political Economy,* as Alan Ryan confirms in his *J.S. Mill,* show no originality. But 'the book secured its privileged standing because of the way Mill tied the discussion of economic problems to pressing social issues'.[27]

There are frequent *references* in *Representative Government* to the poor, the working class, or labour, and what is more a lucid remark to the

---

[26] Sir Isaiah Berlin: *John Stuart Mill and the Ends of Life*, Robert Waley Cohen Memorial Lecture, 1, 1959, London 1962. (My italics).

[27] A. Ryan: *J.S. Mill.*

effect that 'the great difficulty of democratic government has hitherto seemed to be, how to provide, in a democratic society . . . a social support, a *point d'appui,* for individual resistance to the tendencies of the ruling power; a protection, a rallying point, for opinions and interests which the ascendant public opinion views with disfavour'. For, as Asa Briggs notes, Mill would refuse to introduce reforms 'overriding "public opinion"'. Mill believed too much in public opinion to interpret its influence in terms of the clamour of vested interests or the ignorance of people who would not listen to sound advice' concludes Briggs.[28]

Yet the pessimism that *Representative Government* often exhales regarding the future of democracy (in part inspired by Tocqueville) does imply a premonition of the changes that industrial society was going to lead to in the political processes of decision-making and of representation. This is certainly confirmed by the passage in *Representative Government* where John Stuart Mill proposes the elitist change in the electoral system by introducing plurality of votes according to the knowledge and the competence of the voter.

> The only thing which can justify reckoning one person's opinion as equivalent to more than one is individual mental superiority . . . the nature of a person's occupation is some test . . . a foreman is generally more intelligent than an ordinary labourer, and a labourer in the skilled trades than in the unskilled . . . subject to some condition, two or more votes might be allowed to every person who exercises any of such functions.

When this whole idea came to Mill he had already realized the impact which personal competence in the *function* makes in an intrinsically *functional* industrial society. Saint-Simon's vision of the priority to be given to scientists and experts in the processes of decision-making in an industrial society was formulated on the experience of a pre-industrial society. But in John Stuart Mill the proposal to introduce a technocratic plurality of votes in an already fair and valid system of representation can only be the result of a change he himself had noticed in the *point d'appui* of the changing society.

And yet few of these premonitions are reflected in the constitutional treatise. Its main purpose was to ascertain how well the representative system worked, and how it could be improved, in the sense of how could society as a whole participate in the decision-making process. Thus the question of adapting the processes of policy-making of a society because that society has itself been altered as a result of the growing functionalism of industrial society comes into the work only incidentally. There is for instance a passage where Mill suggests that 'in this country, *for example, what are called* the working classes may be considered as excluded from all direct participation in the government . . . When a subject arises [in the

---

[28] Asa Briggs: 'Foreword' to *Autobiography of John Stuart Mill,* New York, 1964, p. xx.

British Parliament] in which labourers as such have an interest, is it regarded from any point of view but that of the employers of labour?' Such thoughts are honourable — but they do not amount to a reconsideration of the policy-making processes as a whole in the light of the change which has occurred in the centre of gravity of industrialized society. Mill does not even consider the possibility that because of the functional cleavages in an industrial society corporate forces might grow to the extent that they would hamper representative government and try to bend it under their socio-economic weight. The reforms he proposes concern details of procedure. One must thus agree with most of his modern commentators that his general conclusions on the government of modern society are 'depressingly banal'.[29]

The almost subconscious refusal of Mill's mind even to consider that the liberal society and state might be turning into an essentially interdependent industrial society, illustrated the contradiction at the heart of Liberal-Utilitarianism. For it was central to the liberal faith that in a society of free individuals, freedom of individual activity would be guaranteed by the constitutional structure, and that the activities of all interests would ultimately produce the harmony or 'identity' of interests. Whereas the consequentialism which formed part of utilitarianism predisposed it towards the checking, adjusting and regulating of society by public authorities (or rather by institutions invested by the public with authority). Indeed in the history of British social and political ideas and institutionalization, utilitarianism *via* Fabianism played as great a part as socialism in the making of the welfare state.

The third dilemma inherited by John Stuart Mill was the antithesis between the materialism of utilitarianism and the individualistic idealism of liberalism. As Tocqueville pointed out, individualism, unlike egoism, is a modern concept. 'Nos pères ne connaissaient que l'égoisme', which is 'un sentiment réfléchi et paisible qui dispose chaque citoyen à s'isoler de la masse de ses semblables et à se retirer à l'écart avec sa famille et ses amis; de telle sorte que, après s'être ainsi créé une petite société à son usage, il abandonne volontiers la grande société elle-même'.[30]

On the fundamental antagonism between materialism and idealism which tore the very fabric of utilitarian liberalism apart from the beginning, John Stuart Mill sided with the materialism of his forerunners as against the 'idealism' reintroduced into 'liberalism' by Tocqueville or T.H. Green. Mill maintained his optimistic belief that provided the economic and political institutions (*Representative Government*) work satisfactorily, the identity of interests will manifest itself, the final result of which will be that the greatest number of individual human beings will receive the greatest happiness. But Green and Tocqueville were pessimistically con-

[29] A. Ryan, *J.S. Mill.*
[30] Alexis de Tocqueville: *De la démocratie en Amérique*, Vol. II, Pt. 2, Ch. 2.

cerned not only with the quality of society, but with the integrity of the individual threatened with absorption into society, with the very survival of individuality. And in so far as Tocqueville was Mill's great friend, and Green his junior and critical, liberal, follower, the contrast between Mill and the other two men is fairly striking.

To take Green first, since he in a sense continues the story of British liberalism after John Stuart Mill. His philosophy is difficult to grasp in its entirety, both because of his style and because of his own failure to indicate to which of his two main impulses he gives priority: to the desire to devote man's efforts to the establishing of justice and equality in society (for which he is more popularly known as the 'idealistic' prophet of an authoritarian state); or to the desire to keep the conscience of the individual alive and intact in materialistic and collectivistic surroundings. But if sympathetically and, as it were, selectively, read, both the *Lectures on the Principles of Political Obligation* and *The Prolegomena to Ethics* (1907) do reveal the possibilities according to the Kantian and Christian philosophies of co-ordinating the two causes to which Green wanted to devote himself. Positive freedom is for Green the freedom of the individual whose conscience, animated by the moral sense of duty, exercises the power of its freedom 'through the help or security given him by his fellowmen, and which he in turn helps to secure for them'.

In order to re-situate liberalism on moral foundations, Green went back to the very origin of the dilemma, to Bentham's double confusion between happiness and the object of life, and between happiness and pleasure. Courageously, he went back in the history of philosophy to the contrast between Bentham and Kant. 'The Benthamists', he wrote, 'repudiate or pronounce unintelligible the notion of an absolute value in the individual person. It is not every person according to him, but every pleasure, that is of value of itself . . .' And speaking of the recognition of the claims of a common humanity Green asserts that 'if it is only the conscience of the individual that brings the principle of human equality into productive contact with the particular facts of human life, on the other hand it is from the embodiment of the principle in laws and institutions and social requirements that the conscience itself appropriates it'.[31] Green draws the conclusion himself:

> Our conclusion then is that it is a misinterpretation of consciousness . . . to regard the idea of a truer or higher good . . . as equivalent or reducible to the idea of a larger sum of pleasure enjoyable by the person entertaining the idea. In the mind at least of those persons over whom the idea has any controlling power, its filling is supplied by ideal objects to which they are seeking to give reality, and of which the realisation forms their prevailing interest. Such an ideal object, for example, is the welfare of a family.[32]

[31] T.H. Green: *Prolegomena to Ethics*, ed. C.A. Bradley, Oxford 1929, pp. 247, 249.

[32] Ibid., p. 268.

Politics and the pursuit of happiness

But the real reconciliation which Green operated between the interiorized moral conscience and the exteriorized conscience of political and social action consists in something else which has been insufficiently remarked in his moral philosophy. Having stated that the ordinary activity of men, regulated by law and custom, contributes to the realization of human capabilities, Green remarks that it is not for this ordinary activity that men who aspire towards some further perfection 'enquire into the ends of living'. Green defines those ends as 'the production of personal excellence, moral and intellectual'. The concept of *personal excellence* already operates the change from the exterior 'felicific calculuses' to the interior assessment of one's moral and intellectual perfectibility, always aspiring towards excellence. How different is this individuality, seen from inside one's own self, from John Stuart Mill's painful, flat, indeed two-dimensional attempt to find, in the chapter on individuality in *On Liberty,* 'the nature and limits of the power which can be legitimately exercised by society over individuals'?

To Mill's legalistic calculations on how to assign limits within which the individual might act without hurting others or the society outside himself, or, vice versa, how to assign limits to the control of society over the individual, Green replies that the solution lies in finding your own excellence within yourself. For the more you achieve your excellence within yourself, the more use will that excellence be to society, and the less will it *compete* with the excellence of others. The jungle of competition is precisely what law, custom and materialistic moral philosophies are called on to regulate. But when Green reminds us that 'there can be no competition between man and man for the realization of the human soul'[33] he offers a solution. For, on the one hand, the markets and streets of social life will then be that much less crowded with men competing to find their excellence there or trying endlessly to improve society itself and the lives of others and their own. And, on the other hand, only when the individual is in full and permanent agreement with his own conscience will he find excellence, which is real happiness.

The general differences between John Stuart Mill and Tocqueville are well known from the many studies of the history of political ideas in the nineteenth century. Here it is perhaps useful to stress one special difference, which is fundamental to the perspective of this enquiry. This is the difference in their attitude towards the mystery of life.

Nothing is more pathetic in John Stuart Mill's *Autobiography* than the passages in which he reveals how the utilitarian education his father gave him deprived him of, one might even say immunized him against, both faith and poetry, the two oases of mystery in man's 'calculable' existence in the Waste Land of the materialistic world. He tells us only too

[33] Ibid., p. 332.

130

frequently and proudly that he did not have to 'throw off religious belief, but never had it: I grew up in a negative state with regard to it'.

Tocqueville instead was decidedly anti-materialistic:

> When one reads Plato, one is bound to remark that before and during his life there were many writers who preached materialism. These writers either have not reached us at all or only very incompletely. The same happened in almost all centuries. The majority of the great schools were dedicated to the spirit. We must not believe therefore, that at any time and whatever the political situation, the passion of materialistic pleasures and the beliefs fostered by it could satisfy a whole people. Man's soul is vaster than we think; it can entertain both the taste for earthly goods and the love of the goods of heaven. Sometimes a people seems to be pursuing only one of them; but soon it will seek the other. . .[34]

And, like Green, Tocqueville had kept his Christian faith. Pascal's influence on him was particularly evident.[35] This is why he concluded his reflections on democracy in America with the characteristically Pascalian remark that:

> Providence has created the human species neither completely free nor completely enslaved. Providence has drawn around every human being a fatal circle, from which there is no way out; but within those vast limits, the human being is strong and free; and so are the peoples. It depends on them whether equality will lead them to servitude or to freedom, to enlightenment or to barbarism, to prosperity or to abject poverty.

And in another passage of the same work he notes:

> Human beings pass through time and disappear afterwards for ever in God's bosom. They can be seen only for one moment tottering over the edge of the two abysses in which they are then lost.[36]

Yet at the end of the day, a thought should be spared for John Stuart Mill's own doubts on the validity and integrity of the ideology he so loyally defended — and so desperately tried to change. Everybody who remembers the dramatic chapter of his *Autobiography* is left with grave doubts about his wishful belief that he had fully recovered from it, that he could have afterwards been fully reconciled with the Benthamite method of promising political happiness. One must conclude this chapter with the haunting passages:

[34] *De la démocratie en Amérique*, vol. 1, p. 15. Tocqueville could not know that Karl Marx was to choose Democritus as the subject for his doctoral thesis.

[35] On Pascal's influence on Tocqueville see Luis Diez del Corral: *La mentalidad política de Tocqueville con especial referencia a Pascal*, Madrid, 1963.

[36] A. de Tocqueville, *De la démocratie en Amérique*, Vol. II, p. 17. (my translation.).

Having first mentioned that 'From the winter of 1821, when I first read Bentham, I had what might truly be called an object in life: to be a reformer of the world', after the 'crisis' he says: 'In this [new] frame of mind it occurred to me to put the question directly to myself: "Suppose that all your objects in life were realized; that all the changes in institutions and opinions which you are looking forward to could be completely effected at this very instant: would this be a great joy and happiness to you?" and an irrepressible self-consciousness distinctly answered, "No" . . . The other important change which my opinions at this time underwent was that I, for the first time, gave the proper place, among the prime necessities of human well-being to the internal culture of the individual. I ceased to attach almost exclusive importance to the ordering of outward circumstances, and the training of the human being for speculation and for action . . . I now looked upon the choice of political institutions as a moral and educational question, more than one of material interests, thinking that it ought to be decided mainly by the consideration, what great improvement in life and culture stands next in order for the people concerned as the condition of their further progress, and what institutions are most likely to promote that'.[37]

[37] J.S. Mill, *Autobiography,* ed. A. Briggs, pp. 106, 107, 113, 129.

Chapter 7

The communist system of political happiness

Communism is the solution to the riddle of history

Karl Marx

The name *Communist* is given here to the third system of political happiness for a number of reasons. The first is that it is the name which Karl Marx himself gave to the ideologized form of his philosophy, as expounded in the Communist Manifesto. It is the name he also gave to those who shared that ideology and were to bring it to its fulfilment: the Communists.[1] Secondly it is the name which Lenin gave in 1921 to the Russian Social Democratic party of the Bolsheviks, and which has afterwards been used by all the parties affiliated to the Third International and linked by Marxist–Leninist ideology, the communist parties throughout the world, whose members are called Communists. The year which marked the complete separation between socialist parties and communist parties was 1921. The German Social Democratic party had been formed first of all and the name Social Democratic had until then been used by the Russian party and by other parties which, together with socialist or 'Labour' parties of non-Marxist inspiration and not bound by Marxist ideology, were united in the Second International. And the Second International in turn had been formed after the inevitable collapse of the First International, unable to reconcile the contradictions between the two major doctrines which co-existed under its umbrella: the anarchists and the Communists (later socialists).

The third reason why the name *Communist* is used here arises from the semantics of this enquiry, as well as from current political literature. One of the constitutive elements of what is described here as a system of political happiness is a pre-existing nation-state (see pp. 67–8) which can be taken over and moulded according to the ideology. A number of states have been thus taken over and moulded by the Marxist–Leninist

---

[1] As for instance in the following statement in the Communist Manifesto: 'To this end Communists of various nationalities had assembled in London . . .', etc.

ideology, and are thus generally called communist states. In contrast, because they respected such liberal principles as the existence of competitive parties based on universal suffrage, private property, and freedom of information, the socialist parties (Social Democratic, Socialist or Labour) which have so frequently been in power in other European industrial states[2] accommodated themselves within the constitutions of the liberal states. There are no socialist 'states' in Western Europe, even when socialist parties from the government. (Yet it so happens that, in the Marxist—Leninist semantics, the countries of Eastern Europe governed by communist parties are called socialist.) The structural changes operated by the liberal states under the combined influence of the socialist and the utilitarian ideologies led to the formation of the '*welfare* states'. But this description does not imply a particular constitutional structure.

In the light of these perspectives we can now distinguish in European industrial society two political systems descending from the original Jacobin proto-system of political happiness: one of them is revolutionary and Marxist; the other groups together the industrial states governed by non-Marxist parties and generally called the *welfare* states.

This being said, let us now turn to the analysis of the constitutive elements of the *communist* system of political happiness.

THE MARXIST PROMISE OF HAPPINESS

Marx's promise of happiness is double — a philosophical promise: happiness through man's reintegration within himself, and a practical, economic promise: 'to each according to his needs' in the future, communist society.

Marx re-establishes the link with Rousseau's search for the integration of man, through the immersion of the individual in the general will. For Marx that integration occurs not in the general will but in the *Galtung*, the human species as a whole seen in its historical development. When human beings have acquired a humanist consciousness this integration will become possible, and it will be effected by Communism. This was solemnly promised by Marx in his early 'Economic and philosophical manuscripts'.[3]

> Communism, as completed naturalism, is humanism and as completed humanism is naturalism. It is the genuine solution of the antagonism between man and nature, and between man and man. It is the true solution of the struggle between existence and essence, between freedom and necessity, between individual and species. It is the solution to the riddle of history, and knows itself to be this solution'.

[2] In the meantime the German Social Democratic party has openly renounced its Marxist affiliation.
[3] Karl Marx, 'Economic and philosophical manuscripts', in David McLellan: *Karl Marx Selected Writings*, Oxford 1977, p. 89.

For this is indeed a promise – and what is more a pledge to action in so far as Communism is the praxis of the theory of historical materialism, the philosophy which will 'transform' the world. Historical materialism visualizes man in the perspective of the history of the relations of production, which determine the human condition. Communist action will 'transform' those relations of production – and by so doing, will also transform the human condition itself. The pivot of the action is the abolition of private ownership of the means of production, which engenders the vicious relations of production.

> This material, immediately sensuous, private property is the material, sensuous expression of man's alienated life. Its movement of production and consumption is the sensuous revelation of all previous production, i.e., the realization or reality of man. Religion, family, state, law, morality, science and art are only particular forms of production and fall under its general law. The positive abolition of private property, and the appropriation of human life is therefore the positive abolition of all alienation, thus the return of man out of religion, family, state, etc., into his human, i.e., social being.[4]

The whole of Marx's system is contained in this seminal passage. His whole work is the development in all directions of this central and particularly complete postulate. Like Hegel's philosophy, Marx's philosophy has an extraordinary unity. The same great oak grows from one acorn, the same theme is repeated in endless variations. But unlike in Hegel's philosophy both the dialectical end and the dialectical means of Marx's philosophy are materialistic. The end is the future transformation of the condition of life of human beings during their material existence (for they are made of matter); and the means is the revolutionary, i.e., political, overthrow of capitalism, or the economic system of private property and the exploitation of private man by private man. For the economic structure is what determines all the elements of the human condition – the political superstructure, culture, even the consciousness of the human being itself. Marx's assertion of the determining primacy of the economy led to what Louis Dumont rightly calls 'the economic ideology',[5] according to which only economic 'science' can find the solution for man's plight. But in political terms, this primacy resulted in the development of the view pejoratively called 'economism' by Lenin, which based itself on absolute economic determinism. 'Economism' held that changes in the economic structure were inevitably bound to happen and would be furthered by 'reforms' of the superstructure (as distinct from the revolutionary overthrow of both base and superstructure).

But can the Marxist concepts of the 'end of alienation' or 'reintegration' be equated with that of happiness? The answer is yes. Man's unhappiness consists of his alienation; a dis-alienated or 'integrated' man is therefore

[4]Ibid.
[5]Louis Dumont: *Homo aequalis, Genèse et épanouissement de l'idéologie économique,* Paris 1980. (English edn, Chicago 1977).

happy — and so is the integrative society. And the Marxist promise although teleological, abstract and essentially collective, as against Bentham's present, sensual and essentially individual promise, is nevertheless a materialistic promise, because like Bentham, Marx reduces the world to the world of matter. 'Man has not created matter itself. And he cannot even create any productive capacity if the matter does not exist beforehand' asserts Marx categorically. The soul of the individual human being dies with that being's material body but sublimates itself through its participation in the history of the species. As in Hegel's philosophy death is sublimated in the spirit and its history. In a more than usually obscure passage, but one of the few in which Marx has the intellectual daring to face explicitly the mystery of man's death, he explains that: 'Death appears as the harsh victory of the species over the particular and seems to contradict their unity; but the particular individual is only a determinate species — being thus mortal'.[6] But then the scattered references to death in Hegel's work are equally obscure and confusing. However while Hegel's 'Spirit' in its mystery, may be immortal, why should Marx think that the human species is and will remain immortal?

Many thinkers have asked the question whether atheism is indispensable to the logic of socialism, or whether it was Marxism which established this strict correlation. Some argue that this correlation was present even in Utopian Socialism. Karl Polanyi for instance insists that the 'fulcrum of Owen's thought was his turning away from Christianity which he accused of "individualization" or of fixing the responsibility for character on the individual himself and its all-powerful formative influence upon character. It was Owen's discovery of society which made him transcend Christianity and reach a position beyond him'.[7] This is not so of Saint-Simon who on the contrary at the end of his social thinking came back to the search for a *New Christianity* and who, in any event, always kept his faith.[8] Owen Chadwick however shows that Marx believed atheism to be the heart of his theory and that the advance of the feeling that atheism and socialism were akin 'coincided largely with the advance of Marxist theory',[9] which he describes as the most powerful philosophy of secularization in the nineteenth century. Although the following passage from Marx's *Critique of Hegel's Dialectics* is a sample of his prose at its most obscure — it is at the same time one of his most complete answers to this question:

In other words atheism is humanism mediated with itself through the supersession of religion, and communism is humanism mediated with itself through the supersession of private property. Only through the

---

[6] Karl Marx, 'Economic and philosophical manuscripts', in David McLellan: *Karl Marx Selected Writings*, Oxford 1977, p. 91.
[7] Karl Polanyi: *The Great Transformation. The Political and Economic Origin of Our Time*, Beacon Paperback 1957, p. 127.
[8] G. Ionescu: *The Political Thought of Saint-Simon*, Oxford 1975.
[9] O. Chadwick, *The Secularization of the European Mind in the Nineteenth Century*, Cambridge 1975, pp. 79 and 67.

supersession of this mediation which is, however, a necessary pre-condition, does positive humanism that begins with itself come into being. But atheism and communism are no flight, no abstraction, no loss of the objective world engendered by man or his faculties that have created his objectivity, no poverty-stricken regression to unnatural and underdeveloped simplicity. They are rather the first real emergence and genuine realization of man's essence as something actual.[10]

Marxist philosophers like Ernst Bloch argue that Marx's atheism is more a de-theocratization (*Enttheocratisierung*) than a de-mythologization. This would amount to saying, in the terminology of this enquiry, that the *promise* of the advent of the happiness-providing communist society is the myth which replaces the religious myths. To that extent, as already intimated, all ideologies are by their very *raison d'être* anti-religious; they try to replace religious faith with the faiths they offer. But it remains undeniable that while the dismissal of religion is, in utilitarian liberalism, implicit, agnostic and permissively tolerant, and in Jacobinism it was anti-Christian but deistic — in Marxism, and in Marxism—Leninism, with all its ramifications, the anti-religious stance is atheistic, militant and unconditional. In the true logic of Marxist Communism, religion and Communism are mutually exclusive. For a man, indeed the 'new man' of Communism, to emerge the old roots of religious hope must be extirpated; and it is only when those 'new men' will compose society that society will be Communist. This is the philosophical promise of Communism.

The economic promise of Communism, which will also be fulfilled with the advent of communist society, is that each man will then be given 'according to his needs'. The formula taken out of its context, and indeed transformed into the popular slogan of communist ideologization, is of course intoxicating. It corresponds both to the profound positive aspiration of human beings towards equality and social justice and to the negative human instincts of envy and jealousy. But in context — that is in the text of the manifesto — it is most explicitly linked with the advent of the communist society, when human beings will produce according to their needs. For in pure Marxist theory the distribution of goods recommended by the different systems of distributive justice, with different criteria of equalization, is relevant only to societies in which private ownership prevails. On this point Marx directly opposes John Stuart Mill: 'Thus it is quite absurd to say as J.S. Mill does for example . . . that "the . . . distribution of wealth is a matter of human institutions solely". The "laws and conditions" of the production of wealth are the same laws in a different form; they both change and undergo the same historical process'.

The goal of Communism is therefore to change the relations of production themselves, which are the dialectic counterpart of consumption — or of satisfaction of the 'needs' of human beings. Abolition of private property is the only means of achieving a just distribution and a true equality.

[10]McLellan, op. cit., p. 108.

To distribute wealth, wealth must first be expropriated. Then men will be able to put an end to the alienation of their existence which is caused by the alienation of labour — and thus reintegrated within themselves be for the first time happy. This fundamental, if abstract and theoretical, promise of Communism was transformed by ideologization into simple slogans, the *leitmotif* of which was the moral principle of egalitarianism. Simplified in this way, Marxist egalitarianism aroused in nineteenth- and twentieth-century human beings both the positive aspirations towards social justice and human dignity and the negative instincts of social envy and jealousy. In the false light of these feelings, the abolition of private property was and still is understood as the simple first act of expropriation.

Marx himself was responsible for these grave ideological deformations in so far as he never explained in detail what would happen in the economic realm after expropriation had taken place and in the political realm after the revolution and the 'smashing' of the state.

By being deliberately elusive on these two questions, the two promises of Communism, Marx encouraged the tendency of Marxist ideologization and of ideological parties to implant in those who fell under the spell of that ideology the idea that the revolution itself and by itself was the 'open sesame', the solution of all human problems; that, in other words, once the (bourgeois) state was 'smashed' and capitalism was 'overthrown' by the simple act of expropriation of private property hey presto! and at once all economic and social conflicts would cease, and so would politics which, in Marx's vision, is only the by-product of those conflicts. Marx failed to explain how and why *after* the revolution and the expropriation of private property relations of production would be transformed overnight; and how the smashing of the state, army and police would by itself bring about at once an institutionless society of spontaneous collaboration. The failure might have been due to his awareness that those questions could not possibly be answered. Nevertheless it was his deliberate intention to lead simple minds to concentrate only on the miracle of the revolution. Marxist ideology and ideological parties have followed, and are still following, this propagandistic strategy with tenacity.

Yet it was precisely these two cardinal promises which were going to be proven false.

IDEOLOGY AND PARTY

The confusions in Marx's thought initially took the form of ideological controversies among his followers. In Germany, the country to which the Communist Manifesto was directly addressed, both Marx and Engels had proudly seen the first 'working-class' party appear — the German Social Democratic party. Moreover in 1875, that is eight years before Marx's death, his close disciples, August Bebel and Wilhelm Liebknecht, who had becomes its leaders, proclaimed that it was a Marxist party. But that was only the beginning of the controversies and quarrels. That the two major promises of Marxism were true, or false, could not be demonstrated until Marxists had succeeded in taking power in one or more states. Thus the controversy now raged on how Marxists should reach power? Should this be achieved by constitutional means, that is to say by the increasing popularity and parliamentary strength of the party and by reforms in the socio-economic structures effected by the influence of powerful trade unions; or by revolutionary means? Or by accepting that in order to smash the structure the superstructure and notably the state must first be smashed, or in other words that a true Marxist system could not be established within the institutions of the capitalist system? To these questions the ageing Marx and Engels answered only in a confused and contradictory way. After Marx's death in 1883 the controversy raged even more fiercely, and by the turn of the century a trend towards 'reformism' or 'revisionism' of the inherent incoherence of Marxist ideology emerged.

As is only too well known the Western Social Democratic, Socialist, and Labour parties gradually abandoned, if they had ever held, the revolutionary position and embarked on the joint socio-economic (trade union) and politico-ideological (party) action towards the 'reform' of society in a socialist sense, which in turn required that the working-class parties should conquer power by parliamentary means. This whole evolution from within the liberal state helped ultimately to create the welfare state, before the war in Sweden and in the impressive, if brief, experiment in the American 'New Deal', and immediately after the war in most Western industrial states. As is also very well known the principles of the welfare state were much closer to those of the liberal John Maynard Keynes than to those of Karl Marx. But the welfare state will be discussed in the next chapter.

Here we must return to the moment when the first open break occurred in a Social Democratic party and that took place in the clandestine Russian party in 1903. The two irreconcilable wings of the party: the minority, in Russian, Menshevik and the majority, in Russian, Bolshevik, split finally and irrevocably in 1912. The leader of the Bolsheviks was Lenin — who had already expressed the view that the working class would come to power only through revolution, specifically in Russia but also everywhere, in his *What is to be done?* published in 1902. In the same book he had already explained that ideology was the principal weapon of the revolution, which arms the ideological revolutionary party — in its very essence a monolithic party. He accused the parliamentary Social Democratic parties of collaborating with the capitalist—nationalistic governments of their countries. The First World War confirmed Lenin's analysis in both respects: the Socialist International, formed by the Socialist parties, which according to Marx should have put the solidarity of the international working class above the nationalism of their countries, collapsed abjectly, almost all the Social Democratic parties backing their own national governments. Lenin was the only leader of a Marxist party who opposed the war. But the war also confirmed his theory that a revolution could take place in Russia – for in November 1917 he proclaimed it.

The trouble was that the Russian revolution was no longer a Marxist revolution. It was a Marxist–Leninist revolution because in the meantime Lenin, the disciple, had given a new interpretation to the doctrine of the master.

If John Stuart Mill made only a partial and uncertain impact on the Benthamite mould of utilitarianism, Marx's most important disciple, Lenin, succeeded in transforming Marxism. Indeed, after Lenin Marxism became Marxism–Leninism. For, what Lenin did was to cut the various Gordian knots of Marx's voluntary or involuntary confusions – and to choose from Marx's many ambiguities one single way of thinking and of acting. It is true that in some respects Lenin's writings were exercises in bringing Marxism up to date and in adapting Marx's interpretations to the world of some half a century later: *Imperialism, the Last Stage of Capitalism*, and *Materialism and Empirio-Criticism* are example of this creative updating of the doctrine. But in many other respects what Lenin did – indeed had to do, faced as he was with imminent problems of action and realization – was to cut through Marx's waffle and imprecision and to put his seal of interpretation on one or the other of the confusing alternatives. In five major respects Lenin transformed Marxism into Marxism–Leninism.

The two first transformations belong to the philosophical aspect of Marx's doctrine. Lenin cut through the Marx–Engels verbiage about determinism and human action by asserting, in *What is to be done?* and in his actual practice in 1917–22, the supremacy of voluntarism. And he cut through the cirumlocutions of the 'young Marx' on the question of idealistic materialism and materialistic idealism. He simply demonstrated that there could not be anything but simple and primitive materialism, that the doctrine should acknowledge and proclaim that everything originated in matter. Without this basic reiteration, he insisted in his important work *Materialism and Empirio-Criticism*, the whole edifice of Marx's philosophy of action would collapse.

The third interpretation consisted in turning Marx's actual definition of the very concept of ideology upside down. Marx's critical definition of ideology as the 'false consciousness' or as 'the *camera obscura* [in which] men and their circumstances appear upside down [because] this phenomenon arises just as much from their historical life-process as the inversion of objects on the retina does from their physical life-process', was changed by Lenin into a definition of ideology as a set of positive principles with which the working class confronts and interprets the reality of the socio-economic situation hitherto blurred by the falsifying interpretations of bourgeois theories. Marxist ideology was defined by Lenin as the principal weapon of the workers in their 'ideological combat' or 'ideological competition' with the bourgeoisie. But, as can be seen, Lenin through his authoritative interpretation had up-ended Marx's definition. What Lenin considered to be a glorification was in reality a degradation. But it was true to life and Lenin's truth prevailed.

Lenin's fourth interpretation was the rejection of Social Democratic constitutionalism. He interpreted Marx's theory of the revolutionary and insurrectional coming to power of the working class as the sole method of bringing about a genuine communist society. Admittedly Lenin's theory was the projection upon Marxism of the revolutionary situation in Tsarist Russia. And because in the original Russian situation there was no demographic justification for the Russian industrial working class to undertake the revolution, Lenin prescribed the 'alliance with the peasantry'. This turned Marxism—Leninism into a revolutionary prescription for under-developed countries and continents. But precisely because of that Lenin was right. For in reality, so vast and abrupt is the abyss separating Marx's vision of the evolution of capitalist industrial society from the real evolution of industrial society, capitalist and non-capitalist alike, as we see it today, that the Marxist theory of an inevitable seizure of power by a pauperized proletariat in highly developed societies becomes increasingly 'Utopian'. Only 'revolution', in the insurrectional, even putschist, sense of the word could now serve the Marxist theory — and such insurrectional revolutions take place for the most part in underdeveloped countries.

The fifth of Lenin's amplifications of Marxist theory is his affirmation of the continuation and the strengthening of the state after the Communist revolution. The intellectual equivocations of Marx on the *Zerbrechen* and *Aufhebung* of the state, and his failure to answer the question on the form which post-revolutionary institutionalization, or non-institutionalization, would take has been touched on in the preceding pages. Faced with a 'communist' revolution which he was going to launch in Russia by insurrection, Lenin damned Marx for not offering a precise answer to this all-important question. Then, with the help of some scattered remarks by Marx and Engels, he constructed in his *State and Revolution* (1917) the theory 'of the dictatorship of the proletariat', for the brief transition from the bourgeois state to the classless society. But by 1919, against the wishes even of the Constitutional Commission which he himself set up after the dissolution of the Constituent Assembly, he had (with Stalin's help) proclaimed and institutionalized the 'state' of the Russian Republic, and in 1922 he was able to constitute for good the federal state of the USSR with practically the same frontiers and a stronger centralistic organization than that of the Tsarist Empire. In that, too, Lenin was a faithful interpreter of Karl Marx for, unlike the anarchists, Marx had always believed in the necessity of the state itself as the key-instrument in the phase of socialism. The truth was soon revealed. The most authoritarian state was created in Russia and 'socialism in one country' — which is equivalent to the rejection of internationalism and of permanent revolution — was established. Stalin, who was to Lenin what Lenin had been to Marx, inherited this Marxist—Leninist legacy.[11]

Finally, in spite of Marx's clear pledge in the Communist Manifesto that 'the Communists do not form a separate party opposed to other working-class parties', and in spite of the fact that Marx himself avoided the name of 'party' and had formed a League (*Bund*) for the political purposes of Communism, Lenin created the strongest, most exclusive, and best honed political party ever known in history. With that party he effected the revolution; he governed the state; and he imposed it as an indispensable model for other communist parties in the world. Yet Lenin was right again. In the materialistic logic of the Leninist ideologization of Marxism, a strong political party was needed to provide the link between the ideology, the revolution and the state.

Lenin did indeed create that party, as he had conceived it,[12] as 'an army of steeled revolutionary communists', 'a small compact core consisting of the most reliable, experienced and hardened workers with responsible agents' (in January 1917 the Bolshevik party emerging from illegality numbered 23,000 men); 'the Party-members will devote to the revolution not only their spare evenings but the whole of their lives'; 'such an organization should consist above all of people professionally engaged in revolutionary activity and animated by a spirit of complete centralistic democracy'; it will ignore 'the parliamentary comedy'; the party is the leader, the vanguard of the proletariat which rules directly'. And with that party he made the communist revolution of November 1917.

But what then?

THE END OF THE PROMISES

In 1916, one year before the revolution, Lenin entered in his 'notebook': 'Marx speaks of the "future state of communist society"?' Thus even in *communist* society the state will exist! Is there not a contradiction in this?'[13] Not only is there a contradiction, this is the crucial contradiction of communist political philosophy. Communism is, if it is anything, the society of communal organization, the society based on communes — territorial communes in the countryside, functional communes in the urban

[11] See also my article 'Lenin, the State and the Commune', in *Government and Opposition*, Vol. 5, No. 2, Spring 1970.
[12] See also G. Ionescu: *The Politics of the European Communist States*, London 1967, pp. 70–4.
[13] V.I. Lenin: The blue notebook, Appendix III to Karl Marx: *Critique of the Gotha Programme*, Lawrence and Wishart, London. See also my 'Lenin, the State and the Commune, op. cit.

and industrial parts of society like workers' councils, or any social or professional organs of self-management. Moreover, the concept of the communes is logically incompatible with that of the state because of the other political contradictions which this incompatibility entails: centralism versus decentralization; self-management versus the state; the withering away of the state versus the 'all people's state'; or real democratic participation versus theoretical democratic centralism.

The work in which Marx analysed the conceptual relation between the state and the commune is the *Class Struggle in France* — which is important not only because it is his one work which might be said to dwell on the future or *post-revolutionary* organization of society, but also because to a certain extent it provided Lenin with the theory of the commune (or Soviet) state on which he afterwards based his fateful politics, both in theory and in practice. The *Class Struggle in France* was in fact the report presented by Karl Marx to the First International after the defeat of the Commune of Paris on 30 May 1871.

In the revived Paris Commune of 1871 the ideology and the aim of the revolution was anti-state, and in 1871 it was inspired by the additional belief that only total territorial decentralization and professional devolution could lead to socialism. Thus the programme of 19 April 1871 stated: 'Unity such as was imposed until now upon us is only despotic, unintelligent, arbitrary centralization. The political unity as Paris wants it is the voluntary association of all the local initiators, the spontaneous and free co-operation of all individual energies'. And on 27 March, one of the fundamental texts of the Commune, the declaration of the twenty *arrondissements*, stated:

> The Commune is the basis of all political states, as the family is the embryo of societies. It must be autonomous, i.e., govern and administer itself . . . keeping its complete sovereignty . . . it can associate with all the other communes, i.e., federalize with all other communes or associates of communes which form the nation. It is the communal idea, followed since the twelfth century, that triumphed on 18 March 1871.[14]

Marx's report[15] is an unhappy exercise in walking the tightrope between Bakunin's assertion that the state, *qua* central organization, had been abolished,[16] and Marx's own conviction that some central organization was needed by the revolutionary proletariat in order to 'smash' (*Zerbrechen*) the bourgeois state. Yet the expression 'dictatorship of the proletariat' was not used by Marx in the *Class Struggle in France*, though it

[14] Henri Lefébre: *La proclamation de la Commune*, Paris 1965, pp. 357–58.
[15] Of which there are two complete drafts — one with the accent clearly put on decentralization, published and released by Peking, as against the third and last, in which Marx's statist theories resurfaced much more frequently.
[16] Bakunin left Switzerland when summoned by the communards of Lyon, and arrived there in September 1870. On 25 September, he and his friends issued in Lyon the manifesto on 'The Revolutionary Federation of the Communes'. Two articles of

was a concept around which Lenin — baffled by Marx's ambiguities on the role of the state in post-revolutionary organization —was to build the entire theory of the Soviet state, and to build the present Soviet state, the most powerful state in the history of mankind. It is true that Marx used the phrase 'dictatorship of the proletariat' in the *Critique of the Gotha Programme*, but it was Engels who filled the blank, in the preface to a new edition of *The Class Struggle in France* in 1891, by connecting the Paris Commune with the dictatorship of the proletariat in the famous sentence: 'Look at the Paris Commune. That was the dictatorship of the proletariat'. Lenin noted again in his blue notebook:

> Engels proposes (1) not to speak of the state at all; (2) to replace this word with community; (3) he declares even the Commune (i.e., 'the dictatorship of the proletariat') 'no longer a state in the proper sense of the word' while Marx says not a *whisper* on all this, but *on the contrary* even speaks of the future *state organization* of the society.[17]

The action prevailed. The moment had come for Lenin to 'transform' the world rather than to 'interpret' it. The war had proved too much of a strain for the tottering Russian Empire; it collapsed in the February 1917 revolution. Lenin forged his theory of the state-which-was-not-a-state soon after that revolution. The *Letters from Afar* (Zürich, March–April 1917) show that the synthesis between the thesis of the need for a super-centralistic state organization and the anti-thesis of the pledge to create the first classless and eventually conflictless and coercion-free society was found in a distorted reactualization of the Paris Commune of 1871 to which was added the experience of the Soviets of 1905. 'The workers have rightly taken the path indicated by the experience of our 1905 revolution and of the 1871 Paris Commune' . . . . 'We need a state but not the kind of state the bourgeoisie needs'.[18] The fifth, seventh and eighth thesis in the *Tasks of the Proletariat in the Present Revolution*[19] define the new state: 'Not a parliamentary republic — to return to a parliamentary republic from the Soviets of Workers' Deputies would be a retrograde step — but a republic of Soviets of Workers', Agricultural Labourers' and Peasants' Deputies throughout the country, from top to bottom. Abolition of the police, the army and the bureaucracy, . . .'[20] and 'It is not our *immediate* task to "introduce" socialism, but only to bring social production and the

---

this manifesto are essential for the argument expounded here. Article 1: 'The administrative and governmental machinery of the state, having become impotent, is abolished. The people of France takes possession of itself anew'. Article 5: 'All the municipal organizations are abolished and replaced in the federated communes by committees of security of France (*comités de salut*) which will exercise their power, under the immediate control of the people'.

[17] V.J. Lenin: The blue notebook, Appendix III to Karl Marx: *Critique of the Gothic Programme*, Lawrence and Wishart, London, p. 70. (Italics in the text).

[18] V.I. Lenin: *Collected Works*, Vol. 23, pp. 324, 325 and 327.

[19] V.I. Lenin: *Collected Works*, Vol. 24, p. 23.

[20] Ibid., p. 23.

distribution of products at once under the *control* of the Soviets of Workers' Deputies' (8th thesis).[21] But it is *Letters on Tactics* (April 1917) which operates the final 'synthesis' in the formula of the commune-state. In answer to Kamenev's assertion that 'a "commune-state" (i.e. a state organized along the lines of the Paris Commune) *cannot* be introduced in Russia "immediately"', Lenin wrote:

> Comrade Kamenev has somewhat over-reached himself in his eagerness, and has repeated the bourgeois prejudice about the Paris Commune having wanted to introduce socialism 'immediately'. This is not so. The Commune, unfortunately, was too slow in introducing socialism. The real essence of the Commune is not where the bourgeois usually looks for it, but in the creation of a state of special type. Such a state has *already* risen in Russia, it is the Soviets of Workers' and Peasants' Deputies. Comrade Kamenev has not pondered on the *fact*, the significance, of the *existing* Soviets, their identity, in point of type and socio-political character with the Commune State.[22]

Coming after the lucid formulations in these three texts, *State and Revolution* was to show only the basic irreconcilability of the concepts of commune and state in Marxism—Leninism.

The new form of political organization was called 'the dictatorship of the proletariat' or even 'the state of the dictatorship of the proletariat', for Lenin had now, that is in *State and Revolution*[23], equated the dictatorship of the proletariat with the commune, the commune with the Soviet and the new Soviet type of state with the 'commune-state'.

And in historical reality after just over one year (for as Lenin had shown in October 1918 in *The Proletarian Revolution and the Renegade Kautski* 'the Soviets arose without any constitution and existed without one *for more than one year*' — italics in the text) the Declaration of 25 January 1918 proclaimed Russia a Republic of Soviets; on 10 July 1918 the 'Constitution (Fundamental Law) of the Russian Socialist Federal Soviet Republic' was endorsed by the fifth All-Russian Congress of Soviets;[24] and on 6 July 1923, just a few months before his death Lenin's work was crowned by the Constitution of the Union of Soviet

---

[21] Ibid., p. 24.
[22] Ibid., p. 63, italics in the text.
[23] V.I. Lenin: *Collected Works*, Vol. 28, pp. 385–492.
[24] The birth of the new Russian state had not been unopposed from within the revolutionary camp. Until the last moment the Commissar for Justice himself, M.A. Reisner, had proposed a Republic formed by five (syndical) federations of 'workers, land-workers, industrial workers, employees of trading institutions, employees of the state and employees of private persons', stressing that 'It is indispensable to keep in mind that territorial organization and territorial federation cannot serve as a basis for the solution of state questions in a socialist republic. Our federation is not an alliance of territorial governments or states, but a federation of social-economic organizations. It is founded not on the territorial fetishes of state power, but on the real interests of the toiling classes of the Russian Republic' quoted from G.S. Gurvich: *Istoriya Sovetskoy Konstitutsii,* Moscow 1973.

Socialist Republics which united the territory of the former Russian Empire again as a 'single state', but federal. This is how the promise of the communist revolution — to smash the state for ever, in order to release a free, dis-alienated society, was betrayed.

The second aspect of the Marxist philosophical promise which alone can put an end to human alienation, namely that Communism, having abolished private ownership will in consequence eliminate exploitation from the relations of production, was also betrayed.

Lenin at first allowed the peasants to take the land and allowed the workers themselves or workers' councils or soviets or factory committees to run the factories. And indeed workers' councils and trade unions maintained some degree of independence and some control in some sectors of industry up to approximately January 1918. But by then disorder prevailed in every branch of industry and the railways were failing signally in the task of transporting food from the countryside to the towns. Suspected of being Mensheviks and of sabotaging the Bolshevik regime, the railwaymen were also mismanaging the supplies to the Red Army quickly set up by Trotsky, and which was fighting not only against the Germans but against the White Russian armies. Lenin realized that the revolutionary government[25] — shades of Robespierre! — must put all industries and essential services under state control if it were to survive. On 20 March 1918 a government decree gave the People's Commissar for Communications 'dictatorial powers in matters relating to railway transport', thus abolishing workers' control in the one industry in which it had really existed. To deprive the government 'of the right of direct control over all the enterprises of the given industry throughout the country', argued Lenin on 2 June 1918, would be 'anarcho-syndicalism, and not communism'.[26] And indeed a decree of 28 June 1918 nationalized all important industries. Nationalization signified here taking industries back from the self-management of the workers and putting them into the ownership and under the management of the state.

From that moment, the relations of production were again officially re-situated in the *permanent* situation in which a sole owner, the state, appoints through its party-government the managers ('what is the good of having a party if it can't appoint the people in the management?' Lenin asked during the crucial debates of the Tenth Congress of the CPSU), who organize and control the labour of the workers, who receive money-payments for their labour as calculated by the owner and management. The mechanism of alienation worked as implacably as ever, regardless of the change of owner. The workers soon noticed the fraud. A 'workers opposition' against the Bolshevik party arose from the trade unions and the Soviets. It was debated at the dramatic Tenth Congress of 1921. Trotsky,

[25] Council of People's Commissars.
[26] 'Remarks on the draft "Regulations for the Management of Nationalized Enterprises".' In *On the Soviet State Apparatus,* London 1909, p. 162.

who had so successfully organized the Red Army (the first apparat of the new state in which centralized command and hierarchical order and discipline replaced democratic consultation) proposed the 'mobilization' of the trade unions like that of the army. Bukharin argued on the contrary that industrial democracy 'should be allowed, and that managers should not be appointed with an eye to their practical staunchness'. Cutting between the two Lenin decided that the party should thenceforwards: 'put the lid' on any opposition including and especially that of workers; use the trade unions as 'transmission-belts', an expression he forged then; and consolidate the absolute control of the state and the party over industrial production, and all the 'relations' it entails.

Simultaneously the opposition of the workers took direct action and dramatic form in the Kronstadt mutiny. The Kronstadt Soviet, barricaded in its own citadel, declared its determination to keep the Soviet spirit alive in opposition to the centralizing, monolithic and dictatorial Bolshevik party and government. Lenin sent Trotsky personally with strong detachments of the Red Army to put an end to the affair. Decimated by the fire-power of the army of the state the Kronstadt Soviet, like the Paris Commune, had to capitulate.

But it was still Lenin whose coffin was draped in January 1924 in the flag of the Paris Commune.

Chapter 8

Dysfunctionalism of the systems and its symptoms

In the two preceding chapters we have examined what kind of happiness each of the political systems promised, one to individuals, the other to humanity. This, we said, corresponded to the progress, and to the faith in progress, engendered by the advance of science and by the prosperity which industrialization had fostered in Western Europe and the United States. The ideologies of political happiness forwarded the development of industrial society as long as the progress was homogeneous — as long as, in other words, human beings felt that the advance was made simultaneously on the material and on the spiritual planes.

When industrial societies were in the process of formation, ideologies seemed to be the continuation, and popularization, of the belief in progress. Progress was the direct consequence of science and of its application to industry. In the first half of the nineteenth century, people were bewildered about what the human mind, and its extension, science, could achieve. Scientific judgement, being essentially a causal judgement and therefore, in the nineteenth century usually regarded as a rationalistic judgement, rejected the tenets of religion. The pursuit of human happiness was the creed of all who fought against intellectual and political obscurantism. It reached its greatest influence in the nineteenth century among those who witnessed the extraordinary changes which were taking place under their eyes. In particular the decades between 1870 and 1914 are rightly considered by historians of civilization like Fourastié, Robert Nesbit or Michael Biddis to be those in which change has been most rapid and most homogeneous in human history. The struggle against the opponents of progress (as for instance in the papal Syllabus of Errors issued by the Catholic Church in 1864 which indicted 'liberalism, progress and modern consciousness') was not only subjectively justified in the eyes of nineteenth-century thinkers and politicians, but also objectively necessary for the accomplishment of these changes. Had it not been for their fight, some of these changes in the human environment and the human condition might have been much delayed, or would not have taken place at all.

The word homogeneous, in the previous paragraph, probably gives the key to the answer sought here. It signifies that the belief which animated the 'progressives' during the nineteenth century seemed then to proceed in all directions of human activity: progress, although essentially material, was equally rapid and pursued with equal intensity in the moral fields: illiteracy was being rapidly reduced, education was expanding and improving in quality, and the rationalistic ethics — or in Britain the Victorian ethics — were, although based on other premises, particularly strict. Moreover, in so far as industrialization, the engine of this train of progress, appeared together with the capitalistic 'exploitation of man by man' and, as early capitalists sought moral justifications for their prosperity, the fight on the social plane for a modicum of egalitarianism was ethically more justified than ever in the progressive ambiance. Finally the orientation of the intellectual climate of the age towards materialist philosophies, on the assumption that this was the epistemology of science, was not disputed by the scientists themselves — on the contrary it was proclaimed by some of them in more exaggerated terms than materialistic philosophers would dare to use. As Owen Chadwick shows,[1] Karl Vogt, notorious in history for his dictum that 'thoughts come out of the brain as gall from the liver or urine from the kidneys . . .' 'did not receive the scientific reputation which his pure science deserved. Twenty-five year later he was remembered only for sayings of biting humour'.

In the economic field also, progress was homogeneous in the sense that more and cheaper goods were available. Finally in politics, the *democratization* hoped for by the progressives was confirmed by a succession of electoral reforms which expanded the franchise in Britain, Germany and France, leading ultimately to universal manhood suffrage. The fact that in the meantime governments and chancelleries were engaged in a fierce rivalry for new markets and new sources of raw materials for the buoyant economy, and were staggering from blunder to blunder, keeping Europe on the brink of war, was one more reason why progressives demanded the replacement of existing governments by democratic governments.

To complete therefore the answer to the questions asked in this section: from its very inception the ideologies of political happiness carried within themselves the seeds of logical contradictions which have now had harmful consequences in and for Europe. But since these ideologies first appeared in the naïve and idealistic formulations drawn from Condorcet's *Tableau Historique du Progrès Humain* at the end of the eighteenth century, down to Ernst Haeckel's[2] cosmology with science as God, at the end of the nineteenth century, they were justified until then by the homogeneity and credibility of progress itself. And it is true that the egalitarian doctrines of socialism or Communism were fully justified in the eyes of the intellectuals, working-class parties and last but not least trade unions, by the

---

[1] Chadwick, op. cit., p. 166.
[2] Professor of Biology at the University of Jena and fervent disciple of Charles Darwin.

inequality created by the advance of progress as they saw it. For progress had been homogeneous until then on all three fronts: material, intellectual (there was no contradiction between science and philosophy) and moral (the same ethical concern for equality should have prevailed now that it was based on rationalistic grounds and that education and civic rights had been extended to 'the masses').

Therefore in spite of the fact that we, with hindsight, now see more clearly that the ideologies of public happiness were mis-oriented from the outset and were bound to lead to counter-productive ends, nevertheless they were integrated into the forward march of progress and helped to extend it. It is only since the discrepancies between the material plane and the intellectual and moral planes have become so glaring that these ideologies have become dysfunctional.

THE DISCREPANCIES

In the first decades of the twentieth century a series of variegated negative developments gave a pessimistic orientation almost overnight to the general mentality of human beings in industrial society. Since this pessimistic orientation was itself the result of the way the ideologies and the systems functioned, we must turn to those developments which aroused people from their previous optimism, and left the ideologies and systems of political happiness suspended in mid-air.

The fundamental shock to the idea of the progress of man's reason, a progress which is interwoven with and dependent on the exploration of the mysteries of human life and of the universe by the natural sciences, came from those sciences themselves. Physics, since the days of Newton, had been the queen of sciences, because it comprised the scientific proof of the relations of causality on which human reasoning and human rationality are based. Yet physics was the first to draw its conclusions. A series of unexpected and distressing discoveries shattered the previous certainties. The basic principle of causality was undermined by the discoveries made by Rutherford and Bohr of the fissility and unpredictability of the atom, until then regarded as the basis of matter; by Max Planck's negation of the law of continuity through his discovery of the essentially discontinuous quantum theory; and by Einstein's theory of relativity, which was based on the principles of the continuum space—time, of the constant and limited speed of light and of the equivalent mass—energy.

As the popular name of 'theory of relativity' suggests (echoing the 'relativization' of values in human ethics and behaviour), Einstein's theory confirmed on a wider front a basic shift in the central concern of physics. Instead of concentrating mainly on the exploration of physical matter, physicists turned their attention to the transformation of the very concept of matter into essentially non-materialistic concepts such as energy or indetermination. Indeed Einstein had himself been influenced by Ernst Mach's 'idealistic' mechanism — that same Mach whose theories had alarmed Lenin, the guardian of Marxist historical materialism. Lenin had soon realized that if materialism — not to speak of rationalism — was to be pulled from under the feet of historical materialism, the whole edifice of the communist ideology would crumble from top to bottom. In his *Materialism and Empirio-Criticism*[3] (1908) Lenin wrote a passionate if un-scholarly defence of the concept of matter: 'a philosophical category is needed for this objective reality and this concept has been worked out long, long ago. This concept is *matter* . . . Therefore to say that such a concept can become "antiquated" is *childish talk,* a senseless repetition of the arguments of fashionable *reactionary philosophy'*, and 'Recent philosophy is as partisan as was philosophy two thousand years ago . . . The objective class-role of empirio-criticism consists entirely in rendering faithful service to the fideists in their struggle against materialism in general and historical materialism in particular.'

Biology was the second science which cast doubt on the element of continuity without which it would be impossible to retrace the origin of human life, as Darwin had proposed, and of life in general. Here, too, previous certainties were undermined by the 'theory of mutation' of De Vries and T.H. Morgan, which first posited the existence of abrupt and complete ruptures in lines of heredity; and now by the theory of 'chance and necessity' of the French Nobel prize winner, the biologist Jacques Monod, who argued at the end of his research, that 'the decisive element [in the origin of life] might have happened *only once* . . . that life might have appeared only once on earth',[4] a conclusion which strikes one as coming nearer to religion than to science. But Monod also draws some conclusions relevant to the present enquiry when he insists that man's thoughts should observe 'the ethics of knowledge' and when he singles out for criticism 'the historical propheticism based on dialectical materialism', which, he argues, 'is based on a total confusion of the categories of values and of knowledge. It was this confusion which allowed it to proclaim that it had "scientifically" established the laws of history which man must obey if he does not want to be sucked into the void'.[5]

Psychology was the third science to discredit man's reason. It was Sigmund Freud who, in *The Psychopathology of Daily Life* (1901), revealed the existence of the subconscious and the unconscious planes behind and beyond human consciousness, the product of the human brain and the motor of human thinking and human reason. The subconscious

---

[3] V.I. Lenin, *Collected Works,* Vol. 14, Moscow 1972, pp. 130 and 358. (Italics in the text).

[4] Jacques Monod: *Le hasard et la necessité*, Paris 1970, pp. 160–66. (Italics in the text).

[5] Ibid., pp. 193–94.

and the unconscious, according to Freud, not only influenced but actually controlled the mechanisms of human reasoning. Moreover these two *anterior* planes, which produced the uncontrollable dreams of the individual, were the locus of all kinds of instincts, from the highest to the lowest, which were systematically repressed and rejected by the plane of the conscious. These repressed instincts develop an unconscious aggressivity in each human being which must be 'liberated' if he is not to succumb to its stresses and end up a psychopath. Freud thus devised a system of psychoanalysis which enabled the patient or potential patient to 'liberate' some of his most 'sinful' desires, more often than not incestuous, by dredging them up from his subconscious and confessing them on the couch of the psychoanalyst.

Thus the conclusions of the only three sciences mentioned here (together with many others) converged on a number of serious issues. These included: the impossibility of finding the answers to the beginning or the end of the mystery of life either through physics or through biology; the negation of continuity and of causality; the negation of the concept of matter and of the materialistic theories which originate from that concept; the negation of determinism and of deterministic interpretations which cannot but be based on the concepts of matter and of causality; the doubts cast on the validity of human reason because of the negation in physics of the relation of causality, and the doubts cast by psychology on the purity and authenticity of the human mind, and hence of rationalism and its philosophical, social, and political ramifications. Science had now placed itself categorically under one principle, defined by the scientist Walter Heisenberg as the 'principle of indetermination', and as 'the relations of uncertainty'.

Since the time of Haeckel, modern science had ceased to associate itself openly with materialist or rationalist philosophies. But some of the latter had claimed unilaterally that they were 'scientific' and expressed the findings of science. These materialist philosophies had now been explicitly warned against any attempt to base progressive philosophies or ideologies or systems on 'scientific' pretences.

The two systems of political happiness whose intellectual and moral foundation was the affirmation of human progress through the progress of science were thus deprived of the right to claim a 'knowledge' superior to that of other systems, philosophies or methods. On the contrary, what Monod called the 'ethics of knowledge' should have obliged the ideologists of both systems of public happiness to reconsider their premises and above all their assumed authority to make promises of happiness based on 'scientifically guaranteed' interpretations. But Lenin and the Marxist system of political happiness decided to deny simply and firmly the new findings of science; while in the liberal system, the mechanism of progressive permissiveness twirled faster and spread more widely as education, information and communication extended throughout society.

Detached from the human intellect, science detached itself from morality and allowed its discoveries to be used both for good and evil ends. Human material comfort, the quality of life, health and longevity were improved out of all recognition, and man pursued his exploration of the lifeless companions of earth. But by a tragic coincidence one of the first applications of nuclear physics was the atomic bomb dropped on Hiroshima and one of the most popular applications of modern bio-genetics is the anti-life, contraceptive pill.

A second pessimistic reorientation of ideas arose at the beginning of the twentieth century as a result of the relativization of values, if still only in the exclusive realm of philosophy, and not yet among the general public. Disrespect for, indeed negation of, the traditional European moral values was by then a commonplace phenomenon. The strongest philosophical denunciation of those morals was made by Friedrich Nietzsche, who died in the first year of the new century. What is striking in Nietzsche's attitude is precisely his total rejection of those moral values, the origins of which he pushed back to pre-Christian times. He accuses Jesus Christ of having introduced humility, compassion and hope. But the real guilt lies in Nietzsche's view with Socrates who sought for the logical perception of the good in human consciousness. What Nietzsche visualized was a tragic humanity of supermen, living their life and dying their death absolutely. Echoing Dostoevsky's lament 'God is dead' (and Dostoevsky was one of the few authors he admired) Nietzsche repeated obsessively that if this was so, then man, or rather superman, should live without any of the restrictions of a so-called conscience, and with no respect for the so-called laws of the gods or of God. The absolute attitude of Nietzsche had terrible consequences for Europe, thanks to its indirect impact on human minds, particularly in Germany. In justice to Nietzsche, however, it must be added that in the first place he actually detested Germans and the German mind; and secondly he never put forward any hypocritical pretence that he wanted to replace old and outdated moral values with new and more satisfactory ones.

Bentham and Marx had also played their part in the relativization of values. Bentham had criticized ascetic Christian values because he found them inferior to the hedonistic consequentialist values of the future; and Marx had criticized bourgeois capitalist religious values which to him masked the brutality of the whole system, because he believed that in communist society, the true, free values of free man would be revealed in their full glory. Both ideologies thus contributed to the undermining of the moral values as Europe had known them for the last twenty-three centuries. But in contrast with Nietzsche, they were destroying traditional ethics in order to replace them with a relativized code of their own invention. And again, in contrast with Nietzsche, whose philosophy was a real one, not an ideological philosophy, they ideologized, propagandized, vulgarized and disseminated their ideology as widely as possible.

Yet another trend played its part in the relativization of values, namely romanticism. In their genuine quest for the real, idealized, self, the romantics rejected and ridiculed what they regarded as the cautious, materialistic and hypocritical *bourgeois* ethics derived from the eudaemonistic values of the eighteenth century. They proclaimed free love in the belief that they were emulating either the Christian romanticism of Chateaubriand, or the rationalistic romanticism of Goethe, the revolutionary romanticism of Shelley or the conservative romanticism of Coleridge. But whereas the inspiration of the post-romantics was weaker than that of their predecessors, they had a sharper critical sense.

It is also true that in the meantime the mores of the bourgeoisie were also deteriorating. Living in a capitalist society obsessed with the making of profits, and actually enjoying the profits they made, the bourgeoisie was becoming harder towards the other social classes, and notably the working class with which it had been in overt conflict at least since 1848. But at the same time it was becoming more lenient towards itself and its own morality. Flaubert's *Madame Bovary*, Tolstoy's *Anna Karenina* and Ibsen's *Hedda Gabler* were the symbols of the bourgeois woman sacrificed in her search for love by a rigid society. Libertinism, in both its senses, was gradually making inroads into the Victorian citadel. The men were obsessed with the wealth they were making, their families with the pursuit of happiness, now finally permissible. This set up a vicious circle, for the more they relaxed their moral values, the more they were criticized; and the more their values were criticized, the more prepared were they to throw them overboard. It is in this vicious circle that the role played by the custodians of the moral values, the clergy and the intellectuals, turned into a *trahison des clercs,* in which the custodians themselves became increasingly caught up in progressive permissiveness.

The third reason for the pessimism which overwhelmed the first decades of the twentieth century was of course the First World War. Two effects of the First World War, ought to be singled out, as directly relevant to this enquiry. One is that in its useless prolongation and cruel loss of life, it was the most brutal denial of human ethics anyone could possibly have imagined.

The fourth consequence, deriving from the third, was the Russian Revolution, the second great revolution in modern history, carrying with it the fervent good wishes of all those who felt that capitalism was breeding war by its own laws of competition and economic rivalry; and also the sympathy of all the progressive human beings who had witnessed the horrors committed in the name of nationalism, with almost no opposition from the socialist parties which were members of the Second International. Lenin was considered by them as the only true internationalist politician in Europe and for a while the communist parties appeared to be the messengers of true working-class pacifism. The Russian Revolution also inaugurated the communist system of political happiness, and thus marked the division of the world between two opposed ideological camps.

The economic depression of the 1930s was the fifth and most depressing development for liberal industrial society. Apart from its immediate social and economic consequences at the time, the crisis left an indelible trauma on the psychology of people living in liberal industrial societies both in Europe and in America. In the atmosphere of mounting disorder, the lack of any semblance of moral or intellectual order in the conduct of the liberal economy further undermined any public confidence in it, and in capitalism in general. Unemployment, inflation, and heightened social tension made the promises of Communism and Fascism seem more attractive to the disoriented people. But how mistaken they were!

For the sixth source of pessimism in the early decades of the twentieth century, surprising though it may seem for the reader who has only just now read about the universal expectations raised by the Russian Revolution, was the miscarriage of the revolution which became evident to all in the 1930s. Like the French Revolution, the Russian Revolution had given birth not to the essentially internationalistic, institutionless, free society of syndical federations, but to a nation-state, soon to become a federal nation-state within the frontiers of the old Russian Empire, with all the paraphernalia of sovereignty, army, flag, government, police,[6] and with an enormous bureaucracy supervised by a national political party. Lenin's successor, Stalin, made quite explicit Lenin's implicit policy of 'socialism in one country'. Soon Trotsky was exiled, and wandered about the world telling how the revolution had been betrayed, and how Stalin was proposing to make Russia into the strongest state which had ever existed. To all those who had once believed that a communist revolution anywhere in the world offered the last hope of creating a system of freedom, equality and peace to replace the oppressive, socially unjust, economically unbalanced and warlike capitalist industrial system, it was becoming increasingly clear that the Russian Revolution had been 'betrayed'.

Finally and by far the worst cause of pessimism in the twentieth century was the advent of Hitler to power in 1933. But in so far as, from the point of view of this enquiry, that sinister event is seen as a) the result of the conflict between the two ideologies and b) as the cause of the first crisis in which *both* systems of political happiness ran the danger of being simultaneously destroyed by another system, Nazism and the Second World War will be treated separately in the concluding section of this chapter.

---

[6] The Cheka or secret police was first organized to arrest the anarchists as enemies of the state.

DYSFUNCTIONAL PROGRESS OF IDEOLOGIZATION

While the 'scientific' foundations of the ideologies of human happiness were demolished by science itself, the process of ideologization launched in the nineteenth century reached its apogee in the twentieth century. For now, in the mass-democracies, with mass-communication media providing unprecedented means of propagation, ideologization was fostered by political means: the ideological political parties which were reaching full fruition only then. Apart from acting directly on their members and voters, the ideological parties acted also by counter-ideologization on the other political parties.

Historically the first ideological party was the *Sozialistische Partei Deutschlands* which declared itself 'Marxist' in 1875, and proceeded to give itself a disciplinarian character. Social Democratic parties were formed in Switzerland in 1876, in Denmark in 1879, and in Spain in 1879, in Austria in 1888, in Germany itself in 1890 when *Socialist* in the name was changed into Social Democrat, in Belgium in 1885, Norway in 1887 whereas the French Socialist party and the British Labour party adopted the system of organization of the SDP but not the Marxist filiation.

The second and decisive moment in the ideologization of parties was the formation of the Third International (Comintern) which made its twenty-one rules compulsory for any affiliated 'Communist Party' and declared its irreconcilability with the Social Democratic parties.[7]

The direct imitation by the Fascist movement, and then by the Nazi movement, of the communist system of political happiness and notably of its two modern components, ideology and party, was the third moment. Both Fascism and Nazism recognized their *negative* affinity with the communist political system. They shared with it a contempt for the 'soft' utilitarian—hedonistic philosophy of life and for its liberal economic and especially political consequences: political pluralism, representative institutions and 'responsible' governments, separation of powers and above all the independence of the judiciary. They also shared a deep contempt for the 'bourgeois' respect for ethics and civic values. At the same time the Fascist parties presented themselves to the frightened Italian and German 'bourgeoisies' as their defenders against the 'alien' Jewish and Russian Marxist—Leninist Communism. But what they wanted above all to copy from the Communists was the model of the revolutionary professional party as the monolithic and terroristic instrument of the ideology, in opposition and in power. In the Communist parties and the Fascist and Nazi parties, ideologization proceeded from their common materialistic

---

[7]This led to such extraordinary consequences as for instance the Communist party of Germany being ordered by Moscow to consider the Social Democratic party of Germany a greater danger to its revolutionary aims than the National Socialist party — thus greatly facilitating the coming to power of Hitler and National Socialism.

and atheistic belief in the voluntaristic transformation not only of society but also of individual human beings, of man, himself. In the confessional or Conservative parties which respected, if for different reasons, the individual human being, ideologization was not applicable. In their case counter-ideologization was at work. For political competition now began to be based on the attractiveness of the promises the political party makes to the electorate. Thus the escalation of political promises changed its character when the ideological parties began to offer future human happiness in their package deals.

The Christian Democratic parties experienced the greatest difficulties in facing the problem of ideologization. Historically the first attempt to give Christian philosophy a political reality was attempted by Bishop Ketteler, in Germany in 1877. This was a clear, if not wholly successful, attempt to induce Christians to organize themselves politically in order to defend the Christian values attacked by the *Kulturkampf,* by secularization in general and by Marxist and Nietzschean atheism in particular, on the political battlefields which by then were becoming a determining test of the orientation of politics in the German state. Christian Democracy, as a political movement originating in the Roman Catholic Church, had no success in Britain or the United States because they were predominantly Protestant countries, but also because the utilitarian and in America pragmatic, mentality had already 'socialized' religion among both clergy and worshippers. The success of Christian Democracy in the Catholic countries themselves was only relative before the war. Much more successful was the revival in the two formerly Fascist countries, Germany and Italy, and in many of the countries which were occupied by them during the war, of the redeeming Christian philosophy. After the war the Christian Democratic parties emerged in both countries as the two most powerful political organizations.

The British Conservative party adapted itself with surprising flexibility to the modern political conditions of universal suffrage and mass-communication. Its organization proved to be one of the most effective in modern European politics; its staff and activists most disciplined and loyal; its techniques of electoral propaganda best prepared for the new techniques of modern publicity and public relations.

Yet this change in form seemed until very recently not to alter the characteristic non-ideological, indeed anti-ideological stance of Toryism. Even as late as 1977, Sir Ian Gilmour, the authoritative contemporary interpreter of Toryism, still explained that by its very nature British Conservatism was adverse to ideologization – and deplored the escalating ideologization of the Labour party. 'British Conservatism is not an "ism". It is *not* an ideology or a doctrine – No British Conservative [thinker] ', he argued after having examined the works of such predecessors as Halifax, Bolingbroke, Hume, Burke or Coleridge, 'has produced a system of abstract political ideas or an ideology'. Moreover he insisted that in spite of the belief that ideology is what gives a party its consistency in action, 'consistency will paradoxically be best presented by the absence of ideology, not by its presence'.[8]

Yet, only seven years later British Conservatism was showing clear signs of ideologization — or of counter-ideologization. This could be detected in the reductionistic, almost deterministic, method by which the new 'Thatcherite' party linked the principal problems of British industrial society with one cause alone: monetary inflation — and declared monetary inflation to be 'scientifically' curable only through the precepts of two 'scientific' authors: Hayek and Friedman. Not surprisingly the first man to be alerted by these symptoms of ideological infection was the author of *Inside Right.* In a new book, *Britain can Work,* Sir Ian Gilmour argued that 'Professor Friedman claims that his doctrine is "scientific" . . . But monetarism's methodological flaws do not discomfort its devotees. Its appeal to many is ideological. For such adherents monetarism is much more than just a theory purporting to explain and predict some economic phenomena. It provides a whole attitude to politics and economics' and later: 'Ideology is not confined to economics . . . Ideology simplifies. And in politics and constitutional matters, to the Tory at least, simplicity is misleading and dangerous'.[9]

But while during the first Thatcher government critics questioned 'monetarism' or 'the monetarist policy' or even the monetarist ideology of that government — after the elections of 1983 a new expression, 'Thatcherism', became rapidly popular. This might indeed surprise students of conservatism. Never in the past had one read of Heathism, Macmillanism, Edenism or for that matter even Churchillism or Disraeliism. The Tory party had never indulged in the cult of personality nor was it famous for devising ideological nicknames. Yet 'Thatcherism' sounded part cult of personality, part ideology. What was now significant was that the nickname 'Thatcherism' was no longer used by the adversaries of the Tory government in a derisive or pejorative way, but proudly by the new party itself — or indeed even more surprising by the Prime Minister herself who in a television interview not only spoke of 'Thatcherism' but declared 'I am a Thatcherite' (thus beating Marx at his own game for Marx constantly maintained that he was 'not a Marxist').

The significance of this change from the point of view of this enquiry lies especially in the new respect shown by political circles to ideology — in the widespread belief that ideology and ideologization are indispensable to the success of modern political organizations. Reflecting upon the phenomena of 'Thatcherism' Peter Jenkins wrote that the fact that Mrs Thatcher 'had been credited with an "ism" is the proof that she is widely perceived as an ideologue, a rare creature among Conservative politicians'.[10] Although the author himself believes that 'Thatcherism is

---

[8] Ian Gilmour: *Inside Right,* London 1977, pp. 120, 111 and 145.

[9] Ian Gilmour: *Britain can Work,* Oxford, 1983, pp. 154–55 and 318–19.

[10] Peter Jenkins: 'The world closes in on the Thatcherites' in *The Guardian,* February 4, 1984.

more properly to be regarded as a style than an ideology' he nevertheless recognizes that 'it has at its heart a highly specific economic doctrine' which also explains why the new Tory leader might be 'credited' with being an ideologue. This change of mentality in the Tory party known for, and proud of, its pragmatic tradition is a clear example of what was described here as counter-ideologization. Even non-ideological parties have now to present a semblance of ideology if they have to win credibility in the eyes of ideologized human beings.

The American Republican party has also undergone counter-ideologization under President Reagan's leadership. Here too — and indeed influenced by the Thatcher government example — the accent has been laid on the 'doctrine' of monetarism and on the 'scientific' authority of the scholars who established it. Yet in the case of the monetarist inspired American administration, public perception of the ideological change occurred almost exclusively in the economic field (even the popular nickname was 'Reaganomics') while 'Thatcherism' is now presented as a complete ideology, with its ethical 'goals' and its 'scientific' methods all wrapped up in one overall belief represented by one leader. The difference between the British and the American cases is due to at least three circumstances. One is the difference in the 'style' of the leaders. Mrs Thatcher takes up a more moralizing and paternalistic attitude towards the public than President Reagan's more familiar behaviour. Then there is the difference between the British utilitarian parochial background, and the real problems of the modern world. The orientation of British politics in Europe around 'le juste retour' was utilitarianism at its worst.

And finally one must remember that the genuine ideological element in American politics is much more prominent in the field of foreign affairs. Because the United States is the super power responsible for the defence and security of liberal industrial society, its public opinion is bound to concentrate more on the strategy of the great international contest. It is in this direction that political leaders are expected to propose to national and international opinion a general view, in which moral and philosophical considerations ought to justify the military strategy adopted, which in turn influences all other policies. But the question of American ideological world-strategy is discussed at greater length in the last section of the next chapter (see below pp. 201–5).

THE FIRST CRISIS OF THE TWO SYSTEMS

If politics is considered to be the activity of regulating the co-existence of human beings, as we have posited in this enquiry, then politics is always in crisis. Mortality implies change. Each generation faces problems different from those which presented themselves to previous generations. The world itself changes, and industrial society changes more quickly than any previous society. The nature of human understanding also changes — not in the Marxist sense that the mind is determined — but in the sense which comes closer to hermeneutic *Verstehen*, of seeking an understanding of a changed society with changing means of perception. People born after the Second World War will have absorbed the new perceptions which the war insinuated into the human mind. To take an example, this new generation, able to make use of new media of communication, and of computerized techniques, must be imbued with a new understanding, different from that of the generation which died before the war. But this does not mean that they will not be able to achieve much more or to seek something existentially different from what all mortals have sought or achieved. So this rhythm of constant rupture, of constant generational reconsideration of values and institutions transmitted from parents to children sometimes sharper, sometimes less acute, according to the magnitude of the changes, gives to political history its sense of crisis, of incessant turning points.

The ideological systems have increased the sense of political crisis in two ways. First, because they bind past, present and future into a historical direction which is called human progress and which each of them interprets in its own way. Secondly, because having thus set, and ideologically maintained, two different indeed *opposite* interpretations, each of them stands in the way of the other, each of them denies the future to the other. The future thus becomes a struggle between the two of them and the world a chessboard on which each of them watches the other's moves. Especially since the end of the Second World War the ideological rivalry between the two 'camps' has led to such fierce polarization that each of the systems, obsessed by the hostility of the other, is now guided by the realization that if the political world is ever to become harmonious, according to its own views of 'harmony', the other system will first have to be 'buried'. This is called the 'cold war', in permanent danger of becoming 'hot' at any moment of decision, in any part of the chessboard. In the light of this terrible reality one can say that the conflict of the ideologies of political happiness represents, at the end of the twentieth century, a serious danger to the happiness of men.

But, and with this we come back to the precise subject of this section and, in time, to the mid-1930s when Fascism and anti-Fascism were the names of the ideological game — there is another possibility of crisis in the world of the ideological systems. This is the crisis in which both systems, each still waiting to 'bury' the other, might both be buried together. Developments which both systems had failed to interpret correctly, either because of the deficiencies of the consequential calculus or because of the straitjacket of historical materialism, and the results of which have been constantly exacerbated by their own blindness, might kill them both off at the same time. As we noted above, while every crisis in the political world since the 1920s has been due to the competition between the two systems, there were two crises in which both systems could have collapsed simultaneously: the crisis of Hitlerism, and the cultural and economic crisis of 1968—70.

The peace treaties which the liberal systems concluded after the First World War carried the seeds of their own destruction within themselves, as John Maynard Keynes foresaw. The punitive obligations imposed upon the German economy unbalanced it. On top of that, trying to experiment with a completely new liberal system, the Weimar Republic faced the inherent difficulties of the beginning of liberalization for a people still unused to it.

The whole history of the Weimar Republic can be symbolically presented as the dress rehearsal for the tragedy of progressive permissiveness. For the republic sank into one of the pitfalls of financial permissiveness, namely inflation (people were reduced to paying for an overcoat with two suitcases full of banknotes); into the extreme of political permissiveness which is civil war (armed Communists and Nazis fought over the dying body of the republic); and into the cesspool of moral permissiveness (Berlin became the capital of vice, of all vices). As in *Parsifal* the sick German community hoped that it would be saved from the evils of either Russian Communism or Anglo-Saxon liberalism, which it had handled so badly, by a saviour of its own. The Germans mistook Hitler for that saviour, and Nazism as the new creed of the Holy Grail.

In this situation ideologies came to dance their infernal dance. Fascism and Nazism both pretended to be new ideologies, but they were in fact the strident revival of the old ideology of nationalism dressed up in a mirror-image imitation of Marxism—Leninism. Mussolini, himself a former socialist, had perhaps rightly foreseen that the structural promises of Communism, that is to say the withering away of the state and the end of alienation in the relations of production were impracticable. More to the point however he also saw that what remained from the Bolshevik victory was the super-structural political organization, comprising a strong ideology to bind men under its commandments; a strong party to coerce them to act according to the ideology and under its discipline; a strong state to control in a totalitarian way (for it was Mussolini who invented the word, thus giving its true meaning to Lenin's *monolithism*) the whole society, with, as both Robespierre and Lenin had recognized to be necessary, state-terroristic means. He thought that the Russian Revolution was the result of these political artifices and he decided to borrow them from Communism – and turn them against it. At the same time he offered to the Italian and European bourgeoisies, frightened by the success of the *ideology* of Communism, an *ideology* to defeat the strong *ideology* of Communism, and the debilitating *ideology* of liberalism. He came to power – and in the disorder of the world of the 1920s as a whole, he seemed to bring order to Italy.

Nazism in turn imitated the Bolshevik—Fascist 'super-structural'

161

artifices: ideology, party- state-totalitarianism and state-terrorism, but with two great differences. One was the addition to the Fascist ideology of a supplementary and most despicable element of hatred (we know already that ideologies must contain a negative element: envy of the nobility, or of the rich, or class-hatred of workers against a capitalist bourgeoisie), namely racial hatred of the Jews accused, in a typically populist way, of fomenting a world-conspiracy. The other difference is that whereas Italy was a semi-industrialized country, and the Italian people a naturally undisciplined people, Hitler (an Austrian, as Napoleon was a Corsican) took possession of Germany, an industrial great power, and of the German people whose major quality/defect is its propensity to accept discipline.

It was after Hitler's consolidation in power that the tragi-comedy of ideological errors began, which we shall sum up as follows. Because no totalitarian ideology can produce happiness in the present, and at home (where it has the effect of stifling the cooperation of the essentially pluralistic, thus anti-monolithic, society), it situates its 'goals' in the future and in the world at large. This is also why the millenarianism of all ideological revolutions gives rise, sooner or later, to military expansionism: Bonaparte's liberation of Europe; Mussolini's liberation of Ethiopia and Albania; Hitler's liberation of Europe and of the world from Jewry; and last but not least Stalin's liberation of Eastern and Central Europe. *Ideologically* then both Mussolini and Hitler were constrained to commit acts of external aggression — which *ideologically* the liberal systems found difficult to stop from the beginning.

The beginning of Hitler's armed aggression was the German reoccupation of the Rhineland on 7 March 1936. It is now known, as a result of historical research, that had France and Britain opposed Hitler's proposed advance with threats of force he would have desisted. And had he given up armed aggression then, he would have found it more difficult to embark on it another time. And, then, probably, the repressed explosive force of a great people divided against itself and of a stifled industrial society, might have reached levels of opposition too strong even for his regime. War was his only way out the dilemma.

But for *ideological* reasons France could not act. The country was torn in two, with the Left in power and the Right in quasi-insurrectional opposition. And if Britain was unarmed, and therefore unable to react with greater strength and authority against the Hitlerite warmongering, this was also due to ideological reasons — partly because of the *ideological* opposition of the Labour party to re-armament, and partly because of the *counter-ideological,* electoral considerations of the Conservative government. Speaking in 1936 Stanley Baldwin admitted that although Hitler's coming to power in 1933 signalled new military dangers had 'he gone to the country', then still influenced by the Labour party's pacifist ideology, 'and said that Germany was re-arming and we must re-arm . . . nothing would have made the loss of the election from any point of view more certain'.[11] This incident although slightly taken out of context in so far as Baldwin was speaking in 1936 of a by-election held in 1933, is highly significant of the moral conflict facing a modern political leader between his duties as a statesman and his duties as a practitioner of ideological politics — which we shall discuss in the conclusions of this book.

In the meantime the ideologies (or pseudo-ideologies) of Fascism and Nazism were making enormous strides, if only because since philosophical ideology had but little body, the process of ideologization on such visceral slogans as anti-Semitism, was much easier to effect. Europe and the world was divided into two international camps: Fascist and anti-Fascist — which came to superpose themselves on to the tragic Spanish civil war, the first ideological war in history.

Now, the systems of political happiness seemed to be reasonably united for once in the same opposition to the *Tertium Gaudens* of Fascism. For Fascism and Nazism were the creations of the two systems: of the Communist system by providing Mussolini and Hitler with the recipe of how to take possession of whole peoples and states by means of ideology and ideological parties: and of the liberal system because of the permissive attitude this system took towards the emergence of these regimes in international relations. But gradually the two systems came to assert an anti-Fascist stand. The whole of European public opinion despised and feared Nazism. The USSR and the disciplined Third International of Communist parties set themselves up as the champions of anti-Fascism, and during the major Munich crisis in 1938, when the liberal systems again failed to react, the Communist power and its ideological camp claimed that it would have acted had it not been let down by the West.

Yet, when the military ascension of Hitler's ideological regime reached its culminating moment and it was obvious that he would attack Poland (though he had been explicitly forewarned by Britain and France that this would be regarded as a *casus belli*) the Soviet Union, followed by communist parties everywhere, gave Hitler the final encouragement he needed by signing the pact of non-aggression between the USSR and the Third Reich on 27 August 1939. The champions of anti-Fascism who had been pushing other countries to resist the Nazi monster by force now held out to him the hand of friendship. A few days later Hitler invaded Poland, and Britain and France declared war.

In these circumstances, the communist parties everywhere, including the French and British parties,[12] were ordered to follow the ideological

[11] When Baldwin explained his statement in 1936 in the House of Commons, his very words were: 'Supposing I had gone to the country and said that Germany was re-arming and we must re-arm, does anybody think that this pacific democracy would have rallied to that cry at that moment? I cannot think of anything that would have made the loss of the election from any point of view more certain'.

[12] The literature, Communist and non-Communist is abundant on the subject. Among the latest books see John Atfield and Stephen Williams (Eds): *The British Communist Party and the War*, London 1984.

line that this was a war between capitalist powers on which the workers must turn their backs since the outcome was a matter of indifference to them. Even when France was later invaded by Hitler, relying on the material and moral help of the USSR, the communist parties, including the French party, maintained the same ideological line, namely that the working class should not intervene in a war which did not concern it. Did they believe, like Stalin, and did Stalin believe when he had decided upon this strategy, that the two capitalist systems would destroy each other in the war?

Hitler's German forces went on to occupy most of Europe, but Britain's lone stand against her enemies in 1940 was the beginning of the end of his uninterrupted victories. After the defeat of his air force, he realized that he could not quickly defeat Britain and he prepared for a much longer war. Though strengthened by his alliance with Japan, and his association with the USSR, he nevertheless needed many more new supplies of raw materials than Stalin would give him. So he simply turned against his accomplice and invaded Russia in the hope of securing the raw materials he needed.

Stalin proceeded immediately to revive his previous anti-Fascist stand. Communist parties all over the world and especially in occupied France, now turned against Fascism. Alliance with the other anti-Fascist powers was sought by the USSR, and intelligently granted by Churchill whose genius had never been obscured by ideologies. Together the anti-Fascists, with the later addition of the USA, defeated Hitler and the monstrous Fascist and Nazi ideological regimes.

This story, which reads like a fable, has three morals. One is that the ideological factor in the ideological systems of political happiness had conduced to gross and dangerous errors of political judgement. The second is that the superimposition of the ideologies of political happiness on the reality of industrial society has divided that society into two irreconcilable 'camps', each of which expects to flourish only after the other has been transformed — but with a notable difference in virulence between the more universally revolutionary communist ideology and the more, pluralistic and therefore more flexible utilitarian—liberal ideology. And the third and final moral, is that blinded by their respective and different ideologies both regimes have faced in the past and might in the future face common and simultaneous extinction.

Chapter 9

Hope and despair in the industrial society

In the history of industrial society the years 1945–80 fall into two sharply contrasting periods. In the first human hopes seemed to ascend to their zenith; in the second they seemed to fall to a very nadir of despair. This contrast was also reflected in the gulf between the generations living in those two periods. Seldom in history has human personality seemed to change so much and so quickly; seldom has history produced such profound mutual incomprehension between parents and children, such an epistemological 'break' between them.

One need scarcely be reminded that the feeling of hope which pervaded Western industrial society was a direct response to the end of the war itself. But there was another cause for hope, which added a moral dimension to the victory on the battlefield, and gave to the human beings who had brought it about a particularly proud place in history. This was the conviction that Nazism in itself, and even more clearly in comparison with any other ideological and political system in the history of industrial society, was the most complete incarnation of the spirit of inhumanity. Both its goal, world domination by the supreme embodiment of the human race, the German *Volk*, and its means, the eugenic extirpation of the so-called inferior races, and the terror of Belsen or Oradour-sur-Glane, were essentially inhuman in that they denied the right to live to multitudes of human beings.

By contrast with, and in opposition to, this ideology of death, the ideologies of political happiness revealed their ultimately common character. They claimed that their goal was the happiness of human beings, even if they sought this happiness so differently. People fought against the Nazis with an added moral sense. In Great Britain, although class-consciousness had been on the increase, all classes joined together in the fight against Nazi Germany (even if for some eighteen months the Communist party of Great Britain portrayed the war as an intra-capitalist conflict). In a different context when the USSR was invaded, the Germans were at first received in some frontier areas as potential liberators from Stalin's terror. But the Nazi determination to exterminate whole populations drew the peoples of the USSR together around Stalin and they fought heroically until the victorious end. And yet in another context in the occupied countries the Resistance kept alive the belief that this was a fight for the survival of the dignity of man. And when America also joined in, the full circle closed against the Axis (Germany—Italy—Japan).

The above interpretation stands only if it is taken together with the seemingly paradoxical proviso that the reunion of the systems of political happiness — forced on to Stalin by the betrayal of his former totalitarian ally — was achieved only by putting what they believed in above what divided them, by forgetting the differences between liberalism and Communism in order to concentrate on the common opposition to Fascism. (Stalin, for instance, quickly dissolved the Third International in 1941, and ordered its former members, the communist parties of the world, to fight on the side of the Allies). Only because the systems had forgotten their ideologies had they been able to join together to fight the third ideology. Moreover since the communist ideology is more dynamic, monolithic and aggressive than the liberal ideology, it was the communist ideology which had to a greater extent to tone down its tenets.

The question after the war was whether the reunion between the two ideologies would lead in the future to a reduction of the tensions they had nourished, and towards the discovery of some 'convergence'; or whether the old antagonistic rocks would emerge from the depths when the joyous tide withdrew.

For a short while it seemed that the positive orientation would prevail. For one thing, some of those who had shared in the experience of war on both sides had emerged from it with a different moral nature. In the allied camp, war had intensified the sense of fraternal mortality, as human beings died together and waited for death together; it had deepened the sense of an ultimately common human dignity as against the total indignity threatened by the aggressor; it had forged a new sense of moral duty as people restrained the pursuit of pleasure and the avoidance of pain in the common effort; and a new egalitarian austerity, as everyone shared in the minimum of subsistence that could then be provided. In the occupied territories people suffered even more, for indignity was added to poverty and death. In the aggressor countries, Germany and Italy, an overpowering sense of despair and guilt led many after the war towards a moral pursuit of redemption. The emergence and immediate success of the Christian Democratic parties in both these countries, as well as in France and elsewhere, testified to the human quest for redemption in the faith which had above all defended the inviolability of human life.

The birth of two political institutions, at the international and at the national level seemed to herald a new era. The formation of the United Nations was, or should have been, a main symbol of new human wisdom. Here again, the USSR proclaimed its solidarity with the other peoples and nations in the search for universal regulations for the conduct of the co-existence of human beings — that is, universalistic politics. This was of course a Utopian affirmation of ideals, and has been treated as such ever since. But the real truth is that such an organization *was* an imperative requirement of practical politics. For it was only too clear in *Anno Domini* 1945, after two world wars and the rise and fall of the League of Nations, that the co-existence of human beings in the age of the interdependent industrial technological society could no longer be regulated except by means of a common perspective from the highest observation point that men could reach for the overall comprehension (in both senses of the word) of the problems facing them.

Already it was clear that in the industrial age federations, that is vast, self-sufficient units of rule, fared better than smaller nation-states which had lost or were losing their overseas dominions. For as Tocqueville had already discerned (and he was not a federalist), 'the judgements of the federal government are wiser and its projects more durable' than those of the states.[1] The accent here is on the quality of the political judgement, on the comprehensiveness of the assessment and the potential effectiveness of the political decision-making process. Two world wars had sufficiently demonstrated in negative terms the domino-like interdependence of the world in the industrial age. There was plenty of evidence that only a global view could hope to provide an adequate political judgement in such a global village. Even now, in the 1980s, it is clear that the perspectives obtainable from the viewpoint of the United Nations, or in economic matters from the World Bank, and, in descending order from the OECD, and the European Commission are more comprehensive than the assessments obtainable from the lowered vantage-points of the nation-states. So it was not so much the idealistic, pacifist significance of the United Nations which deserved to be underlined, as its practical significance as the best possible instrument of modern policy-making. For if the politicians were to see the whole view together, they might draw the same conclusions and be forced to take the same decisions, with the dialectical result that the more they took universally valid decisions the more effective those decisions would be and the more accurate their judgement-in-common would become.

This argument was reinforced after the war by the vast developments made by the natural sciences during and because of the war — and which were bound to have transnational significance. Such an important healing device as the antibiotic was applied for military medical purposes but then become indispensable to world-medicine; such an important destructive device as nuclear fission was first applied for military purposes, but became indispensable for world-energy. Immediately after the war the third phase of industrialization began, the age of electronics which once more revolutionized man's way of life, way of thinking and even way of behaving. It also stretched the interdependence of industrial society to the point of universal simultaneity and interrelatedness.

[1] *De la démocratie en Amérique*, Vol. I, p. 22.

THE WELFARE PRINCIPLE

The second good omen for people as the Second World War was left behind was the advent of something controversially called the 'welfare state'. The welfare principle, which until then had been experienced on the practical plane by means of welfare work and on the theoretical plane by the development of welfare economics, expressed the popular hope that henceforward society would be 'managed' with a sense of social justice, which both economic and political liberalism had until then abandoned too freely to the care of the 'invisible hand'.

Many new factors had by then become too visible to be left to the tender mercies of *laissez-faire*. The 'mixed economy' had replaced the all-embracing market, which had been divided by the rapid evolution of industrial society into a public sector, grouping industries and services of common interest, and a private sector, driven by the capitalistic rationale of the maximization of profit, and providing the 'wealth of the nations'. The contrast between the overproduction of the ever-expanding technological industry and the underconsumption by the exploited working classes was also all too visible. Antagonism between classes had deepened in the capitalist society. Yet it was believed that the welfare principle applied together with Keynes's prescription for demand management could solve the contradictions of capitalism diagnosed by Marx as insoluble. And it was also assumed that the welfare economy would now undertake such social tasks as the provision of basic social security, universal education, and expansion of the opportunities of employment for as large a number of people as possible — and without endangering political freedom.

The political horrors of totalitarianism, as it had been experienced under Hitler and Stalin, served to strengthen men's faith in the representative institutions of the liberal state. But, in Keynesian logic, modern liberalism should be able to prove that the contradictions inherent in capitalism could in reality neutralize each other. If the mechanism of 'demand' could be properly 'managed' in the advanced industrial societies, in which socio-economic groups had by now replaced individuals as the principal agents of the policy-making processes, it would set the economic mechanism going again, whereby growth of production leads to growth of employment, which leads to growth of demand and in turn to growth of consumption. Such a system of perpetual growth would be bound to lead to a constant increase in the standards of living and indirectly, as well as directly, to the attenuation of social inequality.

But in the still heavily ideologized atmosphere of the time — and ideologization became increasingly intense as Communism extended now over an enormous transcontinental expanse from Hong Kong to Berlin — the ideal type of Keynesian economic game was weighed down and hampered by ideological politics. To be sure economic demand management required political instruments to put it into effect. Given the massive presence of socio-economic interests in the new industrial society, other instruments of political representation and participation were required than those which had remained almost unchanged, in Britain for instance, since the nineteenth-century Reform Acts. A new type of representative government designed for an industrial society was needed. Vast interests as employers and labour should take a greater part in policy-making.

But instead the belief took root among the people at large that a new form of state had been created, the welfare state, or to put if differently, the state which provides welfare for society, or for the 'people'. (In France, this state was called by the even more graphic name of *l'état providence*, i.e., the state which providentially provides). This was of course a gross misrepresentation of Lord Beveridge's initial conception of what he had explicitly called the welfare *society*. For it was not the political institution which provided the welfare, but the social and economic forces of society — and it was not the nation-state itself which was responsible for the developments, but the transnational industrial society as a whole. The source of this misrepresentation lay in the typically ideological confusion between the socialist type of state, or even more, the communist type of state (see p. 133—1), and the liberal type of state adapting itself to a welfare society. Ideologically, the object of any kind of Marxist states is to *transform* society. They therefore project their goals into a near, or in the case of the communist state, a far-distant future — although more often that not the goal is the speedy industrialization of the country — and consider themselves authorized to give priority to these future goals, through which the present problems are interpreted. But the liberal state, with the same constitutional definitions, can adapt itself to the society already transformed, and yet find more adequate methods to govern it, that is to say to regulate its activities. For a better co-ordination the new welfare governments had to institutionalize new agencies with the help of which they could, on the one hand, supervise the *administration* of the public sector, but not as in the communist type of state to run that sector as an owner—employer; and, on the other hand, to establish better forms of representation for the productive spheres of an industrial society, without the full participation of which that society would grind to a halt. But these two operations had to be carried out within the liberal state. They were in reality only the modern forms of its essential functions: the provision of adequate mechanisms for the implementation of the economic and social policies decided upon jointly with the productive spheres of society; and of the best conditions of representation of those spheres so that they could engage themselves responsibly in their consultation with each other and with the government on the courses of action to be taken. The state, *qua* state, still remained the constitutional framework within which these new consultations were taking place.

With the new agencies of the modernized liberal state, the modern government could facilitate the exchanges between the real forces of industrial societies, which might be ideologically divided but which are ultimately linked in a direct complementarity — organized labour and employers. Such an approach was clearly illustrated in the first 'welfare' operation ever to take place, namely the *Saltzjobäden* agreements in Sweden, in 1933. Here, a constitutional method was established whereby labour and the employers, together with other groups in society, first agreed on the broad lines of the economic policy which the government would then be expected to legislate on and to implement. The government's role was double: that of arbiter called upon to intervene when the social partners could not reach agreement; and that of partner in the final tripartite arrangements. A similar approach underlies the mechanism of French planning, where it was statutorily enacted that once the plan had been formulated by consultation with the socio-economic groups, Parliament and the parties could not re-discuss it in detail but only accept or reject it as a whole. This was also the object of *konzertierte Aktion* in Germany, the procedure by which all the interests in society 'concerted' together with the government before the latter presented its economic policies to Parliament.[2] The prestige, and the importance, of the political parties in the immediate process of policy-making was reduced. The major groups, employers and trade unions, did not afterwards need political representation so much. This was also the significance of the political changes introduced into communist Yugoslavia in the 1950s, when efforts to create 'true socialist self-management' were accompanied by an explicit diminution of the role of the two principal political agencies, the Stalinist type centralistic state, and the monolithic party.

In the West, the conflict between the two conceptions, that of a Marxist socialist state and that of the liberal state with a welfare legitimacy, became increasingly evident. Those who were inspired by the Marxist ideology objected to the continuation of the 'private sector' within the mixed economy. They pressed for the state to take a decisive role in the management of the economy, and above all, especially in Britain, for the state to appropriate all the major industries and resources of the country as rapidly as possible. They were in fact driving towards the creation of a new, essentially centralistic and bureaucratic 'socialist state', a trend which ran counter to the fundamental pluralism of industrial society. For, in reality in the course of the disideologization required for the proper understanding and conduct of the industrial society, liberalism itself had been disideologized into pluralism. Pluralism, writes Theodore J. Lowi 'did not become public philosophy, but it is the principal intellectual member in a neo-capitalistic philosophy, interest-group liberalism'.[3]

---

[2] But this was not the case in the exclusive bipartite 'social contract' between the British Labour government and the trade unions.
[3] Theodore J. Lowi: *The End of Liberalism,* New York 1979, p. 35.

Although individuals had participated in politics in the past as citizens, many of them now also participated as members of socio-economic groups. This required them to devote more of their time and attention to public affairs than before. This intensified participation had an essentially occupational character in accordance with the functional character of industrial society.

But ideology and ideological semantics gave another twist to this trend. Popular imagination, stirred by the ideological slogans of the pursuit of happiness by individual interests or by the class struggle, gradually altered the meaning of the welfare principle, from an exercise in self-control in industrial societies designed to procure a modicum of equity, into the myth of the 'providence state' in duty bound to achieve prosperity and equality. The fundamental concepts of 'employment' and 'employment policy' were given controversial connotations.

In Britain, for instance, an ideological dimension was added from the beginning to the concept of 'employment'. Even in the title of his book, the founder of the welfare society, Beveridge, presented employment as *Full Employment in a Free Society*. Yet full employment in the absolute and ideological sense of the words was not what had been prescribed even in the Keynesian 'general themes'. 'The lowest level of unemployment he [Keynes] had been prepared to consider was five per cent', according to T. Wilson.[4] 'Full' employment was thus from the beginning an approximate formula. Confusion was compounded when it was transmuted into a political promise. The three political parties, still united in the wartime coalition, though competitors in the promissory system, together promised in the inaugural White Paper in 1944 that 'the government accepts as one of its main aims and responsibilities the maintenance of a high and stable level of employment after the war'.[5]

This promise was admittedly made in the enthusiasm of victory, in the atmosphere of national solidarity created by the war. Because full employment had been achieved during the war, the mistaken belief arose that the compulsory mobilization of all energies towards a single goal could be continued in peacetime, in a freely functioning mixed economy. Hence full employment became a commitment of all the welfare governments of the liberal state. Yet the promise was misleading for three reasons. It was wrong to promise full employment for ever, or at all. There were abundant indications that in peacetime conditions might sooner or later become less favourable for the optimum functioning of the mixed economy, especially in Britain.[6] Labour-saving devices would certainly

[4]T. Wilson, in Frances Cairncross (ed.), *Changing Perceptions of Economic Policy*, London 1981, p. 64.
[5]Cmd 6527, 1944.
[6]See for another view of the post-war problems of the British economy Sir Ian Gilmour: *Britain Can Work*, Oxford 1983, p. 96. See also a recent article by Sir A. Cairncross: 'Is employment policy a thing of the past', *Three Banks Review*, September 1983.

affect the employment of the unskilled; the entry of women into the labour market would double the number of employable people; the territorial advance of Communism in Europe and Asia would shrink the world market; some sources of raw materials would be exhausted, problems of environment might affect growth, etc. In these conditions, to proclaim full employment as the overall goal of the politics of industrial society was inapposite.

Yet because 'full employment' had been proclaimed as the goal, something called employment policy became the backbone of the economic strategy of the welfare governments. This was the second error. 'Employment policy' is not a policy which stands on its own. It is only an aspect, a dimension, and a *consequence* of other major policies such as the financial, monetary, and above all social and industrial policies,[7] which are best grouped under such all-embracing names as 'industrial strategy' or 'economic policies'. The level of employment is a symptom of the effectiveness of the industrial strategy or economic policy of the society. For if the economic policy as a whole fails to provide satisfactory levels of employment naturally, how can employment be artificially created? Sir Alec Cairncross gives a striking description of how this dilemma was perceived from the very beginning. 'The Treasury', he writes, 'was content to see the government commit itself to full employment through a series of devices that were about as adequate for the task as trying to climb Mount Everest on a bicycle'.[8] Of course the government, which is the third social partner, and the regulator in the functioning of the industrial society can and should stimulate that functioning as much as it can when it faces difficult periods. But in the context of liberal industrial policy, or the welfare state 'as much as it can' signifies in the economic sense up to the limit when the public sector crushes the private sector under its weight: and in a political sense it means up to the limit which separates a liberal state with welfare obligations from a Marxist–Leninist state which is bound to encroach on economic and political freedoms.

The third error lay in the fact that the commitment was made in 1944 by the political parties. In a sound industrial society the basis of the economic policy and of the industrial strategy is laid by the three partners or actors: organized labour (social policy); employers (economic policy); and government (or in a supranational organization like the European Community, its Council of Ministers). The nature of the consultations between these groups, leading to the agreement on the regulatory arrangements, can hardly be ideological. When the regulations have been decided upon, then the representative institutions, namely the political parties and above all Parliament, are constitutionally consulted. But cases in which political parties, in the full knowledge that the actual makers of

[7] See Ghiţa Ionescu and Klaus von Beyme, 'The politics of employment policy in Germany and Great Britain'. *Government and Opposition,* 5, No. 1, Winter 1977, pp. 88–107.
[8] Cairncross, op. cit.

economic policy have already agreed on a course of action, would oppose that course of action, are rare. Such a hypothesis is also hardly conceivable from a practical point of view. The political parties represented in Parliament are closely associated, some with the government, some with organized labour, some with the employers. They are therefore hardly likely to oppose a decision which the three partners have jointly taken before consulting the political parties.

The point of view which presides over the above considerations should not be classified as 'corporatist'. In a probably hurriedly assembled list of authors who use *corporatism* 'as an analytical concept to describe global changes in the political structure of advanced capitalist society'. Claus Offe[9] includes my name. This, as might be clearly deduced both from previous books and from this one, is a misinterpretation. To state that in modern industrial society the socio-economic groups, or as I called them 'corporations', cannot be excluded from the policy-making processes does not mean making of corporatism a profession of faith. Right wing Conservatives still use the expression in the connotation of a 'corporate state' which is a contradiction in terms; and Left wing neo-Marxists use it in order to demonstrate that the advanced capitalist society is disintegrating into irreconcilable social and political fragments which will not be put together again until after the overthrow of capitalism. In contrast with these two 'corporatist' interpretations what I say in my books, on both capitalist and communist industrial societies, is that the massive prominence of the socio-economic groups and their continuous growth in industrial society as a whole are caused by the conditions inherent in the functioning of that society; and that as such they must be integrated in the processes of policy-making. This does not seem to be feasible in communist states. After the Soviet occupation of reformist Czechoslovakia, the militarization of communist Poland in order to resist and preclude the pressure of the trade unions is the latest example. But such integration can be achieved in the liberal state by way of the modernization of the political institutions and processes. The representative institutions will thenceforward have to share in the policy-making processes with the organized interests, pressure groups or corporate forces, whatever one calls them.

This of course does entail a diminution of the role of the ideological political parties and of ideology in general. Yet since the war ideologization has continued unabated, adding subjective ideological difficulties to the objective difficulties experienced by industrial society. The influence of ideology on the miserable state of industrial relations in contemporary Britain, and the ideological hostility between the two 'social partners' are major causes of the particularly bad state of the British economy when compared to that of the United States, Japan, West Germany and many other industrial countries. The misunderstanding

[9]'Attribution of public status to interest groups' in Suzanne D. Berger (ed.) *Organizing Interests in Western Europe,* Cambridge 1981, p. 136.

between the British social partners arose because of the lack of mutual trust and cooperation between them. Capital was not invested in the British economy but overseas. An unmodernized industry could not engender productivity. Badly paid workers and indifferent managers lost interest in work. In the meantime the ideologization of the trade unions, fostered in Britain by the close and official association between the unions and an ideological political party, encouraged lack of discipline in the work force and thus estranged capital even more.

The welfare principle expresses the inter-relatedness of political freedom and social responsibility. Only by maintaining this inter-relatedness and by practising balancing or 'fine tuning' can industrial society function properly, that is function in the economic, and last but not least, political, freedom which it requires. The task of politics in industrial society, like in all previous societies, is to regulate the co-existence of human beings with a view to improve it in the present and in the future by proposing courses of action on the basis of exact assessments and of unbiased judgement. The role of politics is to forecast, not to promise, and especially not to 'bribe' people.

In so far as politics strives to improve the functioning of society it does inspire the people who live in it with hope for the future. Yet is is obvious that 'to inspire hope' is at the opposite end of the pole from 'to deceive'. And as long as the hope offered does not grow out of an unbiased judgemet of the problem under examination, the promises made may cause disappointment.

The promises made in 1944 in an atmosphere of international relaxation and confidence, during a truce in the ideological conflict between the two camps, so long united in the war against Fascism, were meant to last. But that conflict was soon to break out again in peacetime, as the 'cold war'.

THE COLD WAR

The high hopes of peace were overshadowed by two bad omens. One was the explosion of the first atomic bomb over Hiroshima, with such devastating effects. In spite of its evident utility in putting a rapid end to the war, it provided the startling evidence that mankind had now discovered how to exterminate itself. Moreover in an ideologically divided world it was very probable that if one of the systems persevered in its dream of organizing the world according to its principles, it could impose its views upon the other system by using or threatening to use this ultimate weapon. It would follow that in such an ideologically divided world the principal object of each of the camps would be to possess nuclear weapons in sufficient numbers to ensure its defence against nuclear attack. The new situation became clear when after three years or so of apparent hesitation

(1945—47) between co-operation with his former allies or the revival of ideological conflict, Stalin opted for the latter course.

The second bad omen which overshadowed the years of hope, 1945—47, was the presence of Soviet armed forces in Eastern Europe.

The origins of the 'cold war', as it began in earnest in 1947, have been disputed. The communist 'camp' has attributed it to the behaviour of the imperialists: and even in the liberal 'camp' revisionist historians have placed under a critical microscope the quid pro quos of behaviour, intentions and suspicions of the Russians and the Western Allies in the three years which followed the defeat of the Axis in Europe and in Japan.

In the first two years after the war, the Western peoples, and undoubtedly also the peoples of the USSR, not to speak of those of Eastern Europe whose countries were occupied and counter-occupied by invading foreign armies, had come to hope that a new spirit of peaceful constructiveness would be established in the world at large. The United Nations seemed to symbolize this hope — and to provide the institutional framework for peace and international collaboration. Yet it was during the war, at the Teheran conference, that the plan of the British Chiefs of Staff to mount an invasion of the Balkans from the Mediterranean through Yugoslavia was rejected by the American Chiefs of Staff and the Russian Chiefs of Staff and Stalin personally opposed it.[10] It was then that the three powers adopted, in the Military Agreement of 1 December 1943, the strategy whereby the Allied armies alone would liberate Western Europe, while the Soviet armies would have the exclusive right to liberate Eastern Europe. The two armies were then to meet 'somewhere in Europe', as the official text put it. And so they actually did along the haphazard line which has since become the Iron Curtain. But at that time, and in those circumstances, too much political significance need not have been attached to these military decisions, considering that it was also agreed that the military occupation on both sides was to last only until the end of operations and that the 'zones' were to be dissolved after the withdrawal of the armies.

It is at this historical junction that revisionist historians have attempted to discern what actually caused the increasing discord and mutual suspicion between the USSR and the Western Allies and when it began. Though the Soviet government pursued its military strategy and extended its political control over its nearest neighbours in Eastern Europe — some Western revisionist historians have still argued that the Western Allies were to blame for refusing to allow the Russians a share in the post-war administration of Italy, which might have encouraged them to reciprocate in Eastern Europe; or for having, once Roosevelt was dead, allowed relations between Russia and the United States to grow considerably cooler. But the

---

[10] See especially US Department of State: *The Conference of Cairo and Teheran*, Washington 1961 and W.M. McNeill: *America, Britain and Russia*, London 1953.

revisionist thesis has not been borne out by history. Michael Howard explains why.

> After the 'Battle of the Books' between the revisionist and counter-revisionist schools, a picture has emerged over which most historians now agree. It is one of wartime understandings between the Soviet Union and its Western allies — understandings based largely on Western illusions, or at best the most fragile of hopes — breaking down within a few months of the end of hostilities. The Soviet Union moved in — economically, politically and militarily — to consolidate, as part of its empire, the territories already occupied by its armed forces. Simultaneously the United States was liquidating its wartime commitments to its European allies as quickly as — some might say more quickly than — it decently could. As a result Western Europe, in 1946—47, trembled on the verge of economic collapse; a collapse which its Moscow-oriented communist parties were fully prepared to exploit. In Germany, and especially in Berlin, democratic political parties fought what seemed to be a losing battle against strong, well-organized and confident communist opponents who for the past 15 years had been preparing for just such an opportunity. There was a widespread fear, not of Soviet military attack on Western Europe but of a disintegration of the whole political and economic structure that would make any such attack unnecessary.
>   It was to prevent such a disintegration that the United States initiated in 1947, the European Recovery program. This program may have had an unforeseen escalatory effect in that it was perceived by the Soviet Union as a threat to its own control of Eastern Europe, and so precipitated those actions in Prague and Berlin in 1948 that were read by many in the West as clear evidence of Soviet aggressive intentions. If the Russians were thwarted in their use of political means for attaining their objectives (so the argument went) might they not use military ones — unless they were deterred from doing so by the clear perception that any such move would bring them up against the enormous latent power of the United States?[11]

Given the transformation by Stalin of the communist ideology into a theoretical justification for the elevation of the USSR to the status of an industrial super power, Stalin visualized the progress of his brand of post-Communism in almost the same terms which Napoleon used to defend his post-Jacobinism: the revolution would advance where the Soviet armies advanced. Already in the 1920s the straight socialist definition of working-class internationalism had been perverted into a demand for a prior loyalty to be given to the USSR — a nation-state — by all communist parties and by all individual Communists everywhere, who must forswear their loyalty to their own country. This also explains in retrospect Stalin's indifference towards the position of the ideology of Communism as an anti-Fascist ideology, when he concluded the Nazi—Soviet pact in August 1939. And it

---

[11] M. Howard: *Foreign Affairs*, Winter 1982—83, pp. 309—10.

explains the premeditation with which he ordered the Eastern European communist parties to be ready to assume power under the protection of the Red Army and simultaneously the order he gave in 1947 to the Western communist parties to launch revolutionary industrial activity in Western Europe. That Stalin's idea of the geo-political or military advance of the USSR was equated in his eyes with the advance of communist ideology, which remained his supreme objective, shows up like a red thread through all the twists and turns of events. The launching of the 'cold war' in 1948 was a deliberate ideological decision — a continuation of the world revolution by other means.

Stalin's action created new attitudes and new motivations, in both systems of political happiness. In both systems global military alliances were concluded — international organizations each led by a super power — in itself an unprecedented situation for the Western European states. And within each system, and in each of the super powers a hard centre of technocratic power of decision-making was formed in what President Eisenhower, at the end of his presidency, called the 'military—industrial complex', a self-explanatory name.

There were moments of high tension, like the Berlin blockade of 1948 and the Korean war of 1951, in both of which the communist camp was defeated. Then after Stalin's death in 1953 a period of calm ensued. In the communist camp Stalin's successors engaged in a long and anxious search for a 'new course' and passed through the traumatic phase of de-Stalinization begun in 1956. In the liberal—welfare camp relaxation was due primarily to an economic boom, during the period from the mid-1950s to the mid-1960s. But because of the deep roots grown by the ideologies of both systems, the lull did not last long. The chances of more lasting, less superficial, improvements in their mutual relations, which these years had offered were missed. More relevant to this enquiry was the fact that it was ideology itself which was the principal cause of the deterioration of the situation in each camp.

In the communist camp Stalin's successors soon realized, if they did not know it already, that the Marxist—Leninist ideology had acquired too strong a grip on the system for it to adapt itself to the changing conditions of a modern industrial society. The drama of the communist system of political happiness is that the Leninist prescription of one party, one leader, one state, had proved, especially under Stalin's strong hand, to be suitable for the mobilization required by primary industrialization. But once industrialization had been achieved, such a monolithic ideology was functionally opposed to the complexity and interdependence of the modern industry. Modern industry, to repeat again, requires a participatory form of management; all those who use their skills in the process of production expect to take part in the making of the decisions on which those processes are based. This functional form of participation in modern industry reminds one, to a certain extent, of the theoretical socialist and communist demand for workers' participation in the management of the industries in which they work — and therefore should have been widely applied in a communist regime. The Yugoslav experiment with workers' councils and self-management, which Stalin tried so hard to bring to an end, was, at least in theory, an authentic variation on this ideological theme. Moreover the Yugoslavs also realized and accepted, at least in theory, the political consequences of socialist self-management, namely decentralization of the state and the curbing of the previously absolute powers of the party.

But in Russia this was not possible. The initial mould of the state created by Lenin and Stalin had hardened too much. Any move made in the economic field, and some attempts were made, notably under Khrushchev, threatened to destroy the overall political control of the party. Moreover Russia's 'industrial—military' complex, composed of the party, the army, the secret police and heavy industry, paralysed any initiative for reform. The state of the dictatorship of the proletariat was a solid structure which either stood as a whole, or crumbled. The drawbacks were only too obvious. In the economy results were far below expectations; scientists protested uselessly against the censorship and control of incompetent party apparatchiks; eminent writers or musicians were reduced to flee the country or were forcibly deported, while eminent scientists were persecuted.

In his attempt to de-Stalinize, Khrushchev only confirmed, in his speech at the Twentieth Party Congress in 1956, the horrible realities of Stalinist Communism. Within Russia there was some reduction of the brutality and arbitrariness of Stalinist police methods. But de-Stalinization was not enough to change the structure of the system. What was required was de-Marxist-Leninization, which could not be effected without bringing down the whole structure. (This is why Khrushchev's attempt to change at least the by now odious name of 'dictatorship of the proletariat' at the Twenty-second Congress also failed).

The ideological unity of the Eastern European communist parties which had only been maintained by means of severe purges and frequent meetings for indoctrination against the insidious influence of Titoism, also collapsed as a result of Khrushchev's speech at the Twentieth Congress. The ideological conflict with the Chinese Communist party in which Mao accused Khrushchev of revisionism and the USSR of being an imperialist power took further the process of the ideological decomposition of international Communism. The veteran leader of the Italian Communist party, Palmiro Togliatti, declared that the unique central source of ideological inspiration had now become what he called 'polycentrism'. Each communist party henceforward had the right to conduct itself according to its own interpretation of Marxism—Leninism. Marxist—Leninist ideology was thus reduced to a pious symbol. Worse still, soon after the congress the Polish and the Hungarian Communist governments took an open stand against the USSR and the CPSU. In Hungary the revolt was openly anti-monolithic, and its leaders proposed the reintroduction of the multi-party system and the withdrawal of the country from the military organization of the Soviet bloc. Khrushchev decided to adopt the Stalinist method of military repression. Soviet tanks were sent into Hungary, a sovereign communist state. The crisis of communist ideology was now reflected in the crisis of the communist system as a whole.

WELFARE AND PROGRESSIVE PERMISSIVENESS

The welfare state was the successful result of the combination of the liberal—utilitarian and of the social—democratic ideologies. From now on it could be argued that the 'greatest number of people' could benefit from, and share in, the material comforts produced by modern technology, as brought within their financial means by the Keynesian approach to public finance. The 'sharing' took place in conditions of obvious discrepancy. There was still a permanent substratum of poverty at the bottom of the social pyramid, and indeed the definition of what constituted poverty became one of the most popular and controversial subjects of research by economists and sociologists. Even in the United States, the symbol of Western affluence, many people continued to live below the subsistence level while at the top of the pyramid wealth reached extravagant heights.

But in between these two extreme levels was the ever-widening stratum of those who in some degree or another did share in a modicum of modern comfort, provided by a lavishly supplied market. Moreover, they were urged to spend by intensive commercial advertising, and by a particularly generous credit system. People began to own at least one car, sometimes two, radios and television sets, all kinds of domestic mechanical equipment, to buy more clothes, to enjoy package deal holidays at home and abroad, and to live in centrally heated houses, their own, or belonging to local authorities, equipped with bathrooms and modern kitchens. The possession of this modicum of comfort engendered a double sense of satisfaction across the whole broad sector to which it was available. Generally known as the middle classes (the colloquial plural used for this socio-economic group is significantly discerning), they shared in the pleasures provided by the use of all these commodities, and they had the satisfaction of belonging to a civilization which had succeeded in achieving a substantial equalization of standards and conditions of living. Moreover, since most people are guided in life by a basic sense of decency and frugality, they were also inclined to be satisfied with what had been achieved and to feel that more material comfort, more luxury, would not increase their happiness. The old saying: 'You can't take it with you' acquired a new appositeness.

Undoubtedly social jealousy and envy still continued to incite men against men — for such is human nature. But, to the dismay of the zealots of egalitarianism, and especially of the modern levellers, social envy and jealousy had now become a kind of intra-class, or rather, intra-middle-class, affair. Within them the middle classes, individuals and groups, wanted to have more absolutely and more relatively, that is more than the Joneses. But fewer and fewer were those who would abandon the citadel of comfort in which they were commonly installed — to go out into the wilderness of the pursuit of universal equality. This was the moment when the German Social Democratic party — the most successful of all these parties — repudiated Marxism for it had clearly realized that the greatest number of the 'working class', its political and electoral clientele, now belonged to the new middle classes. These social and economic re-alignments were not only the ephemeral result of the high wave of prosperity; they were established for good as was shown during the ensuing period of depression, when the moral differences between the employed and the unemployed, the skilled and the unskilled, the ascending and the declining industries were so strikingly revealed.

The increased availability of the means of 'pleasure', to use Bentham's key-concept in this Benthamite context, was accompanied and fostered by the growth of the capacity for enjoying pleasure. The revolution of mores, which happened at the same time though not for the same reasons as the revolution of affluence, provided people with a new feeling of the legitimacy of material happiness. In a sense what happened now, across the whole of society, was the vindication of the counsels of Helvétius and Bentham to the emerging bourgeoisie of the nineteenth century. The pursuit of hedonism was now general — and sexual pleasure being the most intense and at the same time the least expensive of all pleasures, its pursuit thenceforwards took on an almost obsessional character. Sexuality extended its range in all directions. In general people pursued all kinds of enjoyments and entertainments. Never before had human beings shown a greater and more widespread propensity to 'enjoy life' (an apposite expression in this context).

This final remark applied especially to the British people. For in Britain the severe traditions of puritanism and Victorian ethics considerably delayed the change in economic and ethical thinking — and when it occured provided almost violent decompression in both directions.[12]

As the contradiction between the ideological monolithism of the Marxist—Leninist state and the pluralism functionally required by an industrial society was emerging as the central dilemma of the communist dictatorial system of political happiness, so the contradiction between the progressive permissiveness of the liberal ideology and the productive order required by industrial society was turning into the central dilemma of the liberal—utilitarian system of political happiness. For, as monolithic coercive controls grow necessarily tighter to the point when they strangle society, so excessively progressive permissiveness might lead to the point where a society in which it is practised might begin to dissolve into anomie.[13]

---

[12] For similar historical reasons the explosion has been very loud in the Netherlands.
[13] In Durkheim's sense of the disintegration of social norms in a community.

Progressive permissiveness is, we said, the belief pervading a society ideologized by utilitarian liberalism, that most values, and commandments derived from the European ethical heritage might hinder and frustrate the free development of human beings and their ever-improving rationality.

We also remarked that because they were ideologies and therefore both subordinated ethics to their political goals, the two ideologies of political happiness, separately and contradictorily, but simultaneously, attacked the basic values of European society from both sides. For utilitarian liberals these values were too 'ascetic', for communists they were simply 'bourgeois'. Both ideologies claimed that values are relative — and proceeded to relativize them so as to replace them with their own. That relativization corroded values of all kinds, in all directions: personal, social, individual, collective, legal or economic. This process of the relativization of values started in earnest in the first decades of the twentieth century. By the 1960s the symptoms of the undermining of the ethics of society under the impact of progressive permissiveness were already visible.

The main symptoms appeared in the moral and legal fields, creating a paralysis of the moral and legal norms, injunctions and institutions. The formula 'Law and Order' came to be singled out ironically as reactionary. Defiance of moral rules or legal provisions was regarded as a form of liberation. This rendered relations between authority (parents, teachers, police, judges, government) and the 'look back in anger' young men increasingly difficult. Moreover, the more difficult they became the more the demand for permissiveness grew. The political, legal or religious authorities which originally forbade 'immoral' actions or attitudes, were now urged to 'permit' them and encourage them.

The escalation of permissiveness was visible in all states in the system of political happiness from Catholic Italy to Protestant Denmark, from modern republics like the USA to old monarchies like the United Kingdom, from underdeveloped Ireland to the super-developed Federal Republic of Germany — where political violence was particularly acute.

Some of the principal symptoms of excessive progressive permissiveness were, to take them in a haphazard way: in the political field the unprecedented growth of violence and terrorism; in the cultural field the unprecedented growth of pornography and commercial debauchery; in the religious field the slackening of theological, ethical and sacramental norms; in the industrial field, the indifference, or indeed hostility towards 'profits' and productivity, which are criteria of the validity of an industrial operation; in the financial field — inflation ; in the whole social field the relativization of values and of moral criteria. These are all consequences of permissiveness — because, in strict logic, they could all be avoided by an exercise of the private or public will.

But the public will needs custodians to remind people of the necessity of moral laws. Let us therefore turn to the role in the relativization of values played by the custodians of the cultural sphere.

THE FAULTS OF THE SPIRITUAL CUSTODIANS

Given the conditions in which industrial society functions, the diffusion of the mentality of progressive permissiveness may have been irresistible. But a doubt remains whether the custodians of the people's spiritual integrity have fulfilled their duty — or whether, on the contrary many have been guilty of faults of omission or commission, and have thus helped to propagate that mentality.

The custodians of man's spiritual integrity are, in the realm of faith, the clergy, and in the realm of knowledge, the intellectuals. Their faults are of a different order and should be examined separately. To take the clergy first.

Some clerics have shown an increasing tendency to replace the Church's transcendental themes of human faith and salvation with the material themes of human economic, social and political organization.[14]

THE CHURCH[14]

The social mentality of the Church has of late met with some sharp and direct criticism. I shall quote only two examples. One comes from Pierre Chaunu in France, who writes:

> The Churches have felt obliged in the last twenty years or so to renounce ontological discourse for a discourse and an action which are purely secular . . . We are now led towards a doubly secular militancy, one, that of politics and the other, and worse still, that of the clergy itself, who have given up their duty and who jealously see to it that the place they have deserted should remain empty.[15]

The second comes from Edward Norman in Britain:

> In the largest perspective I shall see the politicization of Christianity as a symptom of its decay as an authentic religion . . . Furthermore, [this] is not the consequence of successful assault by its enemies. It is due to the surrender of its unique claims to an understanding of the nature of men made by its own leaders.[16]

The bishops of the Church of England seem to be divided on this supreme question. Some of them use their authority, and their pulpits, to discuss such problems as 'stagflation', relations between the police and

---

[14]What follows are parts of a conversation with Dr Graham Leonard, Bishop of London, published in *Government and Opposition,* **17,** No. 3, Summer 1982, pp. 351 ff.

[15]Pierre Chaunu: *La mémoire et le sacré*, Paris 1978, p. 166.

[16]Edward Norman: 'The political Christ', First BBC Reith Lecture 1978 in *The Listener,* 2 November 1978, p. 567. See also his *Christianity and the World Order,* Oxford University Press 1978.

racial minorities or why Swapo will defeat the forces of the South African government and therefore should be militarily and politically supported. But on the other side, the Bishop of London, Dr Graham Leonard, for instance, answers T.S. Eliot's poignant question: 'Why should men love the Church?'[17] Thus:

'Why indeed, but the irony is that, though men reject the Church when she is true to herself, they despise her when she has conformed to the world. The Church today having lost her nerve shows at times an almost pathetic desire to be loved by the world. So she too is happy to forget life and death with the world and seek for systems so perfect that no one will need to be good. She is hard where the world is hard and soft where the world is soft'. 'Once your own position is weakened, because you are uncertain of it, then you either start to be hard on others, or you lose your nerve. If you do not really believe in eternity and in redemption — the basic elements in the Christian Gospel — you try to find something which *apparently* justifies the Church in the world's eyes.'

'Is this why the Church turns to politics — and replaces the Christian Gospel by the social gospel? If so, how and why did this happen?' — I asked the Bishop.

'Well, I think that there are all sorts of factors here', he answered. 'I am not looking for one scapegoat because I do not think that there is only one. I think there are all sorts of reasons. First, I would put the confusion in modern philosophy. I think that the development of positivism had a very profound effect — positivism had a corroding influence on modern thinking. The result was that people in fact ceased to believe that there was, that there could be, a coherent philosophy of life. From this point of view, it is highly significant that Wittgenstein himself could write "The sense of the world must lie outside the world" and again "Not *how* the world is, is the mystical, but that it is". The second cause was probably the influence on character of the ideologies which derived from the welfare state. What makes me highly suspicious of any kind of political system which is supposed to supply the answer, is the fact that however good it may be — if indeed it may ever be good — it is going to be actually operated by fallible and sinful human beings. T.S. Eliot's superb verse says it all when he speaks of men who . . .

. . . *constantly try to escape*
from the darkness outside and within
by dreaming of systems so perfect that
no one will need to be good.'

[17] 'Why should men love the Church? Why should they love the laws? She tells them of Life and Death, and of all they would forget. She is tender where they would be hard, and hard where they would like to be soft/They constantly try to escape/From the darkness outside and within/By dreaming of systems so perfect that no one will need to be good/'. T.S. Eliot: *The Rock*, Faber 1934, p. 42.

THE INTELLECTUALS

Unlike the clergy who acknowledge one absolute truth which also inspires their faith, the intellectuals can, indeed should, recognize the plurality and relativity of truths. Ideally, the duty of the intellectuals as custodians of spiritual integrity is to search for and transmit the truth as they find it, without and above their faith. Any inflexion of the truth by wilful interpretation amounts to what, since Julien Benda first wrote about it, has been called *La Trahison des Clercs* — the betrayal by the intellectuals. For only by sharing with men the whole human truth or, conversely, the truth about man as a whole, can the intellectual play his role as custodian of man's spiritual integrity. Ideally, therefore, the intellectuals-*qua*-custodians should take their stand *above* society, and avoid being 'distracted' by it and 'attracted' to it.

But this idealized description of the intellectual-*qua*-custodian is hardly realizable, especially in the conditions of the industrial society.

We have seen that when intellect appeared as a new concept in history, in the eighteenth century, it was greeted as the innermost instrument of reason. 'Intellect' was able to find the true meaning of things surrounding man's existence — and of that existence itself. At that time, long before the advent of the industrial society, it was realized that the standpoint of intellect and of the priests of the intellect, those who called themselves intellectuals, should be total impartiality. Like the priests who have to be sure of the purity of their faith, the intellectuals had to be sure of the exactitude and objectivity of their judgement.

With the coming of the industrial society, this position of pure objectivity became increasingly difficult to maintain. Overwhelming social problems faced the three categories of intellectuals in industrial society, namely the creators: scientists, technical experts, philosophers, writers, playwrights, film-directors, composers, painters and sculptors; the educators: academics and teachers; and the communicators: journalists, radio and television commentators, authors, publishers, etc. For such is the pull of the problems industrial society raises for every individual and all individuals together, that many intellectuals have of late become more 'interested' in the problems of the relations between men within society, or between men and society, than in the overall and ultimate problems of man himself, or indeed of the self of man. This concentration on social affairs of increasingly large numbers of intellectuals, which was the inevitable consequence of their contamination with the ideologies, has gradually transformed large groups of intellectuals *into a Western intelligentsia.*

The *intelligentsia* is a phenomenon of Russian and East European social history. The appearance of an intelligentsia is a consequence of the part played by the state in the process of industrialization of the nation-state, and even if industrialization has been effected by society, of the part the state takes afterwards in the conduct and control of the mixed economy.

In under-capitalized countries where industrialization could be effected only with the help and intervention of the state — as Tsarist

Russia — the individual intellectuals formed a social group, animated by the same ideals, but sharing some 'vested interests'. They opposed the state's obscurantism — the combination of conformism, mysticism and censorship of new ideas — and they 'went to the people' instead. But their alliance with 'the people', which in pre-war Russia meant mainly the impoverished peasantry, and the demand that they should be given schools, hospitals, industry and electricity, had a certain ambiguity. For, secondly, these burgeoning professionals had a vision of their social role, and an interest in opening up posts for themselves and for future generations of intellectuals, in the hospitals, schools, universities, museums, theatres, orchestras, to be founded in the wake of development.

The stubborn obscurantism of the decadent Empire forced them to take revolutionary attitudes. Once the revolution was effected, and the functional beehive of the new state was constructed by Stalin's industrialization drive, the intelligentsia came functionally into its own; and Stalin was able to proclaim in 1936 that a new intelligentsia had been born, which was the 'apple of the eye' of the new state. But to Stalin's astonishment even in the 'new' intelligentsia individual intellectuals aspired to freedom and started to oppose the new oppressive regime. Writers like Solzhenitsyn and scientists like Sakharov are the formidable symbols of intellectual opposition in the USSR.

But where, as in England, and the United States of America, industrialization was effected by society itself, or in other words with private capital, the state for some three-quarters of a century observed the attitude known as *laissez-faire*. A free market became the rule for all exchanges of commodities and services: there was thus also a free market for the services of the 'intellectuals'. This was particularly true of the 'liberal professions' (doctors, lawyers, university teachers), and the artists (writers, architects, playwrights, painters, sculptors) who were able to emancipate themselves from their patrons — be they kings, or popes, Medicis or Sforzas — and to find 'clients' in society as an open market. The universities too were able to preserve their autonomy, indeed to become more autonomous in relation to the Church, while not subservient to the state. This sense of 'independence' of the intellectuals strengthened their awareness of their essential role in finding and imparting the *truth* — one of the corollaries of which was the critical stand they had to take in public matters.

But then the welfare state and the mixed economy had an obvious impact on intellectual life. They created a new relation between the intellectuals and the public authorities. Presented with a new patron, the intellectuals were able to offer their services; and many found the new public or national patron more congenial than the mercantile patrons of old. An intelligentsia-like group-consciousness resulted from this new relationship, in which the intellectuals at the service of the welfare state expected it to expand its functions and responsibilities, and to expand within it their own functions and opportunities. They were dominated by a specific social mentality, in which their occupational interests were subconsciously linked with the public interest. The proliferation of institutions of higher education, new universities, polytechnics, research centres, increasingly serving the state, strengthened this relationship of groups of intellectuals with the state. A functional intelligentsia emerged as a new and distinct interest, or socio-economic group, in the liberal—utilitarian system of happiness.

Ideologically however Western intellectuals and the Western intelligentsia remained divided between a very broadly defined Left and Right, and between 'two cultures', humanist and technocratic. The polarization of intellectuals between Left and Right has a long pedigree. In modern times the Left-wing intellectual has been radical, anti-clerical, anti-bourgeois, anti-capitalist and above all anti-conformist. He is therefore opposed in principle to the set of traditional moral values, and the accompanying institutions and tends to become the spokesman of permissiveness and latitudinarianism, often reconciling under the umbrella of an undifferentiating radicalism both the ideologies of public happiness, state-worshipping Marxism and hedonistic Benthamism.

The division between the humanists and the technocrats does not coincide exactly with the division between Right and Left. It can lead to conflict in so far as the humanists fear that the technocrats are creating an environmentally and socially anti-human machine-ridden society. Humanists denounce technocracy as the supreme enemy and oppose industrial society as a whole.

> It is essential to realise that the technocracy is not the exclusive product of that old devil, capitalism. Rather it is the product of a mature and accelerating industrialism. The profiteering could be eliminated: the technocracy would remain in force. The key problem we have to deal with is the paternalism of expertise within a socio-economic system which is so organized that it is inextricably beholden to expertise. And moreover, to an expertise which has learned a thousand ways to manipulate our acquiescence with an imperceptible subtlety.[18]

And they visualize their brothers — intellectuals from the other sides of the barricades, the detested 'élites' — as the Judases of this betrayal of men.

The social tensions created by the increasingly oppressive nature of the relations of production, visibly in capitalist society, secretly in communist industrial society, aggravated by the external tensions of the 'cold war', estranged large numbers of intellectuals from their erstwhile ideal of independence even further. Many of them lost the remnants of that independence by accepting to be ideologically enrolled.

Ideological enrolment consists of the overt acceptance by an intellectual of the interpretative framework of an ideology, and of his pledge to apply that ideological interpretation to all problems and questions submitted to his examination. This amounts to a declaration of faith in the goals and methods of pre-established and pre-conceived tenets — which moreover are

---

[18] Theodore Roszak, *The Making of a Counterculture*, London 1970, p. 19.

subject to unchallengeable exegesis by the hierarchy of the ideology. In this sense, it can be said that the ideologized intellectuals fall back into the position of the 'schoolmen' of the Middle Ages — reviving an ideological scholasticism.

The analogies between the scholasticism of the Middle Ages and contemporary scholasticism are grounded in the fact that in both periods individual minds were of a particularly high quality, the discussion was particularly sharp-witted and subtle and the antagonism between the differing points of view within the brotherhood of discussants was particularly acrimonious and sometimes fraught with danger for one side or another, according to how the argument developed. But in both periods the arguments have been restrained within the parameters of the given belief, beyond the limits of which the discussion itself lost any meaning. It is not so much the fact that in both periods references must be made to, and scholarly authority found in, 'given' books which justifies the analogy; it is the fact that once caught up in an allegiance to a particular belief, the intellect is deprived of its specific truth-seeking, doubt-projecting, function of investigation. The intellectual-*qua*-custodian no longer pursues the integrity of the mind, but, on the contrary, he pursues the integration of his mind into the 'given' truth. The scholastics did try to introduce Aristotelian logic into Christian theology: and Lukacs, for instance, and the post-Lukacsian Marxist—Leninist scholars have tried to introduce modern sociology into historical materialism. But in both cases the incompatibilities have proved too strong. Like the scholastics the ideologically-enrolled intellectuals had, and have, to learn the bitter lesson of ideological discipline.

We have tried to explain why, once an intellectual has espoused one or another of the ideologies, and has thus surrendered his free judgement, he engages in the relativization of the traditional moral values so as to replace them with the tenets of his or her new creed, and propagate them.

But at the same time the free intellectuals, and notably the creative writers, novelists, playwrights, film directors, etc., who continued to rely on their free judgement and reckoned with the direct success of their work with the public at large, had their own difficulties. They were told by commercial entrepreneurs, as well as by 'trendy' critics, that unless their works were 'progressive', the 'modern' and 'emancipated' public of today — allegedly in quest of 'strong' sensations (sex, terror or both) and of radical, 'revolutionary' ideas — would not *buy* them. For, what had been at first, in the last decades of the nineteenth century and the first decades of the twentieth century, the legitimate crusade of writers and artists, educators, communicators and legislators against the taboos and conformism of nineteenth-century societies, has become in the second half of the twentieth century an increasingly profitable industry of pornography and vice. In the nineteenth century the attempt to censor works of art led to the ridiculous trial of Flaubert for the publication of *Madame Bovary*;

and even in the 1930s, *Lady Chatterley's Lover* and *Ulysses* were banned in Britain. But now, some publishers, and theatrical, cinematographic and photographic producers are thriving on pornography and obscenity. Artists and intellectuals whose activities are still based on the market are encouraged by these kinds of entrepreneurs to deliver the products the market allegedly wants. This had led to a vicious circle. The more pornography was fed to a debased public, the greater the demand for stronger stuff; and the more profitable it proved for commercial intermediaries, the more they supplied it. With the help of mass communications the vicious circle spread everywhere. 'Sex' became the new idol of society and the sexual act was separated in this commercialized presentation from its supreme significance, that of procreation, of giving life, and worshipped for its own sake. Giving and receiving pleasure was all that was sought.

Moreover the pleasure-seeking and pain-avoiding spirit corroded many attitudes and mentalities — gradually replacing the sense of duty, respect and discipline. Parents gave bad examples to their children, managers to workers, teachers to pupils and students. Soon the latter paid them back in kind. A general laxity permeated the 'productive' activities of society — with the result that productivity and production itself declined. But the crisis began to be felt at the end of a decade of world-prosperity. The contrast between the past years of indulgence and the coming years of scarcity was going to be sharp.

THE SECOND AND CONTINUING CRISIS OF THE SYSTEMS

At the end of the 1960s and of the economic boom, the crisis suddenly reappeared simultaneously both in the liberal—utilitarian and in the communist—dictatorial systems of political happiness. The year 1968 was a cataclysmic year for both.

The revolt of the 'students' in May 1968 shook the foundations of the presidency of Johnson for good in the United States, and that of de Gaulle in France, and aroused a widespread popularity for a new, radical, even violent 'Left' in the liberal system. In turn, the Czechoslovak 'spring', which opposed two types, if not two generations, of Communists shook the communist system for good. Both types of industrial society were challenged at the same time. Neither of the revolts brought about the outright victory of the revolutionaries concerned in them. But both marked an irreversible turning point in the relations between the two systems, and between the systems and the people within them.

In reality the world has experienced at least eight such crises or critical chains of events, some of which began in 1968, some in 1972. There were capitalist and communist political and cultural crises which surfaced in

1968, and capitalist and communist economic and social crises which surfaced in 1972. None of these eight crises is over yet, and while they are still in progress, they produce a cumulative and continuous effect. We propose to interpret these ongoing crises here as a second crisis (for the first crisis see pp. 159—64) in which both systems of political happiness have simultaneously lost their credibility.

What was really significant in these simultaneous developments, marked by opposing ideological motivations, was that the revolutionaries or reformists active in each system did not want, let alone claim that they wanted, to replace the existing system by the opposite one. Yet this would have been the logical consequence, had the matter consisted of classical 'cold war' ideological conflict. Each of the two ideologies, utilitarian—liberal and communist—dictatorial, thought of itself, and presented itself, as the natural and exclusive alternative to the other, indeed as the antidote, by polarization, to the other. But neither did the Czechoslovak reformers proclaim that their aim was to install, or re-install a hedonistic utilitarian—liberal or capitalist system; nor did the French students seem (for their wishes were less clearly formulated than those of Czechozlovaks) to postulate the adoption of the Soviet sytem.[19] Therefore, if neither of the 'alternative' systems and their ideologies was desired by the other system's opponents, and indeed if both of them were found wanting by the revolutionaries in both camps — it may follow that what was wrong with those systems was what they had in common.

We know that what they had in common, above and beyond all their striking ideological and practical differences, was that they were both of them systems of political happiness. What happened in 1968 was that for the first time in history the promisees of *both* systems of political happiness were taking the promisers to task for having deceived them, each in its own way.

In the following pages we shall try briefly to retrace the grievances and reproaches of the 'revolted' in each of the systems.

Czechoslovakia was in many respects the most mature country in the Soviet bloc. It had a mature industry. It also had a particularly mature national culture. Its genius has best manifested itself in the philosophies of peace and reform and in a particularly mature civic culture. Politically, it was the only country in Central Europe to have preserved a genuine parliamentary regime until it was occupied by the Nazis in 1938.

In 1968 the Czech Communist party presented the Russian Communist party with two straight declarations. The first was that as Czechoslovakia was a mature country it did not need, or at least no longer needed, the straitjacket of the Marxist—Leninist political structure, but on the contrary

---

[19] One of the more programmatic graffiti at the Sorbonne read: 'The revolution starting now challenges not only the capitalist society but the industrial society as well. We want a new and original world. We reject a world in which the certainty of not dying of hunger is conditioned by the risk of dying of boredom.' *Le Monde*, 15 May 1968.

was suffocated by it. The second was a general declaration that Marxism— Leninism was incompatible with an advanced industrial society, indeed increasingly incompatible the further a society advanced. If the USSR wanted Communism to survive in Czechoslovakia it should at once allow the necessary economic and social pluralization and political participation proposed by the theoreticians of 'socialism with a human face'.

The Czechoslovak crisis of 1968 remains the most significant confrontation which the USSR and the CPSU have had to face between the Twentieth Congress and the present time because it brought into the open the discussion of the inadaptability of Marxist—Leninist state structure (or, in our terminology the communist—dictatorial system of political happiness) to the very functioning of an industrial society. 'Most significant', of course, does not mean either the most dangerous, as is for the USSR the confrontation with China, or the most acute, as is now the confrontation with Poland. In the confrontation with China, the USSR and the CPSU were the industrially advanced and mature partners, while the underdeveloped Chinese were still arguing in romantic terms about instant world-revolution, the transformation of man, and the reintroduction of the masses into the mainstream of politics by such nefarious improvisations as the 'cultural revolution'. The confrontation with Poland is still centred on the fundamental incompatibility between Christianity and Marxist atheism. The fact that the conflict has now taken on a third dimension with the entry on the stage of the (Christian) trade unions is of the highest importance and may lead to unforeseen consequences. Yet one must not forget that this industrial aspect of the crisis of Communism could already be observed in Czechoslovakia in 1968 when the trade unions joined fully in the movement for reform. Moreover, in Czechoslovakia, the whole of industrial 'society', the workers, the managers and the planners, themselves expressed their conviction that the communist—dictatorial system was obsolete and therefore counter-productive in an industrial age. So in this case it was the industrially more advanced Czechoslovakia which spoke on behalf of the modern age, to the relatively less developed USSR.

The 1968 'action programme' of the Czechoslovak Communist party made 'maturity' the key-concept of the proposed reform. With due courtesy the Czechoslovaks tried to explain to the Russians that since their economy was now 'mature' it required a kind of socialist market and a responsible participatory system — and, conversely, that a mature economy abhors the system of state-conducted mobilization which, it was alleged, had been suitable for industrialization in the (immature) USSR of 1930. A mature economy must be effective: and to be effective it is necessary for those who make it work at all levels to exercise responsibility, and responsibility cannot go without participation of all those engaged in economic work in the processes of decision-making. The Czechoslovak party insisted that the pivot of their reform was *freedom of information* and declared that they were prepared to trust their politically and civically 'mature' population. They would base their communist system henceforward on this shared responsibility.

The Russians, hiding behind the Warsaw Treaty Organization, answered on 18 August 1968 that the Marxist—Leninist system is built on unchangeable pillars: security and military defence against capitalist subversion; state control of the economy; a monolithic party and above all complete state and party control of all media of communication (*diamat, agit-prop* and censorship). None of these pillars could be shifted without bringing down the whole structure.

The Czechoslovak idea that in a mature society the government can allow its people to discuss all public problems in the press, radio and television was, and for very real reasons, inconceivable to the communist government and parties of the USSR, the Democratic Republic of Germany, Bulgaria and all other communist governments of the world. For their ultimate strength lies in the prohibition by all means of any opinions which do not follow exactly the ideological prescriptions — as permitted in democratic centralism. Once the monolithic party and the totalitarian ideology were challenged in public the whole edifice of coercion would crumble. It was for the defence of this Achilles's heel of the Leninist state, for its indispensable power of coercion, that ultimately the Warsaw Treaty Organization — minus Romania — used their weapons against a sister communist country.

There ensued not only the tragedy of Czechoslovakia, soon to be once more *gleichgeschaltet,* this time by Soviet tanks — but the tragedy of the USSR and the CPSU which had been thus forced to reveal publicly that only a total change of the structure on which the system is based could make Communism adaptable to modern industrial society, and that this change was impossible. The Czechoslovak crisis of 1968 marked, for those who had eyes to see, the moment in history when the advanced communist industrial society served notice to the less advanced, that the entire communist—dictatorial system of political happiness could survive only if it discarded those heavy relics of the past, its petrified ideology and party politics. Otherwise, since this society could not possibly go forward, it was condemned, after a shorter or longer period of immobilism, to disintegrate further or, like the Nazi regime to compensate for ideological failures at home with military victories abroad.

The crisis in the liberal—utilitarian system was also twofold: there was a cultural crisis in 1968, and an economic crisis in the early 1970s. And as we have seen the crises in both spheres could be attributed to the further escalation of the liberal progressive permissiveness.

The cultural crisis was initially a transgenerational crisis. The description which follows applies to the self-appointed leaders of the younger generation endorsed and magnified by the media. A 'silent majority', less spectacular for the media, continued to live much as before, and to hold traditional moral principles. But the self-styled 'younger generation of 1968' seemed suddenly to experience a shock of moral and mental separation from their elders. 'Don't trust anybody over thirty' was their rallying cry. Everything that had preceded them, creeds, mores, institutions seemed alien to them, and they refused to have anything to do with them. They did not know what they wanted so well as what they did not want — and what they did not want was rejected with a peculiar lack of discrimination.

Now the transitions from generation to generation always entail a conflict of mentalities — be it only the difference of views between those who regret to have to leave the world and those who are afraid to enter it. To this, especially since the nineteenth century, must be added the brusque changes in the way of living and even more in the way of thinking offered in good time to the newcomers but too late for the others not only to enjoy, but even to understand. To paraphrase Daniel Halévy, as history 'accelerated' its own unfolding more and more, the misunderstandings between parents and children became more frequent and even more abrupt. The break experienced by the generation of 1968 was one of the most vertiginous in the history of mankind. That generation happened to be one of the most 'pre-figurative' generations in the history of the world, Margaret Mead's expression for the generations of young people who impose their conceptions and ways of life on the elders. Time was out of joint. Everything seemed to change at once — from such matters of daily taste like popular music and styles of dancing, to means of knowledge, now computerized, and orientations of knowledge, now turning towards the extra-terrestrial.

Old and new causes produced the 1968 epistemological break. Let us take the new causes which became manifest just then.

The major new cause was the Vietnam war — for it was the revolt of the American students against the questionable way in which they were drafted to fight in a war they rejected which sparked off the students' revolt in the rest of the world. The Vietnam war is highly relevant to the problem of ideology discussed here because it was the culmination of the counter-ideologization of the United States in the ideological 'cold war'. Carried away by the anti-communist crusading spirit, American political and military circles embarked, at the beginning almost imperceptibly, on a difficult operation in an Asian country without specific geo-political importance for their own country, and against the advice of the Western Allies. It was above all an ideological operation, a wrong utilitarian calculation. And the way in which President Johnson allowed it to grow, or indeed steered it towards outright war, sending multitudes of young Americans to their deaths in a particularly cruel war, without informing the American public and electorate (as he was constitutionally bound to do) of the real significance and import of the operation, was a sad example of how those who practise promissory politics hide the *painful* news from the public, for it is not impossible that American public opinion might have backed the President. But his handling of the Vietnam war marked a particularly low point of credibility. This had a very bad effect on the attitude of the young toward constitutional politics – and towards the older generation of politicians.[20]

A second new cause for the generational break was the love–hate relationship between the young and some aspects of modern science. They seemed on the one hand to worship science because it provided 'scientific' opportunities for escapism, with its extra-terrestrial explorations and the science fictional quality of some of its experiments with robots and genetic engineering. But in contrast with the previous generation the revolted young of 1968 hated the practical application of science: the mental discipline and accuracy required by a computer-ridden society frightened them and the excesses of material comfort provided by science and modern technology disgusted them. The hedonistic appetites of their parents, fostered by the techniques of advertising and marketing, aroused their wrath. The young contrasted the self-indulgence in material satisfactions of the society they knew with the poverty which still prevailed in their own countries, and which dominated in the third world – towards which young people felt a sense of guilt. They also contrasted the application of science in the domestic field to increase material satisfactions with its role in the destruction of the environment and in the multiplication of lethal weapons of mass murder. Their disgust at the uses to which science was put merged into one single revolt against the hypocrisy of advanced industrial society as a whole.

But there were other causes for the epistemological break which also now came to a head. By the time the young came to be taught the moral virtues, there were few traditional virtues and commandments left to teach and fewer still who could teach them; secondly, people still felt a deep shame for the horrors perpetrated by the white race in the name of Hitler, and for the European civilization which had nurtured him; thirdly, there was the growing disenchantment with the results of the Russian Revolution and awareness that yet another alternative of human hope had been closed in the closed totalitarian system, and replaced by the pathetic, post-Trotskyist, post-Freudian, Marcusian pursuit of sexual and social liberation. Above all there was a widespread realization that science was unable to reach a comprehensive understanding of life, including human life; that it could not provide a rational antidote to the overwhelming sense of the absurd.

That sense of the absurd was probably fundamental to the psychology

[20] An earlier example was Lord Beaverbrook's statement to the Royal Commission on the Press that his newspapers had minimized the dangers of Hitler's aggression because the advertisers had asked him to do so. And a later example was Watergate.

and the behaviour of the young of 1968 — and probably the line of thought which influenced them most derived from such prophets of the absurd as Heidegger and Sartre, or the playwrights Becket and Ionesco, who as Jean Marie Domenach observes,[21] found the absurd so absolute that they transformed it from a tragic sense into a comic sense. Their plays, among the most tragic in the history of drama, are comedies, and very amusing too, especially in the case of Ionesco. However the comedies of Ionesco and Becket are different. While the former achieves his aims with witty dialogue, Becket reaches the deeper spheres of emotion, indeed the catharsis of the spectator with his laconic symbolism and mime.

Then there were the prophets of sex. Alleged heirs of Freud and of D.H. Lawrence, these prophets taught men to liberate themselves by consuming themselves on the sacrificial pyre of sexual passion. The theme of the erotic dominated artistic production in all fields in the 1960s. But here, much more and more categorically than in the preaching of the absurd, commercialism took over. Pornography, as already frequently mentioned, became one of the most profitable industries.

Closely associated with the prophets of sex were the prophets of psychedelism.[22] Psychedelism had appeared in modern philosophy when Aldous Huxley had started this experiment with men's minds; and philosophers like Reich or Lacan gave it, each in his own way, further scholarly endorsement. Then it moved into a pseudo-science, as the American professor Timothy Leary experimented 'scientifically' with the beneficial effects of new chemical drugs like LSD on sexual capacity, or rather on orgasmic capacity, in coition or masturbation. Then finally, drugs by themselves, with the object of assisting escapism by hallucination, made commercial inroads into the life of modern society — and especially among the young. 'Drug pushing' is a most important multinational industry which makes exceptionally high profits.

Behind all these causes there lay the original cause of the liberal—utilitarian pursuit of progressive permissiveness. Now that progressive permissiveness had been implicitly accepted by society, toleration of all kinds of behaviour had reached the point when society was required to give explicit, legal or even sacramental confirmation, or financial assistance to some non-normal kinds of behaviour. Judicial authority was for instance given for the supply of contraceptives by doctors to girls under the age of consent, without the knowledge of their parents, and public money was specifically allotted for special cultural centres for sexual deviants. The inherent inclination of more ideologized sections of public opinion in welfare circles towards the marginals and the handicapped, and the concern of social workers with the problem personalities on the

---

[21] Jean Marie Domenach; *Le retour du tragique,* Paris 1967.

[22] Possibly the most perverted words in the extraordinary modern vocabulary are those of *psyche* and *delic,* in the current expression 'psychedelic' — for they wanted to lose their *'psyche'* in the ecstasy of physical pleasure thus doing the very thing which runs contrary to clarity and lucidity — which is the meaning of 'delos'.

social fringe also furthered this new aspiration to legitimize actions previously considered logically and biologically abnormal, outside the norms, *abnormis.*

The escalation of permissiveness was leading to situations which logically and biologically made *no sense.* To take only three examples from a brief glance at a newspaper. A progressive priest has officiated at a wedding between two women. This is nonsense because marriage is the consecration of the right of a man and a woman to procreate. Two women cannot procreate, and even if one were artificially inseminated, the semen would still come from a *man.* The second example concerns the — by now failed — efforts to legitimize the right of 'paedophiles' to have sexual intercourse with children provided the child consents. This too is logically and biologically nonsensical for a child of tender age is biologically unable to take an active part in sexual intercourse and logically incapable of giving an informed consent to any such act. Thirdly the Private Bill to limit the sale of 'video-nasties', given its first reading at great speed in 1983 by the House of Commons, illustrated the new danger of the spread of vice and debauchery *in any private house*, by way of technical reproduction and commercial distribution.

The attempts to prevent the distribution of 'video-nasties' have however still been seen with scepticism by leading modern philosophers. They are sceptical on the one hand, about the ability of the authorities to stop the profitable trade in pornography even should it be banned. This is a reasonable argument — one cannot see how the police could raid private houses and flats to catch people watching 'nasties'. On the other hand, they have serious doubts about the right of the authorities to prevent people from watching horrible films if they 'like them'. This too is a fair point.

But what is lost in the argument is precisely the difference between the margin allowed to the existence of vice in any society and the legal and commercial institutionalization of vice in the liberal industrial society. This difference consists of three clear distinctions. The first is that any previous society, while publicly disapproving of vice and perversions, knew that they could not be eradicated — whereas in the permissive industrial society entire categories of previously disapproved ways of behaviour are 'permitted' and encouraged. This social endorsement of abnormalities made the first difference. Secondly, in the characteristically publicity-ridden industrial society the trend of progressive permissiveness penetrated all strata of the population regardless of their geographical location, social category, occupation or especially age. The knowledge and temptation of vice spread everywhere, benefiting from the all-pervasive publicity and from the moral endorsement of the society. And, thirdly, in the conditions thus created of *permissible* mass-corruption, the commercial profitability of the vice-trade became the overwhelming factor. Organized prostitution and 'chains' of sex-shops, written and video pornography and last but not least drug-pushing became some of the most profitable occupations in industrial society as a whole — and therefore created powerful interest-groups thriving on vice.

By the 1970s there seemed to be no limits to the degeneration of moral rules into the absurd; and society seemed to be reaching the point where, as Stuart Hampshire would put it, people should be reminded that moral commandments should be carried over into a secular morality.[23] That new generations coming to maturity in this moral climate should find society and its rules 'absurd' was only too understandable.

What effect did the revolt of the self-styled 'generation of 1968' have on the young as a whole? What were young people ultimately seeking?

Ronald Inglehart, whose perceptive book *The Silent Revolution, Changing Values and Political Styles among Western Publics*, has already been mentioned here, encapsulates the whole question in one hypothesis as follows: 'the values of western publics have been shifting from an overwhelming emphasis on material well-being and physical security toward greater emphasis on the quality of life'. In order to check empirically on his hypothesis he conducted a particularly well-organized survey of Western European public opinion, on the basis of a questionnaire containing an equal number of questions indicating 'materialist goals' and 'postmaterialist goals',[24] on the understanding that 'emphasis on order and economic stability might be termed a materialist set of value priorities. By contrast, choice of the items concerning free speech or political participation reflects emphasis on two post-materialist values'.[25] Applying the theories of the psychologist A. Maslow to the socio-cultural and political fields, Inglehart found that 'in every case, the materialists greatly outnumber the post-materialist type among the older age cohorts, but the balance shifts in favour of the post-materialists as we move to the younger cohorts'.[26]

---

[23] 'The sacredness of life, so called, and the absolute prohibitions against the taking of life, except under strictly defined conditions, may be admitted to be human inventions. Once the human origin of the prohibitions has been recognised, the prohibition against the taking of life, and respect for human life as such, may still be reaffirmed as absolute. They are reaffirmed as complementary to a set of customs, habits and observances, which are understood by reference to their function, and which are sustained, partly because of, partly in spite of, this understanding: I mean sexual customs, family observances, ceremonial treatment of the dead, gentle treatment of those who are diseased and useless, and of the old and senile, customs of war and treatment of prisoners, treatment of convicted criminals, political and legal safeguards for the rights of individuals, and the customary rituals of respect and gentleness in personal dealings. This complex of habits, and the rituals associated with them, are carried over into a secular morality.' Stuart Hampshire: *Public and Private Morality,* Cambridge, 1978, pp. 17–18.

[24] The first four were: 'maintaining order in the nation'; 'giving the people more say in important political decisions'; 'fighting rising prices' and 'protecting freedom of speech', loc. cit., p. 28.

[25] Ibid., p. 29.

[26] Ibid., p. 32.

TABLE
Value Types by Age Cohort: Combined 1970 and 1971 Data (Per cent of Materialists [Mats] and Post-Materialists [P.-Mats])

Age range of cohort in 1971	Germany			Belgium			Italy			France			Netherlands			Britain[a]		
	Mats (%)	P.-Mats (%)	N	Mats. (%)	P.-Mats (%)	N	Mats. (%)	P.-Mats (%)	N	Mats. (%)	P.-Mats (%)	N	Mats. (%)	P.-Mats. (%)	N	Mats (%)	P.-Mats N (%)	
16–25	22	22	(544)	20	26	(487)	28	21	(757)	25	20	(754)	26	20	(770)	29	13	(508)
26–35	36	14	(895)	29	16	(429)	37	13	(650)	38	13	(726)	25	14	(696)	28	10	(680)
36–45	47	9	(768)	29	16	(473)	39	9	(735)	40	12	(697)	38	11	(717)	31	8	(556)
46–55	47	7	(663)	30	11	(378)	46	6	(710)	43	10	(649)	34	12	(547)	35	6	(796)
56–65	58	4	(593)	36	9	(409)	48	6	(571)	50	5	(533)	39	7	(455)	41	6	(662)
66+	55	4	(474)	46	5	(474)	55	3	(400)	52	3	(700)	52	5	(324)	47	4	(748)
Difference between youngest and oldest groups	−33	+19		−26	+21		−27	+18		−27	+17		−19·	+15		−18	+9	
Total difference	52 points			47 points			45 points			44 points			34 points			27 points		

[a]Results from a survey carried out in 1971 by the British Social Science Research Council are combined with those from our own British sample in this table.
Source: R. Inglehart, *The Silent Revolution*, p. 31.

Inglehart's intelligent investigation suffers from three limitations. One is that it was applied to one generation only, and in so far as the 1968 generation remains singular in history, the conclusions that can be drawn from its study are bound to be limited. In a more recent article Inglehart shows that although what he calls post-materialism still seems to colour the mentality of almost half the people interviewed in the 1970s 'the recession of the mid-1970s also produced significant period effects'.[27] The second limitation suffered by the study is that it examines only the West European industrial states, leaving out of the field of enquiry not only Japan, but the United States itself, which is where the students' protest originated and then spread to the rest of the industrial — and the non-industrial — world. Its findings can thus not be applied to industrial society as a whole. And, thirdly, and more relevant for this enquiry, the concept of post-materialistic is somewhat unclear. Obviously Inglehart does not want to use 'idealist' — which would be the opposite to materialistic. And indeed as far as the moral attitudes of the 1968 student revolt — notably in the United States, France and West Germany — are concerned they were materialistic, indeed hedonistic, in the sense that they worshipped eroticism ('make love not war' was yet another of their slogans) and other pleasures of their own. They rejected the material comfort of their parents, but they showed an even greater avidity for their own kind of pleasures. Their behaviour itself was direct and they were consistent in their denunciation of 'bourgeois hypocrisy'; even their scruffy way of dressing was a form of protest against urban customs.

More than post-materialistic, I would be inclined to describe the students of 1968 as unrealistic. Everything about them, from their political revolutionary actions, to their fundamental inadaptability to industrial society, had a distinct character of unreality. Indeed probably their most salient characteristic was escapism (the 'stop-the-world-I-want-to-get-off' syndrome). Their obsessive eroticism was escapist; their political actions were escapist[28] although authoritarian and violent; many of them were also drug-addicts, which is the ultimate form of escapism. They hated the not particularly attractive reality of the industrial society, but were very far from proposing any real solutions for replacing it 'after the revolution' — to use Dahl's expression — let alone for improving it. They were the dramatic children of progressive permissiveness and of the promise of happiness which through them and with them was now reaching its bitter disenchantment.

[27] R. Inglehart, 'Post-materialism in an environment of insecurity', *American Political Science Review*, 75, No. 4, December 1981. Roberto Cartucci in an interesting article 'I valori post-materialisti dieci anni doppo' in *Rivista Italiana di Scienza Politica*, 3, 1983, remarks also that Inglehart's questionnaires were circulated among 'better read' young people: students and affluent workers more numerous in the new generation.

[28] One of the most relevant documents on the political psychology of 1968 is the 1983 verbatim report of the '7 April' group of Italian university teachers, practising armed terrorism for the achievement of an 'autonomous' revolution.

But soon the reality of the economic crisis was going to put an end to this long spell of illusions.

The crisis which started in 1973 with the rise in oil prices, when inflation had reached alarming proportions in Great Britain and the United States, can be described as though it were a fable: too many people in these welfare states had spent too much and worked too little. A 1983 OECD paper showed that since 1960 public expenditure on pensions, health and other social expenditures had been almost twice as fast as GDP. Society now had to pay and accept considerable restrictions. Monetarism came back with a vengeance, not only as a monetary and financial technique, but also as a new doctrine of government. Political monetarist leaders addressed the public in a reproachful way, as though society was, as it were, expected to repent.

In reality, though, it was the welfare 'state' itself which was at stake — for what might have broken down in the exercise was its balancing mechanism. Indeed, by the end of the period, in the mid-1970s, both from the social and from the economic point of view doubts were expressed about the viability of the welfare state.

From the social point of view, the critics pointed out that the welfare state — especially in Britain — had not produced a single, comprehensive social policy; that the isolated welfare services were still considered to be acts of charity of the state toward the 'poor' — instead of being recognized as the natural function of a compassionate society; that in the absence of a distributive social policy the poor have become poorer and the rich richer; and that even those welfare institutions which survived, notably social security services, were now threatened with being dismantled for 'economic' reasons.

From the economic point of view it was argued that overburdened by public expenditure and hypertrophied by its growing share of total economic resources, the state had become a principal obstacle to the productive functioning of the economy. In turn the deficiency in that functioning affected the welfare potential of the welfare state. Theodore Geiger concluded his expert study entitled *Welfare and Efficiency: Their Interactions in Western Europe,*[29] by showing that most West European countries, with the exception of Germany, 'have been experiencing in different ways and varying degrees the adverse effects of "negative-seen" Welfare efficiency relations in the course of the 1970s', that in other words they had suffered significant losses of efficiency and eventually of welfare as well. Geiger argued that for the first time since the Second World War real income had declined, in the 1970s, with the result that, under conditions of stagflation, a popular attitude developed directed against the system as a whole. This attitude Geiger noted 'manifested itself not in an ideological shift to the Right or to the Left, but in opposition to whichever type of government was in office and hence was regarded as

[29] National Planning Association, New York 1978. See also Pierre Rosanvallon: *La crise de l'état-providence,* Paris, 1981.

199

responsible for the halt in welfare improvement and in the growth of the after-tax earned income'.

So, even in public opinion, the wheel had turned full circle: it was now efficiency which was sought. The economic point of view had reasserted its practical primacy: if production stops redistribution has to stop. But the renewed primacy of the economic point of view had the inevitable effect, as noted by Geiger, of polarizing the attitudes of public opinion towards the extremes: radical monetarist conservatism and radical state-controlling socialism. The room for manoeuvre of the centrist, or bi-partisan, majorities which had characterized the governments of the United States, Great Britain and West Germany during the four decades after the Second World War shrank dramatically after the entry on to the political stage of these more radical postures: monetarist versus New Left.

The monetarists easily won the first round, not only because a mone-tarist government came to power in Britain (and was elected a second time), the United States — Denmark — and the Federal Republic of Germany — but also, and specially, because the socialist governments elected in the meantime in France since 1982, Sweden since 1983 and Spain, drastically cut their electoral promises for increased social pro-vision and adopted monetarist policies. And the electorate endorsed the welfare cuts.

In the whole of industrial society which had been wooed for the last fifty years by the liberal—utilitarian system of political happiness another form of politics seemed to be about to begin.[30]

At the beginning of the 1980s the two systems of political happi-ness — and their ideologies — were submitted to a long hard look by their respective populations.

It is ironical that what still kept them going was the ideological 'cold war' which one had launched against the other, thus forcing both to fight each other, while from within both the ideologies themselves had lost

---

[30] A historical anecdote may serve to indicate how and when the attitudes of modern European policy-makers woke up to the fact that a move away from the old style of politics was becoming inevitable. In a book which was perhaps insufficiently noticed Mr Douglas Hurd (Douglas Hurd: *The End of Promises,* London 1977) who was Edward Heath's Parliamentary Private Secretary during his Prime Ministership and until his fall, affirms that Heath's decision to call the early and, to him, fatal election in 1974, was caused not so much by the need to have a popular answer to the ques-tion 'who governs', Parliament or the unions, but by the need to win a new electoral mandate for new policies, for new information to be given to the electorate, and for a new background to politics to be established. Because of his interest in general per-spectives, further widened by the broad comparative vistas which were opened to him as a European statesman, Mr Heath had, according to Mr Hurd, come to believe that the world had now reached a point where it was no longer capable of satisfying the constantly rising expectations of its constantly rising population. People had to be told the truth — and the British people who had elected him had to be told the truth by him. But this implied a change in the whole style of politics as usually practised in parliamentary regimes — from essentially promissory politics to consultative politics.

their credibility. But here, in the field of geo-politics and the struggle for world-domination, ideologization and counter-ideologization were engaged in an unprecedented escalation. The causes and the effects of the deliberate escalation were however very different in reality from what they were presented as, and were considered to be. As far as the effects are concerned it must be noted that: a) by the 1980s the armaments race presented in the form of 'defence policy' in communist ideologization and in liberal counter-ideologization was beginning to have negative effects: human beings, openly in the liberal industrial societies and mutedly in the communist societies, were beginning to be more frightened than re-assured by the escalating menace of 'defence' and of 'security' their governments bestowed upon them; and b) in reality the proliferation of nuclear weaponry and war-games reached the point where they resembled very closely the eventualities of science-fiction, where in other words the damage inflicted by such a war would result in the physical annihilation of the industrial society.

As for the causes, what was not sufficiently appreciated was that not only were the now dominant communist ideologization and liberal counter-ideologization in the field of international relations typical examples of the estrangement of *ideologization* from its respective *ideology* (both communist and liberal *ideologies* were implicitly and explicitly pacifist and internationalistic); they were now typical examples of the substitution through the same channels and methods of ideologization used in both ways, of a third ideology, which both communism and liberalism had criticized and rejected in the past, namely nationalism. In both cases the rationale of the debate was now merely and simply nationalistic — or indeed *super-nationalistic*.

AN ASIDE ON CURRENT FOREIGN RELATIONS

This was indeed the extraordinary double deformation inflicted on world politics by the two ideological systems: that on the one hand they continued their ideological domination, that is domination by ideological precepts and ideological parties although in the exercise each of them had exchanged its ideology for nationalism; and that, on the other hand, they succeeded in spite of their internationalistic claims, in dividing the essentially multi- and transnational industrial society, which therefore requires *supra*-national regulation of its functioning, into two *super*-nationalistic camps, irremediably opposed to each other in the common belief that the survival of one of them can only be achieved by 'burying' the other, to use Khrushchev's metaphor.

In communist theory and especially in Marxism—Leninism, the revolutionary expansion in the whole world is not only the main ideal, it is also the sine-qua-non condition of its existence. The system itself cannot be established until the whole planet is brought under its control. According to the same theory, as long as the territory over which the Revolution has triumphed is 'encircled' by capitalist/imperialist powers, the Revolution itself cannot develop normally — it has to give priority to the 'defence' of that territory and is therefore forced to distort the advance of Communism for the time being. This theory, or psychology, of encirclement has been strangely confirmed in communist logic (or communist lack of logic) since Communist China has been charged by the Communist Party and the government of the USSR with threatening the USSR militarily along its longest frontier and with an enormous demographic potential for armed aggression.

Liberal theory also requires, at least in principle, the opening up of all frontiers in the world for free trade, free information and free movement in general. For liberalism too the fragmentation of the world into territorial patches of politically and economically hostile states is seen as relatively incompatible with the establishment of a truly liberal economy and polity. (Though it is not so totally incompatible with a liberal system as the continued existence of liberal oases is with communism).

But while this theoretical incompatibility of the two systems, each necessitating world expansion, was first proclaimed in terms of internationalistic rhetoric and logic — now it is proclaimed in nationalistic terms.

An analysis of why and how the ideology of Soviet Communism was diverted from its very inception as a nation-state into the nationalist ideology of 'socialism in one state', and, after taking over the succession of the entire Russian 'Empire' into 'imperialism', has already been offered in this book: (see pp. 142—6); as well as a description of the decline and fall of Marxist—Leninist ideology from its role of supreme justification and legitimization of the system (see pp. 176—9). But what must be stressed now is the effect that this nationalistic ideologization has had on the counterideologization of liberalism. The ideologization prevalent now in matters of national security in the camp of the liberal democracies, and notably in the leader of the camp, the United States, is the result of the 'counterideologization' suffered by that country, in response to the nationalistimperialist Soviet ideology. And the new nuclear escalation is conducted by both super powers in terms of unprecedented super-nationalism.

President Reagan has been criticized both at home and abroad for having introduced this super-nationalism into American foreign policy, for seeing 'the world through the prism not of history but of ideology', for proclaiming that the United States is infinitely virtuous and that the Soviet Union is infinitely wicked' as Arthur Schlesinger put it in one of the early criticisms.[31] Schlesinger then tries to prove his case by quoting

[31] A. Schlesinger Jr., 'Foreign policy and the American character', in *Foreign Affairs*, Fall, 1983.

some of President Reagan's most strident super nationalistic utterances as, for instance, 'this anointed land was set apart in an uncommon way, (that) a divine plan placed this great continent here between the oceans to be found by people from every corner of the earth who had a special love of faith and freedom'; and such flagrant declarations of incompatibility and irreconcilability with the other super power as, for instance, that the USSR is 'an evil empire' or 'the focus of evil in the modern world', the struggle now is 'between right and wrong and good and evil' and therefore 'we are enjoined by scripture and the Lord Jesus to oppose it with all our might'; or in a clearly geopolitical definition of the modern world as a chess-game in which one player makes all his moves in a characteristically offensive way: 'The Soviet Union underlies all the unrest that is going on. If they weren't engaged in this game of dominos there wouldn't be any hot spots in the world'.

The last statement differs from the others in two respects. On the one hand instead of emphasizing again the providential, indeed, almost divine virtues of the American nation and its subsequent right to lead the world — we are told here that America is led by necessity into a world wide confrontation by the relentless global attack of the USSR, the object of which is to use all geopolitical positions and political events in the world to its *strategic* advantage, with one purpose in view: world domination. With due reservations regarding the independent players still active on the chess set of the two super powers (European integration could, if the political will had existed, interpose a powerful independent friend and necessarily pacifist player — and Khomeini's Islamic brigade might still surprise the embattled super powers) — Reagan's justification of America's current attempt to reduce the overall military superiority of the USSR makes *strategic* sense. And if the whole relation between the two camps is now expressed in strategic terms, this is primarily because of the change operated, as we have seen, in the background of the ideologization of the USSR from that of the Communist Party's revolutionary attempt at world domination, to that of the advance of the Revolution through the military might of the Soviet Army. For the Red Army is now an apparat which is gradually influencing the policy-making processes of the industrial-military complex which rules the USSR, and the only sector which shows real progress within the overall decline of the Soviet Empire.

On the other hand, while it is true to say that President Reagan's portrayal, or at any rate ideological presentation, of world-policy as a strategic contest between two camps is particularly virulent — this should not make us forget that the same ideological argument has been used by at least the last four American Presidents and Administrations. President Johnson was inspired by the idea of freedom, one and indivisible, to be defended by democracies all over the world, when he got bogged down in the Vietnam war, the lasting consequences of which have already been examined here. (See p. 192). The Nixon–Kissinger team which had to put an end to the losing Vietnam adventure, wrapped its strategy in *Realpolitik* terms of direct dialogue between the super powers so as to discern their incidental common interests rather than their permanent incompatibility, the military and strategic points of utilitarian adjustment rather than the ideological economic, social and political irreconcilability. 'We were not abandoning the ideological struggle but simply trying — tall order as it was — to discipline it by precepts of the national interest . . . Detente defined not friendship but a strategy for a relationship among adversaries';[32] while Brezhnev like Khrushchev explained 'co-existence' in terms identical with those of Lenin's motivation. But disarmament could have been a common 'interest' had the USSR played fair — under Nixon defence spending dropped from 44 per cent to 24 per cent — and the Salt I agreement is still applied, as is also Salt II, although still not signed. Finally both super powers had a common interest in halting the progress of the European integration — especially after the entry of Great Britain; this has coincided with the great crisis of stagnation and possible disintegration of the European Community, caused mainly by the nationalism of the governments of the member states. Meanwhile Kissinger's *Realpolitik* achieved the master stroke of an opening towards Communist China, the most dangerous strategic and military communist rival of the USSR.

Yet because of the stigma of the Watergate affair into which Nixon had been led by futile but inexorable party-politics, and because of the bitterness of the defeat in Vietnam, the American nation was in greater need of a world-ideology. President Carter came to power by the deeply shocked nation to clear the polluted political atmosphere. He brought with him a refurbished ideology of the American defence of Human Rights all over the world — one of the direct results of which was the heroic unrest in Poland. But the US had neither the political will (President Carter proved to be personally unable to take decisions) nor the military strength to pursue such a policy. Whereas the military-industrial complex which runs the USSR had both the political will (the Soviet Army succeeded in replacing the disintegrated Polish Party with the Polish Army) and the military strength — (the 'liberation' in Afghanistan was the continuation in Asia of the Brezhnev doctrine, until then limited only to Eastern Europe). Just before the defeat of President Carter in the presidential elections of 1980 his principal strategic adviser, Brzezinski had time to give the green light for the first time to the Pentagon 'to prepare for prolonged but limited nuclear war'.[33]

The Reagan Administration came to power on the strong backlash of

[32] Henry Kissinger *The White House Years,* Boston 1979, p. 1049.

[33] 'In fairness to the Reagan Administration Wieselher notes that it was the Carter Administration (on the frantic urging of the national security adviser Zbigniew Brzezinski), and against the opposition of the State Department, that issued Presidential Directive 59 in July 1980, which called for developing a capacity to wage 'prolonged but limited nuclear war'. George W. Ball 'Sovietizing US Policy' in *The New York Review of Books,* 2 February, 1984.

the neo-conservatives and as a result of the real anxiety in the liberal camp about Soviet military superiority. It issued a new 'Defence Guidance', the purpose of which was to ensure that American nuclear forces 'must prevail and be able to force the Soviet Union to seek earliest termination on terms favourable to the United States'. The real nuclear race was now on. Essential to the US, or Western superiority, in the eyes of the American and most European governments (that of Helmut Schmidt, Margaret Thatcher, François Mitterand, to take only the three principal ones) was the deployment in Europe of the Pershing and Cruise missiles. When this was achieved it led the USSR to break off negotiations in Geneva between the USA and the USSR. Super-nationalism was quickly transforming the ideological cold war into what could be called more accurately the hot peace. A moment had been reached, and a situation had been created in which the antagonism between the two systems, qua ideological systems, i.e. which of them will bring real happiness to man-kind, was replaced by the antagonism between two states, the USA and the USSR, in terms of in which of them were human beings happier, and therefore likely to make mankind happy, and which of them had greater strength, so as to achieve universal happiness by obliteratin the other? This was the situation of super nationalism (the very opposite of the supra nationalism required by the industrial society) which has created the tension preceeding the actual confrontation.

Such a changed situation aroused public opinion to the danger of the infernal dance of ideological escalation, which had now been transformed into a super-nationalistic, military and strategic, escalation. The purely ideological 'unilateralist' campaign so widely waged in the whole of Western Europe as long as the USSR still hoped that it would be possible to prevent the arrival of the Pershing and Cruise missiles in Europe, failed. Although the 'unilateralist' campaign was at its highest and noisiest in the two principal countries involved in that operation, Britain and the Federal Republic of Germany, their voters elected conservative governments which deliberately included in their electoral platforms the intensification of collaboration in nuclear defence with the USA.

But this aside on the current ideologization of international relations must come to an end here, and we must return to the overall effects of the ideologization of society in the 1980s.

Chapter 10

Disideologization

So the crisis had resulted neither in the revolution hoped for by the revolutionaries of 1968, nor in the collapse feared by the economists of 1970. Had a Martian looked at the earth through his telescope in the 1980s, he could have seen the human anthill continuing its activity as frantically as ever — indeed more frantically than ever before since the number of people had increased still further, and people were whizzing around the air, the seas and the roads of their 'global village' more frequently and faster than ever before.

Seen from the inside, however, there were many changes, two of which are particularly relevant to this enquiry. One will be briefly noticed, the other will occupy the rest of these conclusions. The first change took place in the mentality of the new generation which was now taking over. The latest technological revolution, that of electronics, had brought in its train a new, scientifically induced, perception which had greatly differentiated the understanding of the incoming children from that of the departing parents. The inner retina of children was suffused with television images perceived before they could understand them, and their favourite toys were now electronic games and baby computers, while most of their parents left this earth without ever having understood how they worked and what they did. As a result, the newcomers seemed more precocious and *blasé* than any previous generation. How, and whether, their new empathetic predispositions were to affect their capacities and the means they would employ to regulate their co-existence in the twenty-first century the people of the twentieth century could not know.

But a change in politics had already occurred as a result of the crisis of the last decades of the twentieth century, and this is the second point on which this chapter will dwell. Ideological politics had reached, in both systems, a critical point from which people in industrial societies could see, behind them, why and how they had followed the wrong paths, and before them, the pitfalls into which the consequences of those errors might lead. People in the utilitarian-liberal system, notably the middle classes which now included also the skilled workers, wondered whether the mentality of progressive permissiveness was leading their society to economic and moral crises. People in communist dictatorial systems had been able to witness most spectacularly since the crisis in Czechoslovakia in 1968 and the crisis in Poland in the 1980s the functional incompatibility between the ideologically and politically monolithic system and the essentially pluralistic, interdependent and participatory industrial technological society.

Moreover everyone could observe, at the dawn of the 1980s, after the Soviet invasion of Afghanistan, how the 'cold war', an exclusively ideological affair, was hotting up, as the nuclear armament race took on an unprecedented rhythm, and the super-nationalism of the super powers led to unprecedented tension. The thousands of 'conflict-spots' scattered around on the planetary war-board of the systems became so many potential Sarajevos. Modern man had thus many reasons to reflect on the dysfunctionalism of the ideologies, as he watched with mounting anguish the local developments in each trouble-spot, from Nicaragua to the Chad, from Beirut to Sakhalin, wondering when and where the finger would pull the nuclear trigger of ideological war.

Now, as already intimated at the end of the last chapter, the systems had shown, in the light of their simultaneous crises, how dysfunctional ideological politics had become even for professional politicians. In consequence they had begun to tone down some of their most ideological accents. In the communist–dictatorial system, both the ideology and the party were eclipsed. A regime like that which obtained in Poland, the core of which was a Petainist military dictatorship trying to reach a *modus vivendi* with the Catholic Church, was still unjustifiably described as a communist state. Nor could the Hungarian, the Chinese, or the Cuban regimes be regarded as representing Marxist–Leninist thought. Rather, the immobilism of Soviet political ideology represented the true situation of that thought. For, in general terms the millenarian promise of a world-revolution was now actually replaced by the expectation of the ultimate military victory of the Soviet forces in the cold and hot war they were waging against the other system.

In the utilitarian–liberal system, as we have also intimated, austerity-minded governments, conservative as in Britain, the United States and the Federal Republic of Germany, or socialist as in Sweden, France and Spain, were trying to steer the wheel of welfare in the direction of economic effectiveness rather than social providence, and the wheel of the mixed economy towards the private rather than the public sector. That three socialist and three conservative governments should follow almost the same policies was yet another proof of the extent to which the sharp light of the crisis had led to a fading of the ideological tints. And the fact that the sober frankness of these governments went down well with the majority of their peoples was also proof that by then those majorities enjoyed a comfortable average standard of living and were now integrated in a way of life which they wanted to preserve even against their own further hedonistic appetites.

But that was still not enough, first, because to take the most popular example, the excessive rise in unemployment illustrated clearly how active was the principle of social involvement, of almost automatic interdependence, in industrial society. All felicific calculi went wrong; their programmes were rejected by the implacable computers; their principle of the greatest happiness for the greatest number was made to sound merely cynical. The dilemma of the interdependence of socio-economic factors was illustrated by the contradiction between the growth in welfare expenditure and the rate of unemployment.

A gulf had been opened, and grew increasingly wider, between political circles and the different spheres of society. New governments were elected in the welfare states without an absolute electoral majority.[1] Significantly the more ideological parties, like the British Labour party, were the main losers. Socio-economic groups were seeking emancipation from their traditional political tutelage, notably the members of trade unions. Large numbers of the generation of 1980 were aroused by the dangers of nuclear war as a possible result of the ideological confrontation of the two systems. The centres of regulation of industrial societies had now become particularly unstable.

Yet the fragmentation of the tight processes of policy-making, characteristic of an advanced industrial society, is what most hinders its proper functioning, which is based on the functional interdependence and the involvement of most individuals. Every unemployed person is dependent upon society, and each employed person involves all those who are linked by a functional chain reaction with his work.

As outlined in the Introduction, the answer to the political involvement which an industrial society engenders is the demand for political participation. This demand was made quite explicit in both systems in the crisis of 1968. Its fulfilment in the communist—dictatorial system was of course out of the question — the techniques of mobilization still replace participation in that system. But in the utilitarian—liberal system, political participation was not only feasible, it was also particularly necessary if the society as a whole was to function at all. The fact that political participation was being withdrawn or dispersed, and that signs of political apathy were appearing, was a bad omen for the liberal system which thrives on its self-regulatory mechanism.

Yet the reasons for this change to the worse were clear. People were disappointed with the promissory techniques of ideological politics, once the promises had been shown up as illusions. The belief that 'all politicians cheat' or that 'politics is just lies' spread very easily. In order to restore confidence and re-activate the sources of participation a political effort to

---

[1] In the last three general elections in Britain.

tell people the true facts and to let them judge for themselves was necessary.

In other words what was required was disideologization, or the return of politics to a more neutral role. And this necessitated the modification of the promissory techniques. Some of the political parties began to make the effort to speak to the people without ideological parables. But people who had been brusquely awakened to the realities of industrial society demanded a far greater degree of disideologization. It remained to be seen whether this could be provided by the ideologized political personnel, and by the also ideologized and ideologizing 'media'. Would a new type of regulatory agency and agents have to emerge in liberal society to manage these changes? Above all, could disideologization succeed? Could politics leave behind the obsolete form of ideological politics?

There are three ways to achieve disideologization: institutional disideologization, political disideologization and moral disideologization. They will now be briefly examined.

INSTITUTIONAL DISIDEOLOGIZATION

Law, and notably constitutional law, established political institutions and processes so that they should be accessible to all the people in a unit of rule, generation after generation. Some fundamental political institutions are permanent because they are essential in practice. Representation, that is representation of different communities at different times, is the sole alternative to consulting all the citizens, whether they are interested or indifferent, knowledgeable or incompetent, by keeping them together permanently in one single gigantic arena. One of the reasons why the Greeks, to whom Rousseau always referred us, did not practise representation was that they preferred not to, otherwise how could they exclude the women and the slaves? Another practical and long-lasting political institution is the separation of powers, the political form of the division of labour in a society, and at the same time the institutionalization of three successive phases of decision-making — the stuff of politics: formulation in the legislature, implementation in the executive, verification in the judiciary.

Nevertheless, law in its perennial moral function and the political institutions and processes which it sets up need to be adapted by successive generations to changes occurring in the way of life and therefore of co-existence. No greater change in the way of living has ever been recorded than the change from pre-industrial to industrial society — 'the greater transformation'. And yet the political institutions and processes in which the industrial society still functions have not been transformed sufficiently to make them fit the industrial technological society instead of confining it and distorting it. Since, as previously argued, it is an essentially participatory society, it needs to be disideologized for two important reasons. One is in order to obtain a reasonable political participation. The other is in order to match the functional character of industrial society by a functional interpretation of developments.

The word 'reasonable' in the expression 'reasonable participation' must be taken in a twofold sense. The political participation of the human being or the attention he gives to the regulation of his co-existence should be *reasonable* in the sense of proportionate to the primary attention he gives to his self-realization as a human being. ('Love thy neighbour as thyself.') And secondly, reasonable, like rational, means 'made with reason'. A man involved in public affairs should be able to form his own judgement on those affairs by using his reason in assessing the issues which are submitted to his decision or advice. His judgement should be as free and impartial as possible in assessing goals or methods. It follows therefore that if political participation is to be reasonable, it must be kept free from the influence of ideology, the role of which is to absorb the whole man into the sphere of politics and to lead his judgement away from the actual issues into global reasonings which are alleged to lead towards a final and unique goal: the changing by politics of the materialistic human condition.

Even a brief reflection will show that the alternative, and main, obstacle to reasonable political participation on the basis of policies for issues is ideological political participation, the participation exacted by the ideological political party. The following is a clear presentation of the ideological point of view by Mr Robin Cook, Labour MP for Edinburgh:

> The one thing the Labour Party has in abundance is a catalogue of policies. The difficulty is that they are presented precisely as that, without any attempt to identify our priorities or describe how each policy relates to the others. Marx would have recognized in our recent manifesto a parody of all the faults to be expected in a reformist party . . . What is our idea of Utopia? That is not a question which can be answered by reference to a policy on import penetration or ceilings or a description of the national economic assessment. (*Guardian*, 1 July 1983)

Surprising in this context is the reference to Marx and his critique of a 'reformist party', that is a party which does not bind together all issues and problems into one *single* goal: the revolution; and after the revolution, the single orientation of all policies towards one single goal again. This goal is candidly described by the author as 'Utopia'. Ideological argument requires the subordination of all issues to one overall priority, and it requires that this priority should be a Utopia. The advantage of a Utopia for all ideological policy-makers is that it is by definition unattainable.

On the other hand, a reasonable political participation favours the presentation of the problems of human co-existence as issues, which can, logically and morally, be *related* to each other by the 'goal' of making that co-existence as smooth as possible. For only when that smoothness is achieved can the society acquire the flexibility needed for its adaptation to future developments.

Issues themselves can be divided into retrospective issues, that is to say the examination of past performance, and prospective issues, namely the examination of problems in the light of foreseeable future developments. In this sense, it is clear that prospective issues offer more scope for normative approaches. Historians[2] remind us that in the history of British politics during the period of the consolidation of political parties, after 1832, the issues put before the electorate were frequently retrospective: the government presented its record in power and 'submitted to the judgement of the people the propriety of past policy'.[3] The practice[4] was presumably based on at least two assumptions. The first of these is the assumption that a positive experience in the past justifies the hope of a repeat performance in the future. As a corollary of this the second is that problems and issues repeat themselves because of the unchangeability of the essentials of the human condition. Successive generations face the same problems in the regulation of their co-existence, within changing contexts. These contexts had been constantly improving in the material sense in the first century or so of the industrial revolutions. To that extent therefore people were justified in thinking in terms of progress.

Because the issues were presented separately to the electorate or to public opinion, if such expressions can really be used for the small and restricted groups of the eighteenth century, they in turn were meant to assess them as such. Moreover in the mediaeval parliaments, and even until the seventeenth century the decisions taken on these issues had strong analogies with a 'sentence' passed after a judgement, as in a judicial instance. While they were taking stands meant to be for or against the issue, the Members of Parliament were 'judging' them. But this is because, as George Haskins reminds us, in the Middle Ages it was the law which 'was sovereign, and not the community'.[5]

But around the time of the Reform Bills, political parties started to co-ordinate issues together in 'programmes' presented to the new electorate, in order to supply information and an indication on how to use that information. The independent logic of each separate issue was then necessarily bent to fit the general logic of the programme, and the general argument was different in the programme of each of the competing parties. But it must be added in defence of the political parties that the periodicals, pamphlets and books supplied by them were, until the

---

[2] See especially Cecil S. Emden: *The People and the Constitution,* Oxford 1933.
[3] Ibid., p. 237.
[4] Ibid., pp. 237, 251.

[5] George L. Haskins: *The Growth of English Representative Government*, Pennsylvania 1948, p.100. Haskins provides also this illuminating quotation from H. Finch: *Law* (London 1627, p.233) 'And alle Decrees are as judgements and if the Parliament it selfe doe erre (as it may) It can no where be reversed but in Parliament'. Ibid., p.98.

beginning of the twentieth century, the principal sources of political information for a public opinion expanded in quantity and in political efficacy by the enlarged franchise. The obverse side of this dissemination of information through political parties was that the information inevitably reflected a partisan approach, or to put it more precisely, thanks to the pluralism of political parties, several partisan approaches.

Already partisan (in the sense that it reflected the general viewpoint of a political party) political judgement became ideological when ideologization started to make its rapid progress in the industrial societies in the second part of the nineteenth century. Separate issues were squeezed together according to the principal 'goal' of the ideology. In turn, the 'goals' themselves, once implanted in the reasoning of the policy-makers, became promises with the corollary of bribing the electorate, that is the clienteles of given parties, with pledges of future advantages.

Yet paradoxically, while ideological judgement gradually became the typical way of thinking politically, that kind of judgement was becoming less and less appropriate to the specific problems of an industrial society. There are two reasons for the obsolescence of ideological judgement in industrial politics. One is that because of the essentially functional character of industrial society, issues had once again asserted their importance. Scientific, social, economic and cultural issues required to be approached separately by experts in each field. Separate policies, each corresponding to one of the principal issues, alternated in the limelight of the attention of public opinion in liberal industrial society. Each of them, when thus actualized, had to be considered on its merit. The consideration must be made within the context of the problems which it posed and corroborated with the other issues and policies. But to subordinate all issues and all policies, to one single future goal, as is done in exclusively ideological thinking, only results in mixing and squashing all of them into a muddle of illogicality.

The second reason is that the political parties in industrial societies — now of course ideological parties — no longer had a monopoly of information. The political parties, even Parliament itself, among whose duties Bagehot had listed 'to inform', had by now lost the power of informing the nation directly. This duty had been largely taken over by 'the media'. But on the other hand, the formidable transnational spread of information and its equally formidable ubiquity, its presence in almost all homes in almost all corners of the world, had led to an unexpected result. The impact of information coming from so many different sources, more often than not ideologically opposed to each other and therefore neutralizing each other, achieved an objectivity of its own which ran directly counter to the ideological orientation of the political parties. The discrepancy between ideologically loaded information and the objective reality of the events and issues became more visible not only in communist systems, where it made a sharp contrast between obvious lies and stifled truths, but also, more subtly and indirectly in the liberal system where it created a kind of crisis of credibility.

Disideologization is necessary not only in order to render political participation reasonable. It is also imposed by the functional nature of industrial society. The main relation of co-existence of human beings in industrial society is occupational. The industrial society itself is a gigantic grid of professional qualifications, closely enmeshed. It follows then that the individual is doubly involved in political participation: as a human being required to share in concern with general problems, and as a professional required to examine prospective decisions in his own exclusive field, that is, decisions which could not be implemented without his occupational consent.

Because they are functional, technical and diversified, occupational and professional problems offer little scope for ideological assessment. In comparison with promissory ideological goals, the goals of occupational and technical problems are essentially neutral in the sense that they transcend the particular 'interests' of contemporary human beings. In a previous chapter reference has been made to science's indifference towards human happiness which has amply illustrated the discrepancy between the two kinds of pursuits. Even if one were to take one of the professional or occupational categories which comes nearest to ideological approaches, medicine, education or the arts, the ultimate impulse to professional, or purely intellectual, action goes against the grain of ideology.

The politics of industrial societies should try to unite functional deliberations with general political deliberations as well as it can. One of the most widely discussed problems in liberal industrial societies has been the creation of new institutions of joint consultation and decision-making, bringing together professionals (i.e., skilled workers, technicians and experts of all kinds) and politicians.

In the context of industrial society, the 'corporate forces' or 'socio-economic interests' or 'groups' acquire a direct, extra-constitutional influence on policy-making which runs parallel to that of constitutional representative institutions. Political participation in the formulation, approval or implementation of public policies is not achieved by voting alone. 'There are' writes Parry, 'students of politics who hold that the act of voting under modern representative government is connected in so remote a fashion to political decisions that it is not to be ascribed any political quality. Voting is hence not political participation. In their view for an act to be described as political participation there must be a more direct relationship between the act and the outcome.'[6] This leads to one of those curious conjunctions of opposites. For in the liberal system of political happiness, which is constitutionally based on electoral representation, the modern corporate forces declare the representative system to

[6]G. Parry (ed.): *Participation in Politics*, Manchester 1972, p. 3.

be insufficient for the exercise of their real strength in the conduct of public affairs, and demand direct access to the action of governing, at least in the economy. Whereas in the communist system of political happiness, which is constitutionally based on the theory of government by social institutions, and which rejects the principle of parliamentary representation as a typically bourgeois façade, large groups such as trade unions, farmers, technicians, demand free political consultation above all, indeed 'free elections'. This contrast underlines the necessity in *all* modern industrial societies of joint functional–representative institutions of decision-making, of new methods of government decision-making by means of which in liberal industrial societies the representative institutions would be able to consult the productive forces of the economy at an early stage of the policy-making process.

Most of the observations on institutional disideologization made in this section, converge also into a general observation on the role and usefulness of the principal political institution: the party. As we have seen, political parties are now, in varying degrees according to the political culture of the respective liberal industrial states, ideological political parties. But after the Second World War it became evident that the ideological political parties were gradually losing, because of the development of the industrial society, several of their previous *raisons d'être*. It was, for instance, obvious that the political parties had lost their function to inform public opinion. In the nineteenth century by their written (party-publications) or oral (party-meetings) means, the political parties had kept people informed in their interpretative way, of the 'state of the nation' and of that of the world and its developments. But now mass-media are pumping continuous information into every house, into every village of the liberal industrial states. Now, however, it was the political parties, and their electoral fate, which depended on the mass-media. Ideological parties, like for instance the British Labour party, saw with despair how impossible it had become to 'sell', and therefore keep alive, party-controlled publications – let alone a daily national newspaper or a radio or television-station. Extremists in that party demanded that, as in the communist industrial states, the party-state should take over the information-media.

Secondly, the political ideological parties were gradually losing their tutelage of the interests, or socio-economic groups, which they were meant to 'represent' in Parliament and in government. The direct impact made on industrial society by the 'interest' itself – because of the 'direct action' it could take which could bring the functioning of society to a halt, and because of the procedures of direct consultation, established in many European states between governments and interests above the political parties and even above the Parliament – rendered the political 'patronage' of the party increasingly superfluous. And the new, functional, assessments of the given problem, or situations, as made by the groups themselves in the course of the necessary participation in the processes of policy-making, made the ideological interpretation, as practised by the party, seem less and less relevant.

Thirdly, national and international constraints were felt in the policy-making processes of the industrial state much more intensely than in the liberal state. Interdependence was the name of the political game of the industrial society. And power-sharing — social power-sharing with the interests, international power-sharing with other states — was the necessary technique of government in such a society. This left very little room for sweeping ideological promises for the future. The *present* problems, with national or international causes, but affecting the very functioning of the society, kept the policy-makers under constant pressure. And as the elbow-room for alternative or optional policies was shrinking, so the promissory techniques of the ideological parties were being reduced to precious little. For, on the contrary, those parties which persevered in making far-fetched, futurological promises of 'general happiness' to their electorates, and were trying to divert their attention on to the vast 'goal' or 'goals' of the ideology, had to suffer rude awakenings to the present reality; and gradually but irremediably lost their credibility.

For all these and many other reasons the ideological political parties had to come back from the supreme ideological positions which they had occupied, to more menial, pragmatic, disideologized, functions. The political party as an institution, had to change if it was to survive.

The reader will now be offered a hodge-podge of suggestions put forward at various times by particularly perceptive thinkers concerned with the ideological malformation of politics in industrial societies. These suggestions for new institutional structures vary greatly in their object, approaches and motivations. but they all point directly or indirectly towards disideologization. They might, therefore, in their various ways, help the reader to see how wide the range of disideologization can be.

One such proposal was *Saint-Simon's* early, almost prophetic idea of a multi-cameral European Parliament[7] in which 'producers' would meet 'scientists' (or scholars) to debate the issues and elaborate a plan of policies. A kind of European Parliament has already been formed, but it is of the wrong kind since it is based on political parties, and even worse, on national political parties. But no functional chambers, of the kind Saint-Simon envisaged, have yet been created, although the idea pops up frequently in most unexpected quarters. *Sir Winston Churchill* proposed in 1930 the creation of a second, economic chamber. The Yugoslav Constitution of 1958 established a socio-economic chamber, a cultural chamber and a chamber of nationalities — the draft bills of which had to be approved by the fourth and supreme federal chamber in order to become law. As in Saint-Simon's vision the three special chambers prepare the plan. In the 'welfare states', moreover, as we have seen, governmental

[7]See my *The Political Thought of Saint-Simon.*

institutions for direct consultation with the socio-economic groups have been created. But no state has yet gone so far as to introduce socio-economic groups into the legislature. Not even the twentieth-century European Parliament has responded to the obvious need for more functional representation of and participation by European industrial society in its debates. The only arena is the anaemic Economic and Social Committee of the EEC, the weakest of its institutions.

A second proposal is that of *John Stuart Mill*, which has already been mentioned in this book (see pp. 127–8). He suggested that there should be plurality of votes, namely that additional votes should be granted according to the education and professional qualifications of the voter. It can be argued that this is an ugly and unfeasible 'élitist' electoral reform. But it can also be argued that John Stuart Mill's prediction was concordant with the principle of the industrial society – a society based primarily on *knowledge*. In this sense knowledge could ask to be given institutional recognition also in the political processes of that type of society.

Proportional representation, as advocated now by the *Liberal party* and the *SDP* in Britain would help to break the traditional mould of the alternation in power of two parties, a system which has so far confirmed people in the belief that the two parties represent opposing class ideologies.

Clearly and deliberately anti-ideological is *F.A. Hayek's*[8] idea of a legislature independent of political parties, which should be given the privilege of avoiding both the promissory scrimmage of the parties, and the clientelism–patronage which prevails in the present form of political representation. Candidates would be at least forty-five years old, and they would be elected for at least fifteen years; annual elections would be held to fill vacant places. The electorate would be formed of people of a given age, who would vote only once in their lives. Hayek's proposal is much too rigorous for the participatory politics of an industrial society, but some such idea could nevertheless be linked with the establishment of the kind of super-chamber required by a multi-cameral Parliament.

Also disideologizing is the ultimate purpose of at least two of the four proposals made by *Sir John Hoskyns*, a former head of the policy unit in the Prime Minister's Office, in a lecture at the Institute of Directors in September 1983[9] for a 'radical reform of the [British] political and governmental system'. He proposed first that the Prime Minister, in forming a government, should no longer be tied to 'the small pool of career politicians in Westminster'; and, second, that adequate numbers of high-quality outsiders should be brought into the Civil Service. Sir John Hoskyns's own preference for finding new political and administrative leaders in the ranks of business obviously arose from his concern with the constant decline of the British economy. But the general idea of replacing

[8]In the article 'Whither democracy' (1976) in *Three Australian Lectures*, Sidney 1979.
[9]See also article by Sir John Hoskyns in *The Times*, 22 November 1983.

old professionals, and in government especially, the members of the 'small pool of career politicians' with outstanding individuals from other walks of life, amounts also to a quest for people with non-political and non-ideological mentalities and approaches.

Michael Young's idea of the representation of consumers *qua* consumers in the processes of policy-making introduces an entirely new functional element into those processes. Producers of all kinds are in the centre of attention of industrial society, first, because they are credited with supplying the society with what it needs, and, second, because they are by now able to make their influence felt through direct action: more often than not by withdrawing their labour, or, in other words, by halting production. The fact that all human beings in industrial societies are also consumers is more easily forgotten because, at least until now, consumers have not found a way to participate in the decision-making processes of an industrial society. But the defence of consumers by organizations fully represented in those processes is increasingly justified in the advanced industrial society where the 'invisible hand' of the market has been replaced by the 'marketing' and 'advertising' techniques of oligopolistic enterprises. Spontaneous attempts to set up organizations of consumers — like the Nader movement in the United States[10] or the Consumers' Association in Great Britain — have made a certain mark on political attitudes.

Collective actions by consumers, such as mass-boycotts or mass-abstentions, or consumer reactions to producers' industrial actions, or mass-planning of consumption so as to indicate the consumers' own priorities to the planning enterprises of the state have not yet materialized. Nor is consumers' political representation recognized as such, with few exceptions as for instance in the consultations of the European Commission.

In the same order of ideas we can also note the suggestion that just as local authorities explain in percentage terms how the rates raised are expended, so the Inland Revenue should explain in its tax assessment forms the objects on which the revenue raised is spent and in what proportions. Both rate and income tax demands should invite taxpayers to indicate their preference or their order of priorities on how their taxes should be spent: defence, education, health, environment, sport, etc. Such an annual consultation of the preferences of the taxpayers could provide the government with a more detailed and pragmatic opinion poll than those based on political or ideological attitudes or general elections.

Mr Edward Heath's idea that non-party candidates should be encouraged to stand for election to the European Parliament could also be extended to national elections. In view of the strength of the national

---

[10] A recent summary of the American movement can be found in Michael Pertschuk: *Revolt against Regulation — the Rise and Fall of the Consumer Movement*, University of California 1982. But for the consumers' attitudes in public life as a whole see especially A.S.C. Ehrenberg and F.G. Pyatt: *Consumer Behaviour*, London 1971.

organizations, bureaucracies and financial resources of political parties, the possibility of a non-party personality being elected in a constituency is very remote. Non-party candidates recommended by committees of citizens at the local or national level could be supported by official funds.

Theodore J. Lowi's theory of juridical democracy has been left to the end of this list of suggestions, because, together with the following one, it readily admits that the causes of the malfunctioning of the modern liberal state lie in the obsolescence of its institutional structure. Lowi argues in favour of strengthening the juridical principle, indeed in favour of a juridical democracy.

The separation of powers, *de jure* as in the United States, France, or the Federal Republic of Germany, *de facto* as in Great Britain, is the cornerstone of the constitutional structure of the liberal state. It is significant that in European history law was first enacted through the administration of justice – for it was on this supreme ground that people acceded directly to the king, one of whose principal functions was to redress wrongs and grievances; and it is equally significant that when totalitarian dictators begin to suppress a democracy, the first measure they embark on is to abolish the independence of the judiciary, as Hitler did with the proud German judiciary.

However there is a difference between the independence-from-politics of the judiciary as for instance in Britain, and the policy-making function of the judiciary as in the United States or Germany where the Supreme Court or the Constitutional Court, as the case may be, makes policies, or in Hamilton's words 'must . . . declare all acts contrary to the manifest tenor of the Constitution void . . .'. Whereas the Legislature has the supreme power to change the Constitution, the Supreme Court has by now a fully established right to invalidate political decisions which run counter to the spirit or to the letter of the existing Constitution. In this sense the High Court of the United States or the Constitutional Court of the Federal Republic of Germany do have a political role; and by their decisions they also orient public opinion in matters of political judgement, especially when majority and minority opinions are published. The same is true also of the European Court.

Inspired by the positive political role of the judiciary in the USA – although the record of the High Court contains many errors – and worried by the transformation of liberalism into 'interest group liberalism', as he puts it, Lowi advances the somehow moralistic idea of *juridical democracy* as the alternative to interest-group liberalism. His principal arguments for the change are that:

> Interest group liberalism cannot plan, juridical democracy can. Positive law guides; positive law moves in known ways . . . Interest group liberalism cannot achieve justice. Juridical democracy can because its actions derive from known principles and therefore can be judged. Requirement of rule of law leads to a justice-oriented politics . . . While

pluralism eliminates justice from all consideration, the juridical approach does not eliminate pluralist patterns of principles.[11]

In spite of the fact that Lowi's argument against pluralism as such runs counter to the assertion in this enquiry that industrial society must necessarily be pluralistic and that its functioning depends on the participation of all individuals and groups, two of his arguments coincide with the point of view expounded here. The first of these is that interest-groups, and *interest* itself, an essentially relative, materialistic notion, chase out justice, an essentially moral and absolute notion (see pp. 107–9 and 114–18). Lowi's second argument, namely that what liberalism needs in order to be saved from its inevitable 'end' is *justice-oriented politics*, will be presented from the standpoint of this enquiry in the section entitled 'Political judgement'.

Karl W. Deutsch, and many other political scientists working with him either at Harvard or at the *Berlin Zentrum für Internationale Wirtschaft* on studies of international society[12] have now completed their examination of the interrelatedness of the domestic and the international processes and the socio-economic and the political processes of policy-making. The extent of the transnationalization of politics and the gradual evaporation of national sovereignty through the merging of welfare 'nation-states' into welfare 'communities' (as in the case of the European Community) and regional continental units has been amply illustrated in these studies. Moreover it has also been shown that the validity of political judgement in transnational industrial society depends on the extent to which it is founded on the transnational perspective, or to put it differently, the feasibility of a course of action must be assessed from as all-embracing a transnational view as can be obtained. The distance in intellectual ages between a cosmonaut circumnavigating the earth and a nationalist terrorist, be he Irish or Basque, is bigger than the distance in miles which separates them.

In Great Britain, the *Minority Report* of the Royal Commission of the Constitution[13] has also underlined the dual trend towards devolution in modern Britain, towards local government on the national plane, and towards European integration on the international plane.

And finally, if local decentralization and functional devolution are not singled out here it is because on the one hand they are the basic means and ends of the intensification of participation industrial society needs; and on the other hand because devolution towards the local or functional base of the unit of rule is the dialectic twin of devolution for overall co-ordination

[11] Theodore J. Lowi: *The End of Liberalism,* New York 1979, p. 311.
[12] See especially Richard L. Merrit and Bruce M. Russett (eds): *From National Development to Global Community, Essays in Honour of Karl W. Deutsch,* London 1981.
[13] Royal Commission on The Constitution, 1969–1973, Vol. II *Memorandum of Dissent* by Lord Crowther-Hunt and Professor A.T. Peacock, HMSO 1973, Cmnd 5460–61.

towards transnational centres of policy-making — there is decentralization in one direction, centralization in the other.

THE DISIDEOLOGIZATION OF POLITICAL JUDGEMENT

Reasonable participation, as defined here, entails the good use of reason. The feasibility and effectiveness of a course of action depend on the political judgement which preceded it; and in so far as in industrial society, more than in any previous form of democracy, policies cannot be made and decisions taken without prior consultation with all concerned in them, it follows that the political judgement of each and all those concerned should have the qualities of clarity and impartiality inherent in any good judgement, let alone good political judgement.

Ideological judgement, in the sense, let us repeat again, of a judgement moulded on pre-established interpretative methods and oriented towards pre-selected goals, cannot be impartial. It is, on the contrary, partisan, even party-bound. Pre-ideological judgement, that is the kind of political judgement exercised by people before the advent of the nineteenth-century ideologies, was also partial, but in the sense of being incomplete. People had neither the feeling of public power, with its corollary, public responsibility, which awakens political judgement, nor the information on which to base judgement empirically, and with the help of which alone they could have obtained a 'representation' of the thinking of all the others concerned with the same issue. (Here, it will be observed, representation in its logical sense fuses with representation in its political sense.)

The republics of Athens and Rome form the exceptions to this historical description in that their citizens did have the feeling of public power and the sense of political responsibility — but, on the other hand they excluded multitudes from their logical and political 'representation'. Christian political judgement although all-embracing in its fundamental fraternal 'representation' was partial in the sense that it gave only partial and secondary attention to worldly problems, to that which was political and belonged to Caesar. But then, within its self-imposed limitations, Christian political judgement had, by virtue of its intrinsic detachment, greater possibilities of being disinterested and impartial in worldly and political matters. Moreover neither Greek nor Christian political philosophy ever separated political judgement from universal moral judgement. In his refreshing study on *Political Judgment*,[14] Ronald Beiner contrasts Kant's eminently moral concept of political duty with Aristotle's *phronesis*, political wisdom, in which the political judgement of a man must necessarily comprise the impulse of friendship towards other mortals.

[14] Ronald Beiner: *Political Judgment,* London 1983.

But although Beiner understandably leans towards Aristotle, he himself shows that the Aristotelian concept of friendship, of human sympathy, was based on a shared sense of justice, that only just men could be friends. As Aristotle put it, 'friendship and the just deal with the same objects and involve the same persons'.[15] It is this link between the political philosophy of Aristotle (and for that matter of Plato) and that of Kant, through justice and virtue as the imperatives of politics, which makes them together so different from and opposed to the ideological philosophies. For whereas classical political philosophy purifies political judgement, ideological political philosophy vitiates it. It vitiates it directly by narrowing it down to an exclusive goal; and indirectly because in general it puts *interest* (individual or collective interest) at the origin of political thinking and action.

The exercise of political judgement, or at any rate of good political judgement, requires therefore that it should emanate from a sense of responsibility, which implies a share of power in political decision-making; how, in Athens, could slaves or women have made the effort to exert a political judgement when they were not involved in politics? Good political judgement should also be motivated by virtue, that is to say it should have the intention of doing good, jointly with those who have the same motivation. It should be impartial, and therefore totally disinterested – a political judgement associated with interest is perhaps better defined as 'political argument';[16] and it should be exercised by someone who can make a valid judgement about other matters in general.

What remains to be seen however is how the classic pre-conditions of political judgement can be fulfilled in industrial societies and how they accord with the liberal system of public happiness (a comparison with the other system would be difficult because Marx rejected absolute virtues).

Obviously, in an industrial society, it would be easier to comply with the first and the fourth conditions, the sense of responsibility and the capacity for judging. Indeed as far as the capacity to judge is concerned, the fact that illiteracy has been reduced to an absolute minimum in all industrial societies, and particularly in Western industrial societies, coupled with the abundant information provided, indeed imposed by the media, which is actually available to illiterates as well, should enable everyone to have a better understanding of political issues than ever before. (There is of course no question that this is a double-edged weapon – it can spread the poison of totalitarian regimes.) As regards the sense of power and responsibility, it has often been argued in these pages that the specialized knowledge and the interdependence which characterize industrial societies give to its members a particularly highly developed sense of their functional competence, whence they derive their political power.

The spirit of democracy in its general sense has not only helped to

[15] Ibid., p. 80.
[16] Brian Barry: *Political Argument,* London 1976, especially the section on interest, pp. 173–87.

develop this sense, it has been the historical agent of this fundamental change in the regulation of the co-existence of human beings. But when democracy degenerated, after it was corrupted by ideologies, it also corrupted both the individual's sense of responsibility and his capacity to exert an unvitiated political judgement by situating interest in the centre of affairs and by reducing judgement to that of a 'citizen' or a 'comrade'.

The sense of virtue and the sense of duty should only have been enhanced by the way industrial society functions. Those involved in it are necessarily imbued with the reality of their role in the whole process. The very fact that they demand a greater say in the conduct of the operation in which they are involved is only the counterpart of the sense of duty which it awakens in them. And the reality of interdependence, of necessary enmeshment with others, known or unknown, in the enormous national and transnational grid which is the modern process of industrial production, can only illuminate the blind mentalities of parochial interest and thus conduce to a more general sense of virtue — for as Aristotle would put it, the constructive motive of the good is ultimately a stronger motive for human action than that of evil, of destruction.

But here is where both systems of political happiness ran counter to the moral nature of human association and to the functional nature of industrial society. For, in order to promote their own 'values', both systems set out to undermine the lasting values of European civilization. The classic sense of virtue and the sense of duty were described in Marxist–Leninist ideology as the class façades of hypocrisy, and in utilitarian–liberal terms as obstacles to the pursuit of human happiness. Thus, on behalf of its ideology, the Marxist–Leninist system monopolized the exercise of discipline in society for its party alone, and subjected the whole of society to the arbitrary rule of the party; while the utilitarian–liberal system, following the precepts of the hedonistic pursuit of happiness by means of progressive permissiveness, helped to gradually eliminate the commandments, the 'imperatives' of duty and virtue, from the moral fabric of society.

Finally, classical philosophy argues that true political judgement can be exerted only in conditions of total 'disinterestedness'. From the Greeks to Aquinas, to Kant, philosophers warned against the danger of allowing judgement to be vitiated by interest. For, if one wants to think for all, which is the object of political judgement, if one tries to 'represent' in one's own thinking the possible thinking of all the others involved, one must achieve a degree of mental transparence which cannot be attained if the entire operation is envisaged in the chiaroscuro of one's own interest. This is where in strict logic, and in ethical logic, utilitarianism went wrong, and it 'vitiated' the whole operation of political judgement. For while it did counsel that all actions should be preceded by a rigorous 'calculation' of all its consequences, the overt purpose of the calculation was the ultimate interest of the calculator himself; and the final aim of the entire arithmetical calculation was to deduct from whatever pains the action could cause to others the marginal happiness it could produce for its initiator. Obviously, in such an exiguous calculation there is no room for duty; and in such a normative consideration any idea of virtue on its own is subordinated to the sovereign interest. On both counts utilitarian judgement fails to provide a perfect political judgement. The utilitarian method may illuminate the motivations of political ambition but it obscures those of political impartiality.

Ideologies are therefore suspect of being essentially opposed to the exercise of political judgement; and since the lack of political judgement is the cause of most of the evils of modern society, the conclusion of the syllogism is that what should now be sought, is the disideologization of political judgement, at least in the utilitarian—liberal system, whose saving grace is the ability to reform itself.

This process could be embarked on at two levels, the mental and the moral. Mental disideologization is easier to describe. This is because the capacity of judgement is reflected in the independence of judgement. *A fortiori* in political judgement, which has a public finality, the independence of judgement should transcend all subjective factors. The stronger the capacity for judgement, the greater its need for independence. The weaker the capacity for judgement the greater its need to be guided. The stronger the capacity for judgement, the deeper its search for disinterestedness and detachment, in order to reach a position of impartiality necessary for a free political judgement; the weaker that capacity, the greater the danger that the judgement will be deformed by personal criteria, and by ready-made methods of pursuing happiness. Ideologies and ideological parties hamper the individual's aspiration to use his or her own political judgement in so far as they provide a surrogate judgement with methodical answers to most questions, once the method has been learned; and they attach the person to politics by linking the sense of personal interest to the political judgement or action of the person or group.

To paraphrase President Kennedy's widely quoted maxim from his inaugural address, in this context one might describe the people who exert an independent political judgement as those people who ask themselves what they can do for the community, not what the community can do for them. Ideologies and ideological parties, and more generally speaking the promissory political techniques have turned this principle upside down. The very concept of interestedness, 'what is there in it for me?' — on which they are all based turns the political participant into a client.

At the mental level therefore, the greater the capacity for judgement, or the stronger the effort of the individual to improve his capacity for judgement, the less successful the hold of the ideologies on the individual. Whereas these efforts are reduced to a minimum in the communist—dictatorial system (where people or groups who detach themselves from the ideology become what is called there 'internal exiles', or are actually exiled) the advantage of the utilitarian—liberal system is that its inherent pluralism provides, *could* provide, the antidote to ideological conformism and uniformity.

For commercial and other reasons the media create an atmosphere of materialistic *distraction* in the sense given to this word earlier (see pp. 32–3). Yet the 'freedom' of society offers ample opportunities to the man who seeks not to be distracted in the formation of his judgement. The crux of the question lies in the individual's determination to concentrate on his own truth, by providing his judgement with the 'representation' of the points of view of others — the spectrum of which is easy to establish. The very pluralism of industrial society makes it easy to obtain samples. Every library or decent bookshop displays on its shelves not only the classic works which provide direct initiation into the practice of proper judgement but also a whole range of works expounding various ideological positions which in the main neutralize each other. Every newsagent shows the same range — the criterion for the choice of the more positive newspaper being the ratio of news-items to pictures of nudes or accounts of crimes packed into one page of type. Every transistor now provides in the language known to the listener the different interpretations of the same news-item by the BBC, or Radio Moscow, or Radio Vatican or the Voice of America or Radio Tirana.

It is at the moral level that the detachment from ideological politics poses a much more difficult problem. For the initial, functional role of political parties was to enhance political participation, to make people aware of the importance of public issues and of the necessity to seek their solution through the participation and the *judgement* of all those concerned. Ideologists might argue cunningly that if people do not come to the forum for the sake of their own interests — 'what's in it for me?' — they will not come at all. The danger of a community dissolving itself by ascesis is according to utilitarians as great as the danger of dissolving itself by gluttony. At least the latter brings the people together, makes them compete, makes them *act,* and action is the principle of life. Take, if you can, interest away from human intercourse, and it will be reduced to sheer elementals. If it is true, as ideologists argue, that men participate in public affairs only when their interest is involved, then disinterestedness would result in social apathy and indifference, harmful to the proper functioning of any democracy.

But this argument of the ideologists is fallacious, both for the past, and for the present and the future. For the past it should be remembered that 'interest' is an eighteenth-century concept and communism a nineteenth-century concept, whereas politics, even if not under that name, has been a perennial feature of all societies. It is obvious that whatever *actual* participation those past societies have achieved was not set in motion by materialistic concepts. On the contrary, such participation was inspired only by ideals, idealistic ideals to be precise. As for the present and the future industrial society, as this enquiry has shown, and as will be demonstrated in the rest of it, the increasing inadequacy of the materialistic promissory solutions proffered by the two ideologies for the immediate problems of industrial societies is now so blatant that as a result they have toned them down in their respective domestic politics. For if they did not, the ideological parties would run the risk of losing their credibility and their electoral popularity.

MORAL DISIDEOLOGIZATION: FRUGALITY AND CONCERN

This enquiry into the involvement of human beings in the politics of industrial society has been conducted from an ontological standpoint. Although its subject is the *politikos zoon*, it posits that man is both a *zoon* and *politikos*. In other words his political condition is moulded by his human condition, and not the other way round. It is therefore only natural that, having reached the ultimate question, which is how to ensure the political participation of human beings without the lure of ideology, relying instead on the sagacity of a disinterested political judgement, our search for an answer should take us back to man's condition as a human being, as a whole human being.

A whole human being is that being who exists between his unexplained birth and his inevitable death, and who in the *meantime* co-exists with other human beings whose life-span coincides with his. The mystery of his existence forms of necessity the background to all man's thoughts including his thoughts on his own co-existence with others. This is for his own good, for he would not be a whole human being had he not comprehended by means of his own judgement the wholeness of his existence. And it is for the good of his co-existence with others, for it is only when he has understood himself — *gnosti afton*, — and what he can expect from his life-span, that he can understand others and what they can rightly expect from him. He has a concern *for* the others, not an interest in them. 'Love thy neighbour as thyself' and not 'love thyself as thou lovest thy neighbour'.

The cross, devised as an instrument of death, before Christ's death, and for him, was predetermined to become a symbol of life after his death. Its vertical axis symbolizes the ascent of man from his birth on earth and through death to heaven, while its horizontal axis symbolizes the fraternity with all those who inhabit the earth. The parable, moreover, clearly implies that if the vertical axis was not erect, the horizontal one could not be affixed to it. Man has first to live his own life, to stand upright, before he can stretch out his arms towards other men.

It we start the 'calculus' of man's existence in the form of a countdown from the average duration of the life-span (at present usually taken to be three score years and ten) and not as might seem more natural by measuring from zero to infinity, man can assess the parameters of the human condition more adequately. This has the ultimate effect of colouring his outlook with what is called in a different context a 'sense of proportion' or in yet another context, 'common sense'. 'Make the most of your life' and 'you can't take it with you' are typical expressions of common sense.

Between these two sayings lies the concept of frugality[17], of a frugal life. In the better-known concept of moderation the stress falls on control by reason of man's pleasurable actions, or indeed of any kind of actions. But in that of frugality the accent falls on two other considerations. One is contentment in sufficiency (the German word for frugality is *Genügsamkeit*, enoughness) or to quote another English saying, enough is as good as a feast. Contentment is not produced by the quantity of goods to be enjoyed. It resides in the quality of the enjoyment, in the way in which particular enjoyments fit into one's integrity, into the whole of the life of one human being. Hence the precedence of duty over happiness, for it is duty which maintains integrity, and integrity conduces to happiness. On the contrary, satiety soon spoils pleasure. Insatiability engenders vice. The deliberate and sole pursuit of pleasure is equivalent to distraction, leading on to escapism and to dissolution. Frugality, on the contrary concentrates man's life on his sense of achievement, and gives him the rewarding feeling of being always himself, within himself.

Secondly, *frugalis* derives from the Latin *fructus*. It follows that the contentment provided by frugality is the contentment with the fruit of one's work. No moral or physical effort required by work can spoil the legitimacy of the contentment of a man enjoying the fruit of his work. And no amount of dependence entailed in the conditions of his work can affect the ultimate independence of a man who has ensured his self-sufficiency.

Obviously this type of classical bucolic reasoning no longer responds to the conditions of an industrial society. But the proposition that a man can be contented with the fruit of his work is as true in an industrial society as in any other kind of society. What has made industrial labour so ugly since the introduction of large-scale mechanization in the first industrial revolution is the squalor of the place of work, the idiotic monotony of the repeated physical effort contributed by the individual worker to the collective chain of production, and his imprisonment in that chain and in that place. And what made industrial labour morally ugly was the glaring contrast between the escalating profits of the 'capitalist' owner, and the insufficient wage paid to the worker, insufficient in the sense of failing to

---

[17] In a previous essay I described frugality as follows: 'In Latin the word *frugalis* (which comes from *frux*, fruit) has two meanings: the first is 'pertaining to produce' and the second: thrifty, economical. The logical link between the two meanings seems to be formed by the self-contentedness of the frugal man or household with the products of his or its work. Frugality is the opposite of greed, envy, excess and insatiability and, on the other hand, is different from privation, austerity and even economy. *Frugalitas autem pauperitas volutaria est,* observed Seneca.' In F.F. Ridley (ed.): *Studies in Politics*, London 1957, pp. 258–59.

provide him with a basis of existence which would allow him to preserve his independence.

The struggle waged by working-class social and political organizations in the first part of the twentieth century, and the industrial and cultural development of capitalist society have brought about a situation in which skilled industrial workers receive for what is generally cleaner, safer and more intelligent work, rewards which enable them and their families to be self-sufficient: while proper representative government can grant them equality in political action. Modern miners, engineers, or electronic workers, or white-collar employees of service industries have now the opportunity to enjoy frugal contentment. (This is the *embourgeoisement* so deplored by professional revolutionaries).

The disturbing feature of the new technological revolution, associated with the microchip and the increasing predominance of the service industries, is its possible impact on employment. The new machinery has an inbuilt capacity for increased productivity. As a result industries can dispense with much of the labour force previously serving the machines. If automation leads to unemployment more people may in future find it even more difficult to find work and therefore to acquire that minimum of self-sufficiency and independence necessary for human dignity. From another point of view, new class divisions have appeared in society today and they are the divisions between the self-sufficient skilled employed worker and the unemployed worker and more often than not, unskilled. If this new division were to be perpetuated it would lead to a society sharply divided between full human beings and marginals.

The more reassuring fact is that automation is not the only cause of unemployment. If it were it would not explain the sharp differences in the percentage of the unemployed between such a homogeneous group of countries as the ten 'welfare states' which are members of the European Community. The existence of such national differences proves that other factors must be playing a determining part in setting unemployment trends. Among the economic factors, the national index of productivity is probably the most significant; indeed at the level of an individual enterprise, productivity has the same rationale of self-sufficiency as it has for the individual human being. Among the social factors, the principal ones are a system of distributive justice which does not run counter to the economic rationale of efficiency, and the successful working of a social security system which does not overload the public sector in the mixed economy. Among political factors, the intensity and relevance of political participation are, as has only too often been said here, the best indicators of the quality of politics in industrial societies. Moreover, a moment's reflection shows that political participation has evident repercussions on the economic and social factors of a society.

Like all things political, political participation in industrial societies can have positive or negative consequences according to the way it is oriented.

Intensive political participation originating in the naked pursuit of interest and the maximization of personal or 'group' satisfaction, leads only to conflict, and fragmentation which might make the interdependent society grind to a halt. *Unreasonable* political participation hinders the functioning of society, and therefore the more intensified it is, the more harm it does. The sense of negative power, fortified by world publicity, has sometimes led political participation to degenerate into political agitation — part of this agitation being the continuation of the international ideological 'cold war' in national politics. So the negative domestic political participation forms a vicious circle with the negative international politics.

Reasonable political participation originates in the industrial society not from the interest of the individual, but from his *concern*. Because industrial society is functional, pluralistic and interdependent, and it *involves* almost all human beings living within it in its functioning, it gradually changes 'interest' which was once regarded as the impulse of political action and participation into 'concern'. In less politically involved societies interest and interestedness might still provide a valid or plausible motive for political action. Not everything affected everybody; society was made up of loosely connected, or unconnected activities or fields of action which did not necessarily always cross or influence each other. Given the relative political latitude of the pre-industrial society and of the classical liberal state, as long as politics did not interfere with his activities (wars or revolutions) a human being might or might not have in the past an 'interest' in politics. The motive of interest in politics accorded with the definition of interest itself as an optional faculty of 'participating', taking part in an action, in this context political action, or bypassing it, according to whether such action had or did not have any 'utility' for him.

But in industrial society the interrelatedness is such that everybody is *involved* in everyone else's actions. Participation, particularly political participation, remains of course an essentially voluntary action. If it is not voluntary it is not political participation but political mobilization. But the individual motivation for participation is no longer an optional interest — it is an inescapable concern. Since man in industrial society is concerned with everything that can happen everywhere and can affect his own part in the way society functions, he must with deep *concern* take part in all developments which involve him. But then concern is at the opposite pole to interest. Instead of generating conflict it generates understanding; instead of distracting man it concentrates him on his ultimate *raison d'être*; instead of leading him to pursue happiness outside himself, it teaches him to defend his own frugal happiness; instead of driving him to ask the community to give him more in satisfaction of his own interests, his concern for the society of which he is a part leads him to contribute as much as he can to society.

It is at this point that we can detect better how detachment from society and attachment to society make up one single proposition. For the more attached (involved, etc.) man feels he is to his society, the more detached he must be from it — morally by not expecting his happiness to come from it, but on the contrary, being in possession of his own independent self, and mentally in order to place himself at the distance which disinterestedness will give him, enabling him to act positively and in his integrity.

The ideologized human being in industrial society sees his relations with the others, in one kind of ideology, in the context of a calculation of their utility for him; in the other kind of ideology, as the means by which mankind as a whole is conducted towards the future promised to the human species in eternity. A disideologized human being sees his fellow men again as an integral part of his existence — seeking together the improvement of that condition for their own sake and for the sake of their children.

The industrial society requires more organization than any previous society known in history. But this can only be achieved by men who put more into society than they expect to take out of it — more contribution than distribution and more general concern than personal or particular interest. And this can be achieved only in political regimes the principle of which is to stimulate the sense of free creativity of the human beings, that is of the humans *being*.

Conclusions

Politics is a sphere of activity situated at the intersection of the other spheres of social activity. As such it is perennial and like other spheres it has to function if society as a whole is to function. This enquiry did not therefore question either the importance or the necessity of politics; it asked whether it functions satisfactorily or not, in accordance with the various historical periods and the styles, and in particular whether in the present historical period politics is helping or hindering the functioning of industrial society.

Unlike other activities the activity of politics was concealed in the past (with the partial exception of Greek and Roman times) until the end of the eighteenth century behind the religious, legal or military functions of government. Politics was the obvious means, but was not acknowledged under that name as the purpose. But politics became autonomous when it associated itself with the 'people'. Democratic politics — politics with, by, and for the people — this is how both systems describe their politics. The question thus becomes whether the politics of industrial societies has helped or harmed the people in those societies, which it was pledged to serve, absolutely or relatively, that is to say by comparison with other functions and spheres of society. And the answer which one must reluctantly give is in the negative: politics has not served the industrial society as well as the other spheres of activity have served it. Politics has taken the wrong path.

The proposition that the politics of industrial societies have gone astray is justifiable in both relative and absolute terms. In relative terms it is obvious that the performance of politics has been far inferior to the performance of science, technology, culture or economics in the last hundred years or so; while in absolute terms twentieth century politics have led to some of the most horrific developments in political history. An age in which the natural sciences have explored the furthermost outposts of the macrocosmic physical universe, and the minutest elements of the biological microcosm, in which they have enmeshed the whole planet in a web of instant communication, and have provided ample resources for welfare politics in industrial societies, has produced the First World War, the most perversely organized systems of human oppression and destruction ever recorded in human history, and then the Second World War. Now ideological politics has so kindled and fanned all domestic and international conflicts that this last generation is living in an atmosphere of generalized social conflict and under the appalling threat of a third, nuclear war. The growing popular protest against the state of international politics and the danger of war provides clear proof of the political distress of the peoples.

This failure of politics to fulfil its promises has conduced in the liberal-democracies to the spread of the most depressing doubt of all, namely to the impression that the participation of the many in the conduct of public affairs is responsible for the incompetence and incoherence of governments in the liberal-democracies. Such is not the conclusion drawn by this inquiry. On the contrary, it was constantly argued here that, given the interdependent character of any type of industrial society, the functional and political participation of each and all of its active members in the process of decision-making must be statutorily intensified. It is not the principle of political participation which has failed. In communist societies political participation has been devitalized by ideological monolithic control. In the liberal societies the trouble lies in the distortion which this principle has suffered because of ideologization. By means of the glittering promises of political happiness, ideology and ideological politics have first obscured and then entirely falsified the conception of democratic participation. Or in the ironic formulation of the American political theorist, Gary Thom: 'The democratic-pluralist conception is that we are more democratic to the extent that we enable more people to get more of what they want, more of the time, through the political process'.[1]

Moreover, ideologies have disoriented human beings themselves. Too many people have been distracted by ideologies from the concentration on their own selves, and have been provided by ideological systems of thought with new means of trying to find out, on their own, what life is really about.

It is only since the nineteenth century that education, or to put it more precisely, ideologization has been undertaken in the spirit of the pursuit of individual or universal happiness and the avoidance of pain, and especially of the supreme pain. It is only since the nineteenth century that ideological education has not only condoned but actively encouraged the instinct of weak mortals to escape from the tragic sense of life.

> They constantly try to escape
> From the darkness outside and within
> Dreaming of systems so perfect
>   That no one will need to be good . . .

T.S. Eliot's verses, already quoted in this enquiry, sum up the whole story of the emergence of modern 'systemic' political escapism. But while

---

[1] Gary Thom: *Bringing the Left Back Home — A Critique of American Social Criticism*, Yale, 1979, p. 191.

the poet describes that escapism from the point of view of the addicts, or to put it in our political terms, from the point of view of those who abandon their own selves in order to be absorbed in ideological politics, here we have concentrated more on the ideologizers themselves, on the purveyors of the illusion of political happiness.

At the same time, we have also distinguished between the normal presentation of ideas, programmes and courses of action, which lies at the basis of the linkage between political leaders and political followers and the abnormal, ideological demand for the 'commitment' of the followers to the 'moral' and 'philosophical' constructions of the respective systems. The exchange of political ideas and of political promises between politicians or political organizations and their followers forms the bloodstream of democracy. The public opinion of any society must be informed of the proposals for which its support is sought. Hence, the need, in the age of industrial society, for mass organizations and mass publicity. But ideological politics 'purvey' entire happiness-promising conceptions of life, whereby the followers should commit themselves to conduct their lives according to the respective method. Such followers are no longer masters of their own judgement and of their power of choice; they have become 'members' of a system which thinks for them and 'liberates' them from the painful necessity of understanding themselves.

After the examination of the first, albeit brief, operation of ideologization to emerge, namely that of the Jacobins, we stressed that full ideologization only appeared after the victory of the allegedly scientific materialistic philosophies. These philosophies promised to seekers after escape from their anguished selves that they could attain individual happiness by following their down-to-earth interest in one system and their materialistically conditioned class-consciousness in the other. Essential to the success of ideological politics based on materialistic philosophies in the last hundred years or so was the ability of these philosophies to distract people from their meditations on human fate, and attract them in the pursuit of one or other illusion of materialistic happiness.

The ideologization and counter-ideologization of the industrial world divided it into two 'massive' camps, each of them blaming the other for the failure to bring about the kind of happiness which each had promised so freely. This rivalry led in turn to the present political, military and, above all, psychological tension with its obviously dangerous consequences.

There are now many signs that increasing numbers of people, frightened by the irresponsibility of ideological politics, are trying to find their way back, through processes of interiorization, to the problems of personal responsibility — even if some of the means they adopt, such as joining communes, following new and exotic cults, or taking up allegedly non-political causes only estrange them still further from themselves. The true processes of interiorization lead to the integration of the individual's sense of his own life in the human condition as a whole. For only when man sees himself in the whole of the human condition does he see in true perspective the potentialities of his own life.

When and if this perspective is reached, it has been argued here, hedonistic gluttony will change into frugality, that state in which man is content with the 'fruit' of his work. The human being who reaches the state of frugality will not expect others to provide him with what he needs, and he will rely on his own resources to supply most of his needs. The more human beings absorb themselves in, and love, their work, the more energy they devote to developing themselves, the more resources they will find in themselves; and the greater their resources, the greater the help they will be able to offer to others. The translation of these ethical considerations into modern economic, social and political terminology is only too easy.

Seen also in this new perspective, interest — individual or sectorial interest — the poverty of which is so clearly reflected in the classic question: 'What's in it for me?', or 'for us?' is replaced by concern. Concern is by its very nature universal. Everything which happens anywhere concerns me. The two classic definitions of concern, battered though they may be by frequent usage, recover their full freshness in this discussion. One is Terence's 'humani nihil a me alienum puto' the other is John Donne's *Devotion*: 'Any man's death diminishes me because I am involved in mankind; and therefore never send to know for whom the bell tolls; it tolls for thee'. Here again, there is no need to underline the appropriateness of the concept of concern for the unprecedently *interdependent* industrial society.

Donne's lines bring us also to yet another concept, namely that of fraternity. Fraternity is what interdependence means in human terms. It was noted earlier in this inquiry that the Jacobin soon dropped 'fraternity' from the revolutionary triplet, which they then limited to 'liberty' and 'equality'. Since that time, all systems of political happiness have given a much more concrete connotation and greater imperativeness to equality. The real reasons why the systems have subsumed fraternity into equality are first that while equality is practicable from without, that is 'systematically' and politically practicable, even if only by the easy technique of levelling down, the terrible results of which have been so evident since the Russian revolution — fraternity emanates only from within. Secondly, fraternity is essentially a tragic concept, and is thus out of harmony with the key of happiness in which the hymns of the systems are written.

For to come back to Donne, why should he have started his meditation on universal concern with the thought of the death of any man, if it were not for the fact that the only incontestable equality of all men is in the face of death? There is no equality in birth, since man's arrival on earth is a matter of chance and circumstances. But we are all in the end equal in death, 'the great leveller'. And it is this tragic sense of equality in fate which makes those men who are imbued with the tragic sense of humanity find the material inequality of men so outrageous. and leads them to struggle against material inequalities in a spirit of fraternal compassion.

Because of the cunning, indeed perverse way in which Marx labelled true and original socialism as 'Utopian', too many people have forgotten that both the religious and the philosophic origins of socialism were idealistic. But while Marx proudly proclaimed that his social philosophy was materialistic, because he assumed that science was materialistic, he did not, as he should in all fairness have done, call the social philosophy of his predecessors by the apposite and opposite name of idealistic, but by the polemical and pejorative name of 'Utopian'. Yet, as it is so easy to see now, the change he operated was not a change from Utopianism to science, but from idealism to materialism. His semantic bluff was called only a few decades later by the history of ideas. When science repudiated materialism and therefore also scientific 'historical materialism', on the basis of which Marx had heralded the happiness of the species, the rug was pulled from under his feet. When his successors still clung to the materialistic fetish, this became worse than a Utopia, it became a deception. Marx's disalienating revolution became in historical reality the most oppressive state; and his internationalism turned into the most virulent imperialism. This metamorphosis confirmed that the principal premiss having been falsely posed, everything that ensued from it was bound to go wrong.

Industrial society has now begun to show its abhorrence of the ideological approaches which distort and corrupt it. The evident consequence of this is disideologization, the fact that all political parties in industrial societies begin to feel the burden of carrying an ideology increasingly heavy in practice. As they converge together in the liberal camp towards the centre of the essentially empirical industrial society, the former ideological differences between modern socialism, liberalism, and modern conservatism, become increasingly blurred in the search for lasting answers to the still unsolved problems. Meanwhile in the communist camp, ideology is now mostly used for imperialistic purposes. A functional centripetalism should now replace the centrifugalism of the ideologies and ideological parties if worse confrontations are to be avoided. The materialistic ideologies which were based on such principles as 'interest' or 'class consciousness' and have so long postured as the pursuit of ideals, should now be driven out by the true ideals, ideals which are nurtured by the tragic sense of life.

Index